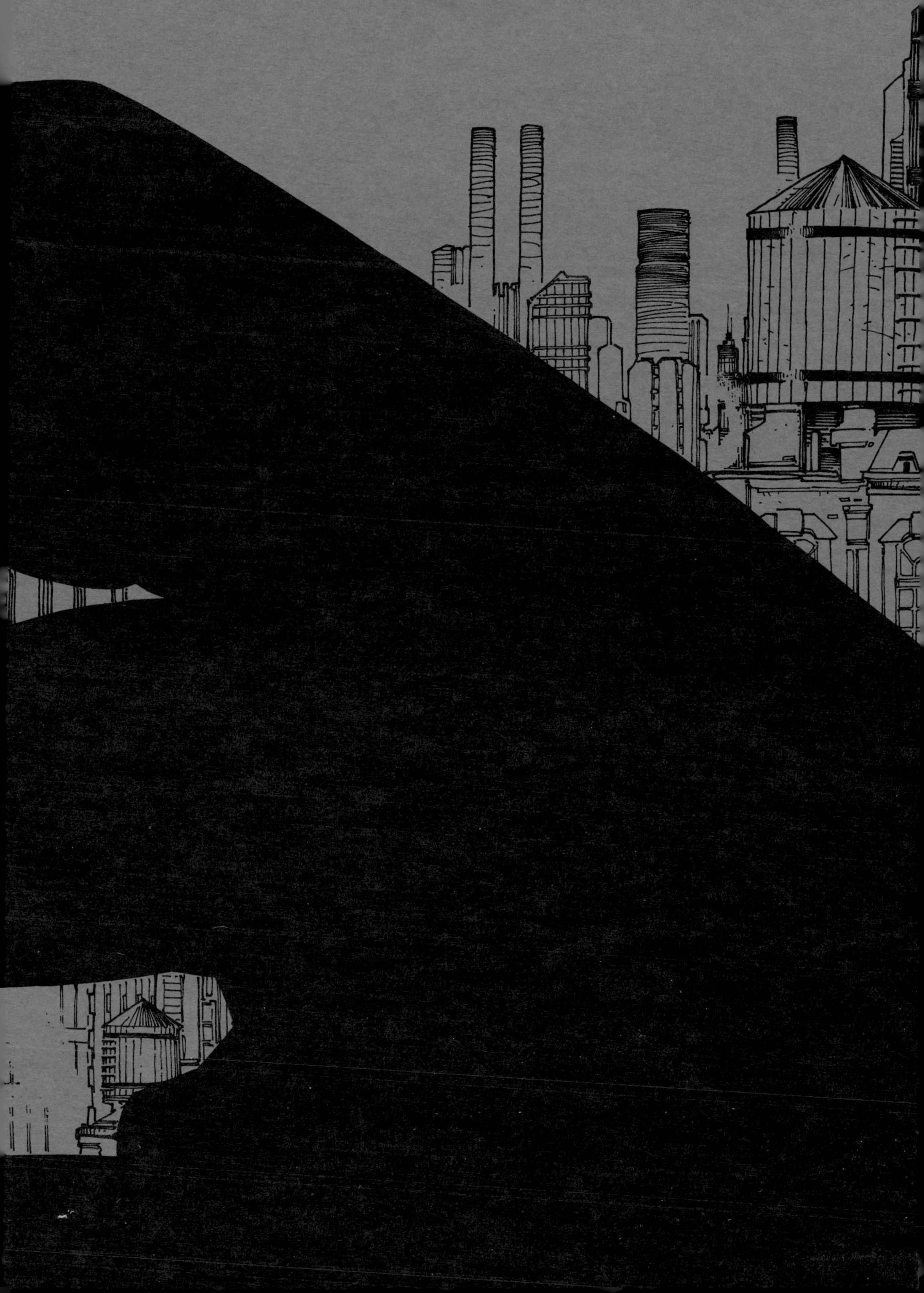

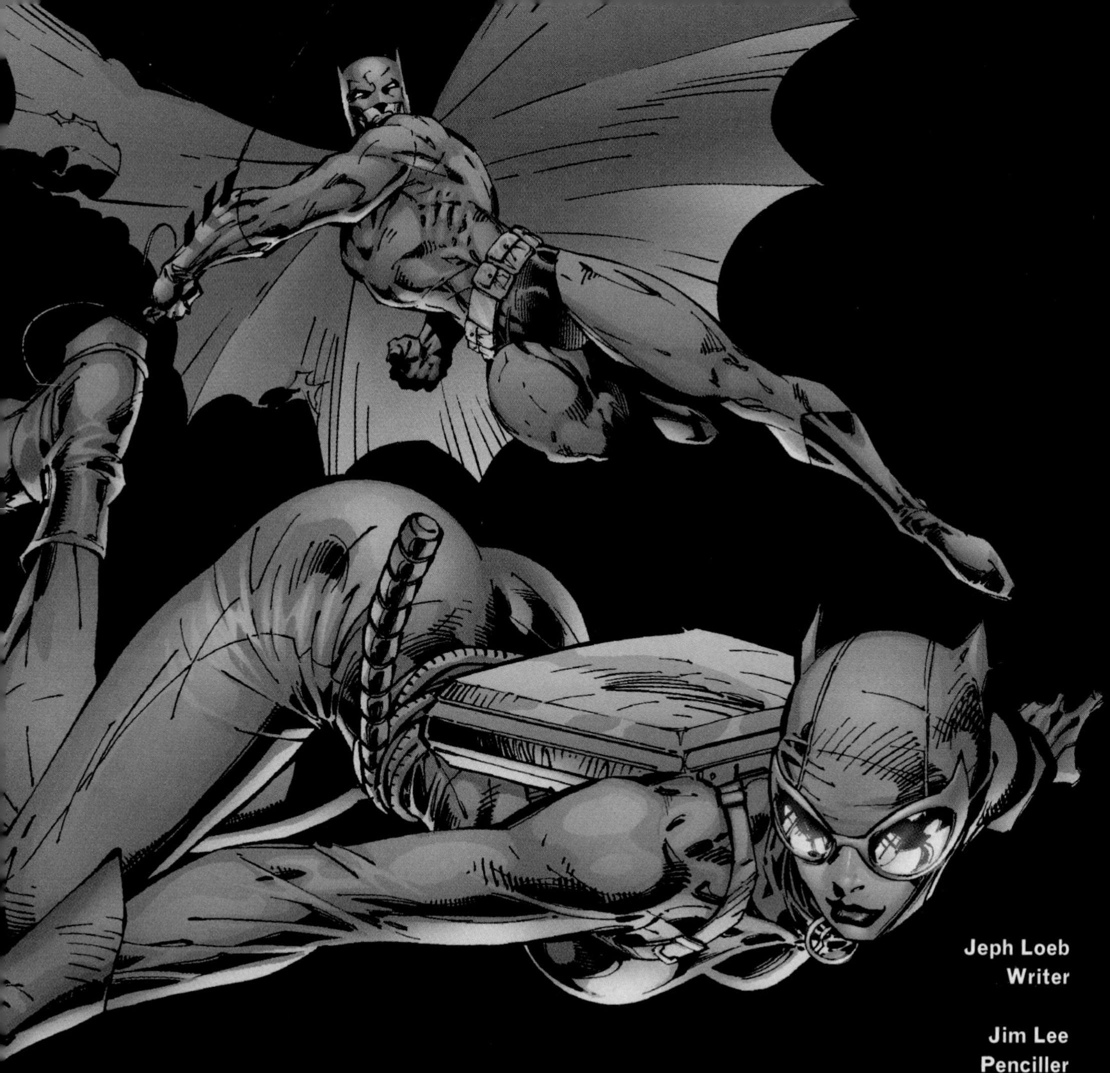

Jeph Loeb
Writer

Jim Lee
Penciller

Scott Williams
Inker

Richard Starkings
Letterer

Alex Sinclair
Colorist

Jim Lee & Scott Williams
Original Series Covers

Batman created by Bob Kane

BATMAN HUSH

VOLUME ONE

Mike Carlin
VP-Executive Editor

Bob Schreck
Editor-Original Series

Bob Greenberger
Senior Editor-Collected Edition

Robbin Brosterman
Senior Art Director

Paul Levitz
President & Publisher

Georg Brewer
VP-Design & Retail Product Development

Richard Bruning
VP-Creative Director

Patrick Caldon
Senior VP-Finance & Operations

Chris Caramalis
VP-Finance

Terri Cunningham
VP-Managing Editor

Dan DiDio
VP-Editorial

Joel Ehrlich
Senior VP-Advertising & Promotions

Alison Gill
VP-Manufacturing

Lillian Laserson
Senior VP & General Counsel

David McKillips
VP-Advertising

John Nee
VP-Business Development

Cheryl Rubin
VP-Licensing & Merchandising

Bob Wayne
VP-Sales & Marketing

BATMAN: HUSH VOLUME ONE

DC Comics
1700 Broadway
New York, NY 10019

A division of Warner Bros. -
An AOL Time Warner Company
Printed in Canada.
First Printing.

Hardcover ISBN: 1 4012 0061 3
Softcover ISBN: 1 4012 0060 5

Cover Illustration by Jim Lee
and Scott Williams.
Cover color by Alex Sinclair.

When I was a little boy my family would get together in my father's den every Wednesday and Thursday night at 7:30 pm to watch a new television show called *Batman*. Twice a week, Adam West and Burt Ward would BIFF! BAM! and POW! with some of Hollywood's most notables playing The Joker, The Riddler, etc. While I'd like to lay claim to remembering best Julie Newmar's sleek cat outfit as my strongest memory, it only ranks a close second. My most vivid memory was actually of my father's backside blocking the television. You see, *Batman* had a very distinct message at the bottom of the screen below the logo: IN COLOR. My father had purchased a brand-new RCA color television and spent most of the show getting up and adjusting the reds and greens (it was a very colorful show) in order to get it, as he would say, "Just right." It didn't matter that the rest of us couldn't actually tell the difference each time he got up and twisted some knob; for my Dad there was a world of difference.

What does all this have to do with HUSH? Glad you asked. On a bright and sunny California afternoon, in the parking lot of the Warner Bros. studio, I met with Mark Chiarello (DC's Editorial Art Director), who had traveled out from the not so bright or sunny New York City to see if I would be interested in writing BATMAN on a monthly basis. Mark had the good (mis)fortune of being my editor on BATMAN: DARK VICTORY, the follow-up to my other Batman opus BATMAN: THE LONG HALLOWEEN, and despite having lived through that experience still wanted to gauge my interest.

JUST RIGHT

INTRODUCTION BY JEPH LOEB

Before I answered, I asked (as I always do) the most important question any comic-book writer can ask before he takes an assignment. I don't care if you grew up reading every issue of *The Adventures of Pow Wow Jones* and this is your only chance to prove to the world that you and Pow Wow were made for each other, you have to ask:

"Who's going to draw it?"

Because, my friends, no matter how good a comic-book story is, it is still a visual medium. We don't write short stories, or novels, or poetry for that matter. We write stories that someone has to draw. And if you find yourself stuck with the unlucky reality of having someone draw your story that doesn't suit what you've got in your head, it's a little like trying to listen to a song you wrote for a piano played on a tuba. It's your song all right, it just doesn't sound ... well... "Just right."

I had a pretty good ace in the hole when I asked. I had only worked on Batman with Tim Sale, who is something of a master illustrator and has made me look better than I am on more than a few occasions. Mark knew Tim was busy. Who could Chiarello possibly come up with who was going to match my ace?

"Jim Lee."

The guy who, at a very young age, sold more copies of a single comic book than anyone else in history. (A record he still holds today — at about 8 million).

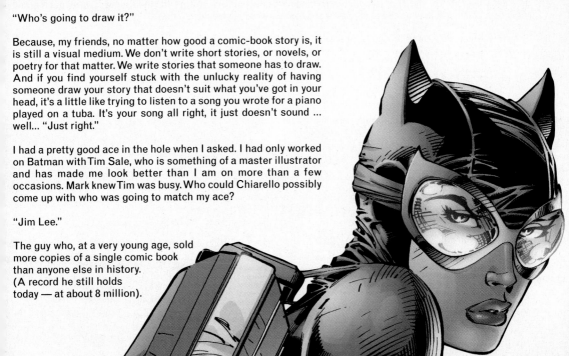

I gulped. If I had the Ace of Hearts, Mark threw down the Ace of Diamonds. Now, we can sit here until tomorrow morning and argue who was better — Michelangelo or da Vinci, but let's save the time and accept that they are both great artists. Different but, no question about it, brilliant. That's how I feel about Tim and Jim.

So, I did what any writer would do without asking how much the job paid. I said "Yes."

Now I had a bigger problem. What story was I going to tell? The greatest challenge a comic-book writer faces is making sure that the story suits the artist's strengths. (Don't forget about that tuba!). Tim and I had only told stories that took place in the mythical "Year One." This is where Batman is starting out and has no Robin or Nightwing or Oracle as part of his cadre. He makes mistakes because he's learning his detective craft, and he has an uneasy alliance with the Gotham City police force.

Jim and I were going to be working in the "Present Day" continuity of Batman. The Dark Knight's at the top of his game now, having inspired a Robin or three, Nightwing, two Batgirls, and an Oracle. Kind of like the dozens of artists who followed Jim's spectacular rocket to comic-book stardom. Gotham City is now his to protect, and he does a damn fine job of it. Kind of like the comic-book industry as a whole, and the contribution Jim has made to it as both a creator and a publisher. The trick is, when you're that good, you need a bigger challenge. Kind of like... Jim.

Where Tim works well in the shadows and ink, Jim demands that you see it all. The magic is in the details. What glorious details! Backgrounds and Batmobiles and babes! Catwoman! Poison Ivy! And... a certain Man of Steel!

I'll let you in on a little secret. No, it's not who or what is the mysterious person in the bandages who seems to have something to do with Batman's plight. This is better. Jim doesn't do his wizardry alone. Nope. He has help.

Scott Williams has inked Jim for longer than either of them likes to admit. If Jim ever needed another arm, it's Scott. Jim's pencils are good, mind you, but Scott has a way of making them glimmer. Scott is more than an inker — he's a partner and advisor. When I've asked if something looks "Just right," we've often deferred to Scott.

He just knows, um... righter.

That only gets us to the black and white of it all. Jim's handpicked colorist is Alex Sinclair. The result is the spectacular vibrancy of color you'll see throughout these chapters. If comics have made a single gigantic leap in the last sixty-odd years, it's in the area of color. Look inside and see what Alex has created!

In fairness to Jim, I can't do anything with my story without help as well. My advisor and "partner in words" is Richard Starkings, who, along with Wes Abbott, has lettered these chapters with such style that even the offbeat notes sound like sweet harmony. As you read the story, take a moment to look at the words themselves. That's Richard's gift.

None of this is possible without the amazing Bat-editorial staff, led by Morgan Dontanville and the Keeper of The Cave, Bob Schreck.

Here's the best part of all. What you hold in your hand is only part of the story. It's the first arc. We've got a grand adventure planned following these chapters and look forward to seeing you there.

Hopefully, when you've read this collection you'll sit back and relax and say to yourself, "Yep, they got it just right."

— Jeph Loeb
New Year's Day, 2003
Los Angeles, California

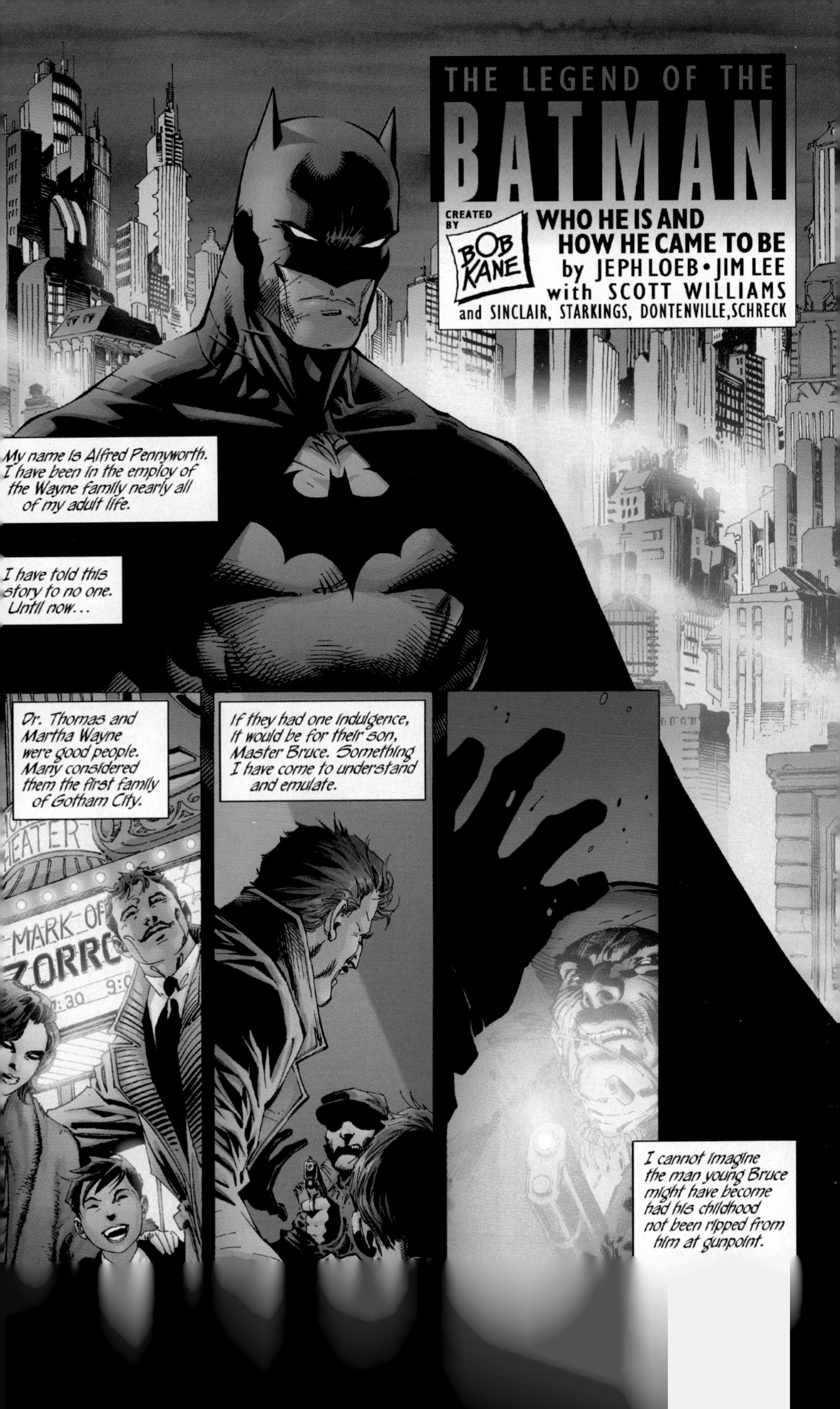

THE LEGEND OF THE
BATMAN
CREATED BY BOB KANE
WHO HE IS AND HOW HE CAME TO BE
by JEPH LOEB • JIM LEE
with SCOTT WILLIAMS
and SINCLAIR, STARKINGS, DONTENVILLE, SCHRECK
My name is Alfred Pennyworth. I have been in the employ of the Wayne family nearly all of my adult life.
I have told this story to no one. Until now...
Dr. Thomas and Martha Wayne were good people. Many considered them the first family of Gotham City.
THEATER
MARK OF ZORRO
If they had one indulgence, it would be for their son, Master Bruce. Something I have come to understand and emulate.
I cannot imagine the man young Bruce might have become had his childhood not been ripped from him at gunpoint.

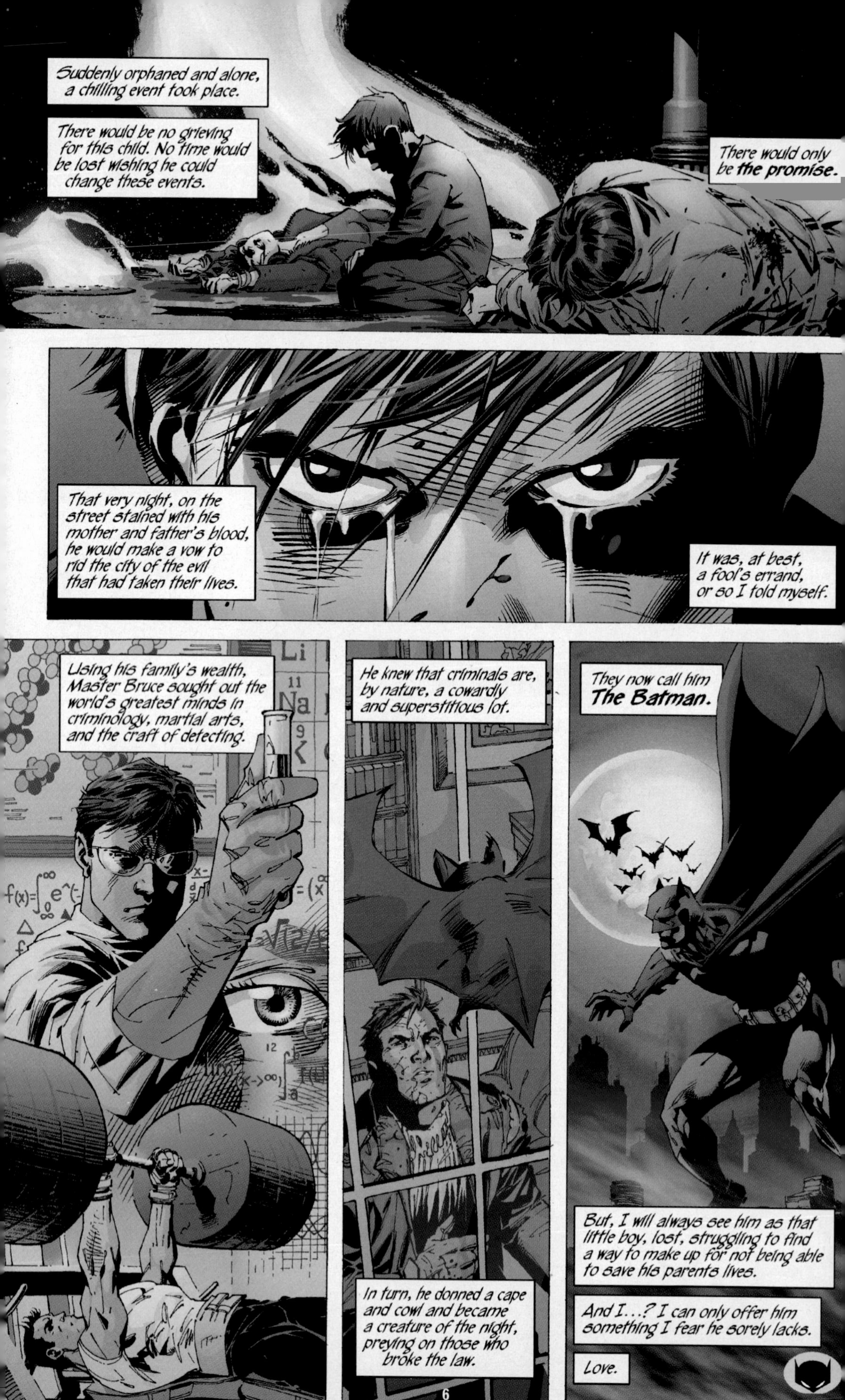

Suddenly orphaned and alone, a chilling event took place.
There would be no grieving for this child. No time would be lost wishing he could change these events.
There would only be **the promise.**
That very night, on the street stained with his mother and father's blood, he would make a vow to rid the city of the evil that had taken their lives.
It was, at best, a fool's errand, or so I told myself.
Using his family's wealth, Master Bruce sought out the world's greatest minds in criminology, martial arts, and the craft of detecting.
He knew that criminals are, by nature, a cowardly and superstitious lot.
In turn, he donned a cape and cowl and became a creature of the night, preying on those who broke the law.
They now call him **The Batman.**
But, I will always see him as that little boy, lost, struggling to find a way to make up for not being able to save his parents lives.
And I...? I can only offer him something I fear he sorely lacks.
Love.

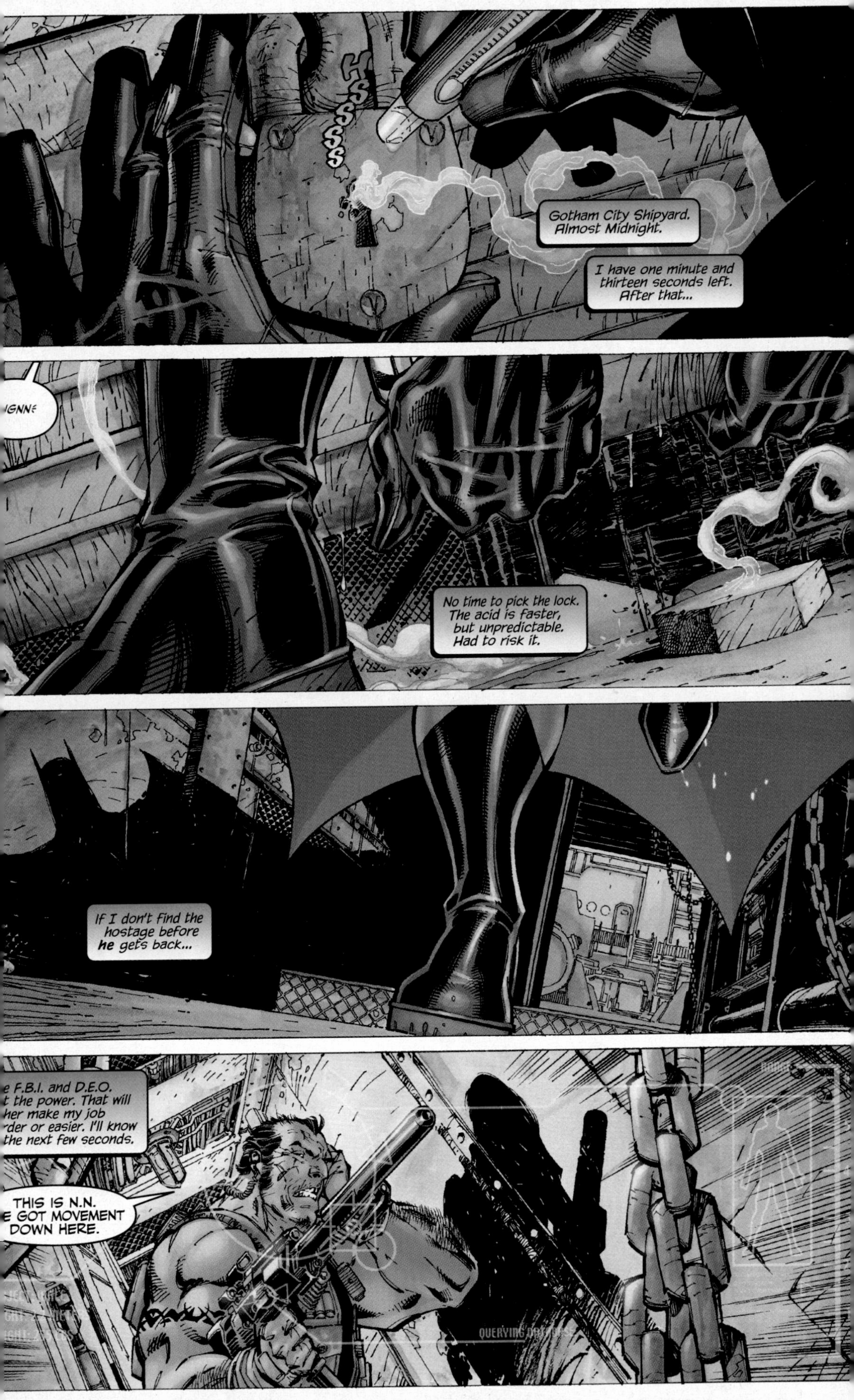
HSSSSS
Gotham City Shipyard. Almost Midnight.
I have one minute and thirteen seconds left. After that...
No time to pick the lock. The acid is faster, but unpredictable. Had to risk it.
If I don't find the hostage before **he** gets back...
e F.B.I. and D.E.O. t the power. That will her make my job rder or easier. I'll know the next few seconds.
THIS IS N.N. E GOT MOVEMENT DOWN HERE.

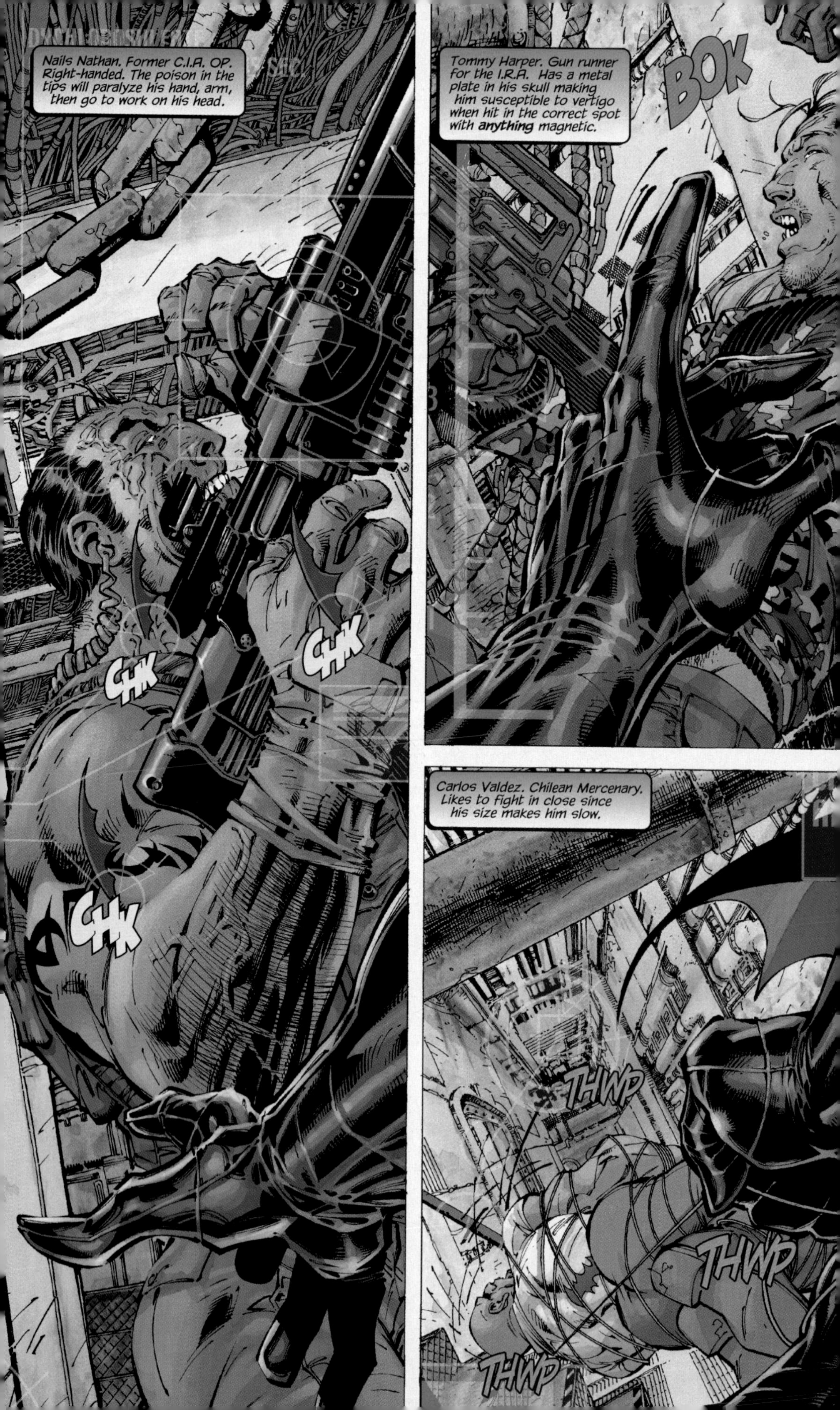
Nails Nathan. Former C.I.A. OP. Right-handed. The poison in the tips will paralyze his hand, arm, then go to work on his head.
CHK
CHK
CHK
Tommy Harper. Gun runner for the I.R.A. Has a metal plate in his skull making him susceptible to vertigo when hit in the correct spot with **anything** magnetic.
BOK
Carlos Valdez. Chilean Mercenary. Likes to fight in close since his size makes him slow.
THWP
THWP
THWP

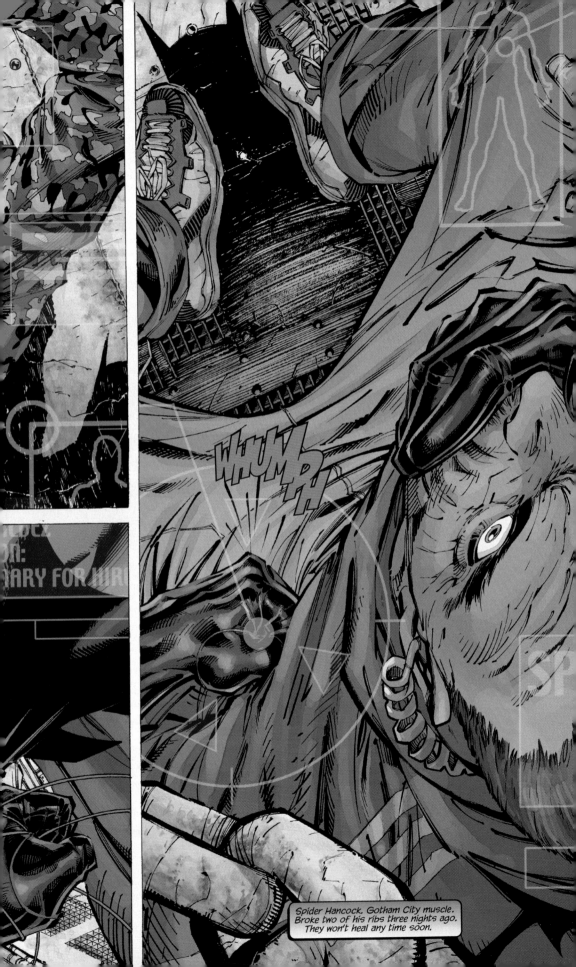

Spider Hancock. Gotham City muscle.
Broke two of his ribs three nights ago.
They won't heal any time soon.

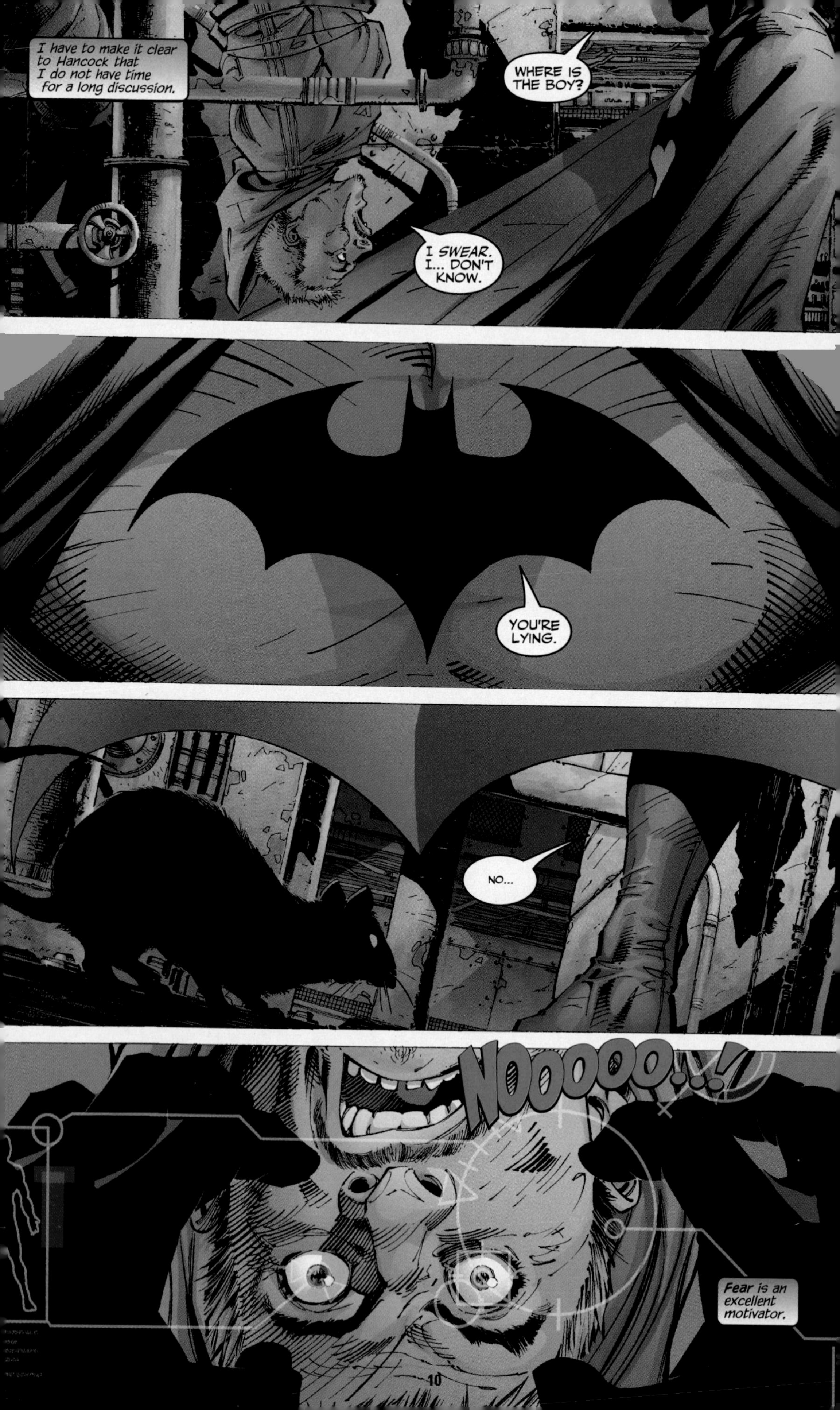

I have to make it clear to Hancock that I do not have time for a long discussion.
WHERE IS THE BOY?
I SWEAR. I... DON'T KNOW.
YOU'RE LYING.
NO...
NOOOOO...!
Fear is an excellent motivator.

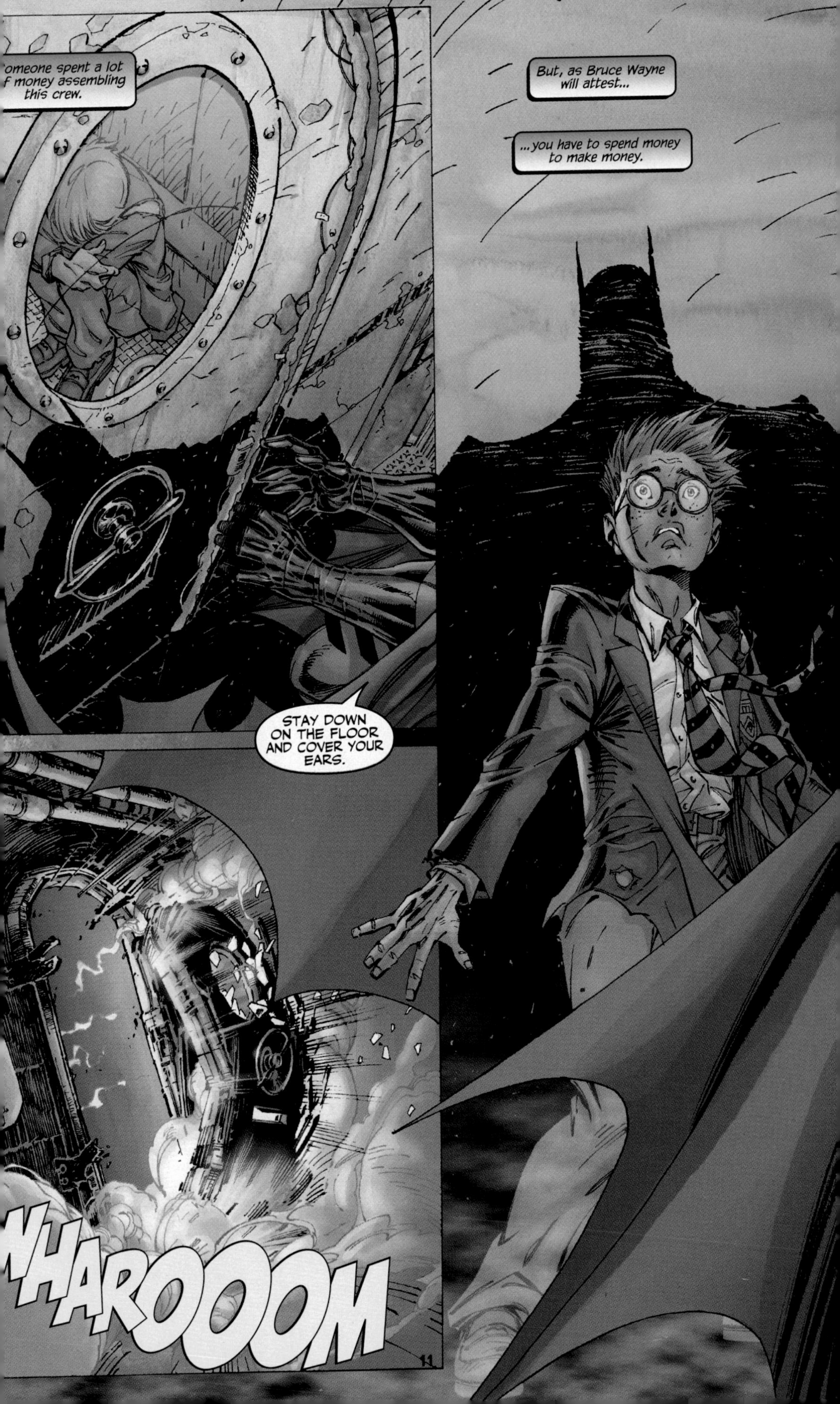
omeone spent a lot
f money assembling
this crew.
STAY DOWN ON THE FLOOR AND COVER YOUR EARS.
HAROOOM
But, as Bruce Wayne will attest...
...you have to spend money to make money.

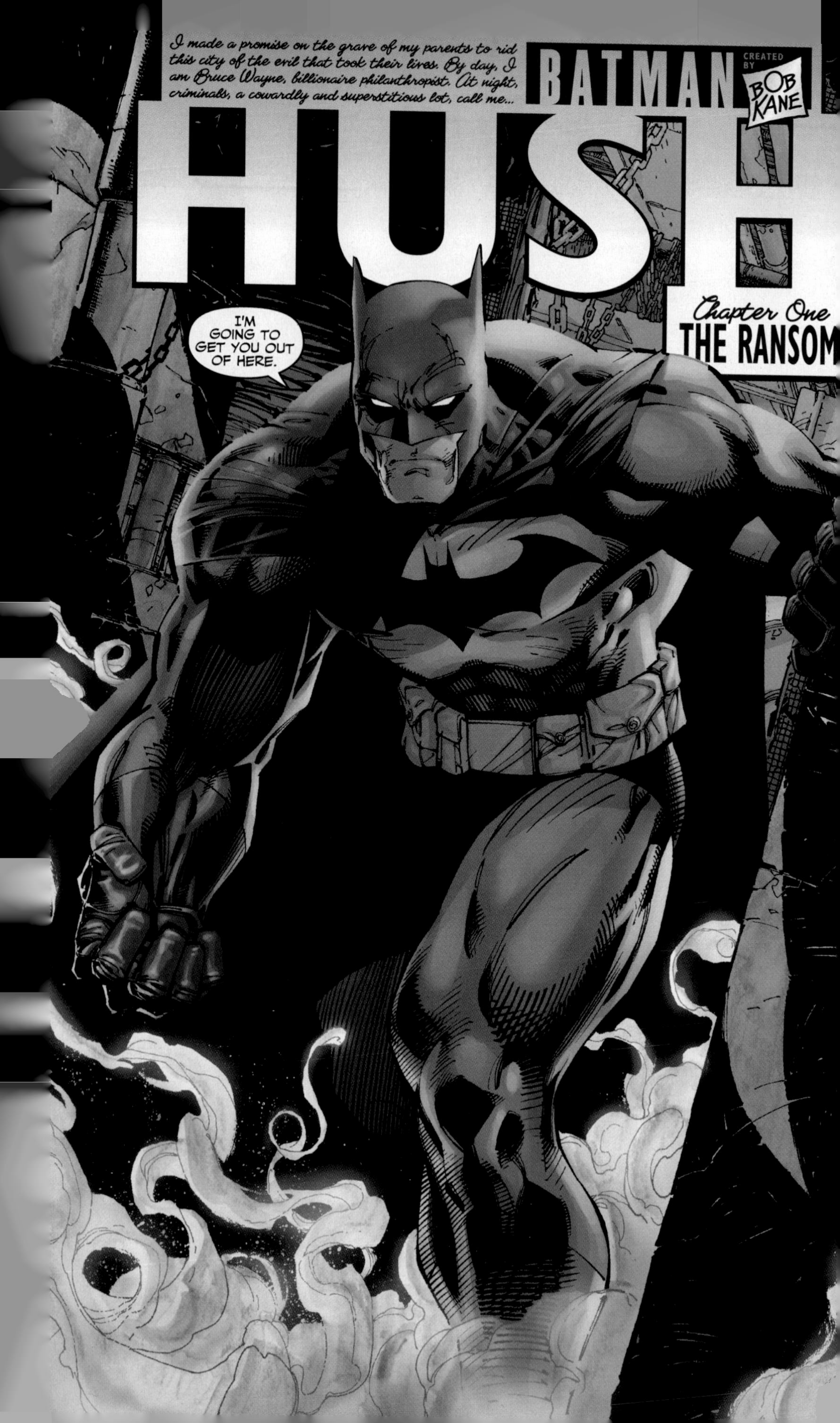
I made a promise on the grave of my parents to rid this city of the evil that took their lives. By day, I am Bruce Wayne, billionaire philanthropist. At night, criminals, a cowardly and superstitious lot, call me...
BATMAN
CREATED BY BOB KANE
HUSH
Chapter One
THE RANSOM
I'M GOING TO GET YOU OUT OF HERE.

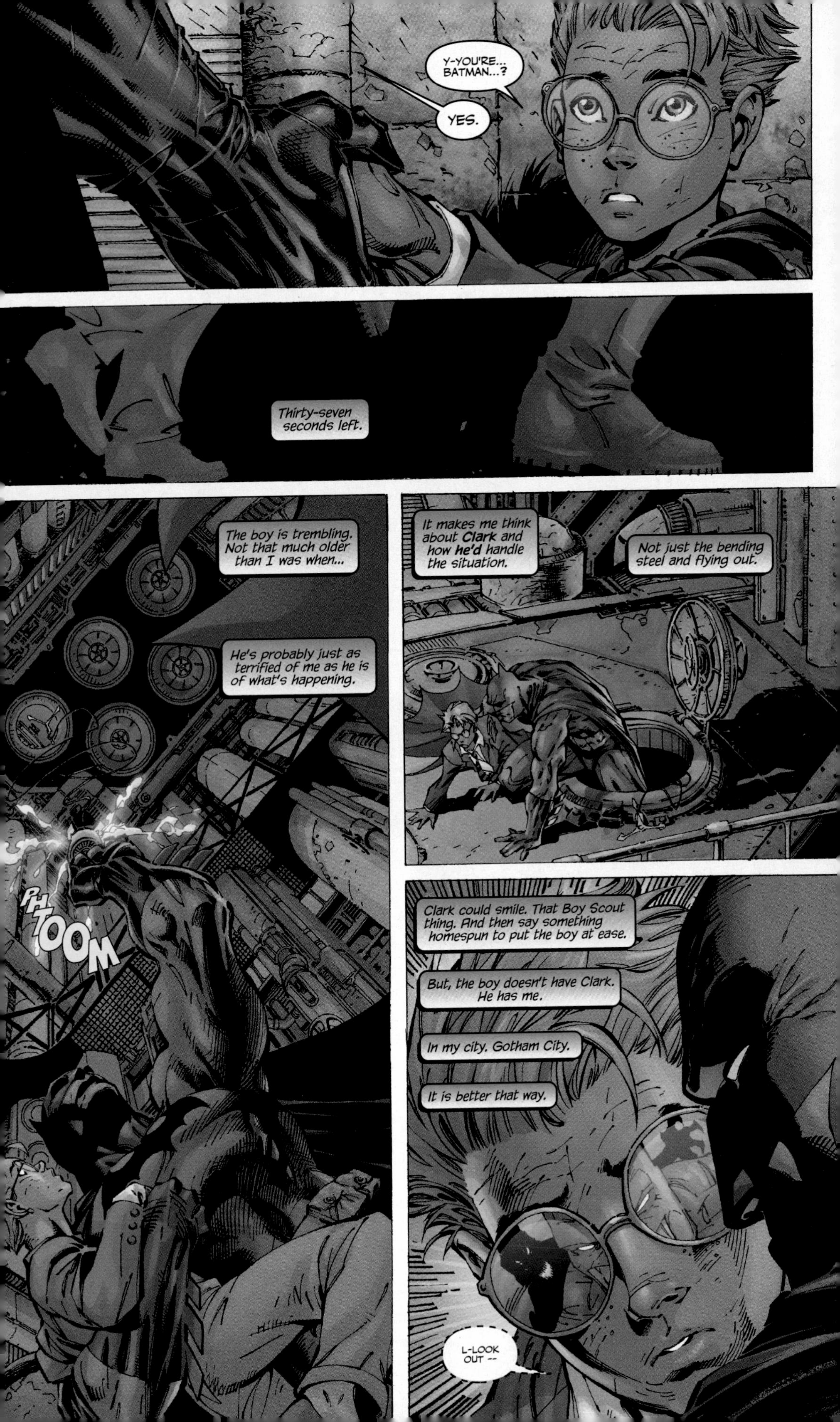
Y-YOU'RE... BATMAN...?
YES.
Thirty-seven seconds left.
The boy is trembling. Not that much older than I was when...
He's probably just as terrified of me as he is of what's happening.
PHTOOM
It makes me think about Clark and how he'd handle the situation.
Not just the bending steel and flying out.
Clark could smile. That Boy Scout thing. And then say something homespun to put the boy at ease.
But, the boy doesn't have Clark. He has me.
In my city. Gotham City.
It is better that way.
L-LOOK OUT --

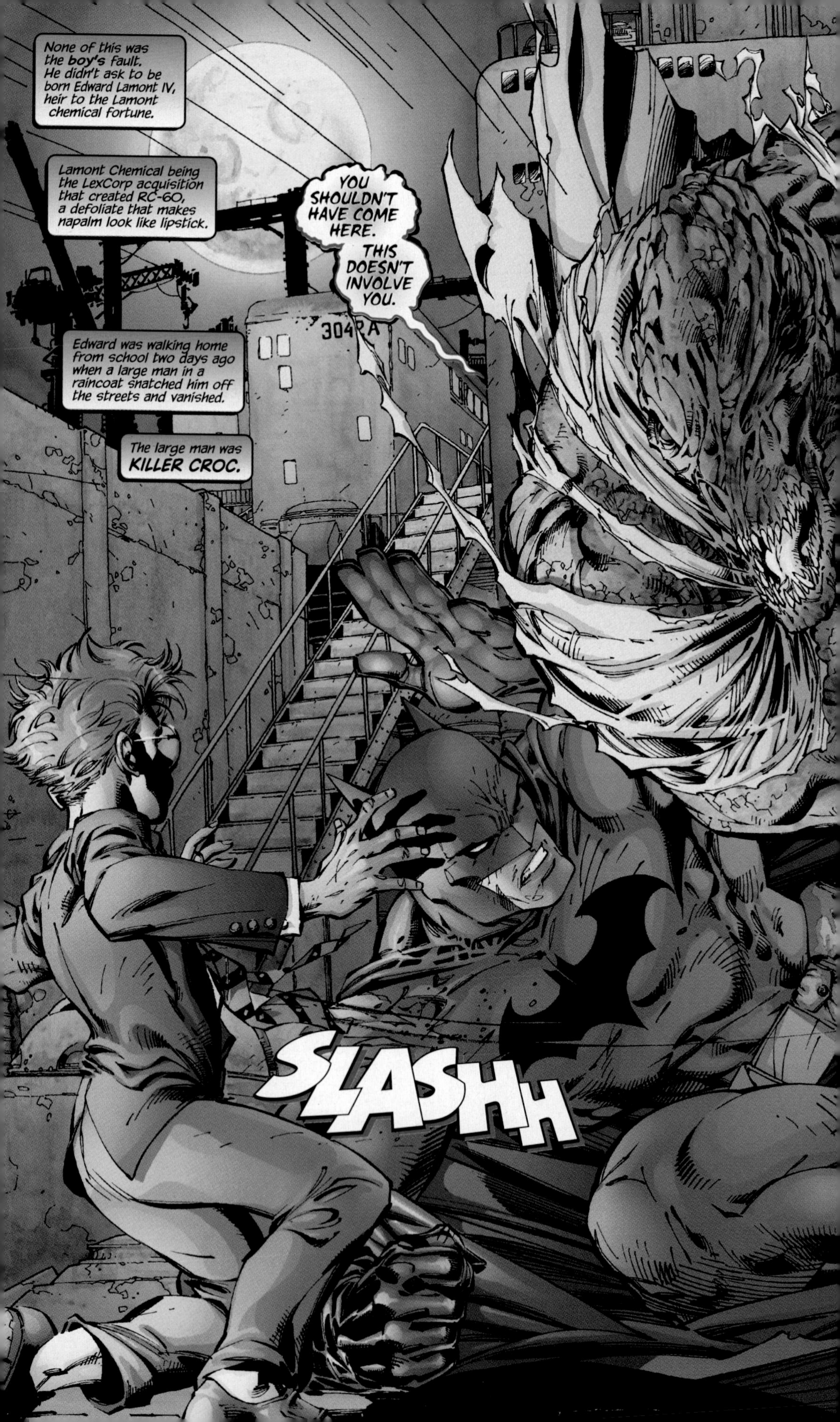

None of this was the boy's fault. He didn't ask to be born Edward Lamont IV, heir to the Lamont chemical fortune.
Lamont Chemical being the LexCorp acquisition that created RC-60, a defoliate that makes napalm look like lipstick.
YOU SHOULDN'T HAVE COME HERE.
THIS DOESN'T INVOLVE YOU.
Edward was walking home from school two days ago when a large man in a raincoat snatched him off the streets and vanished.
The large man was KILLER CROC.
SLASHH

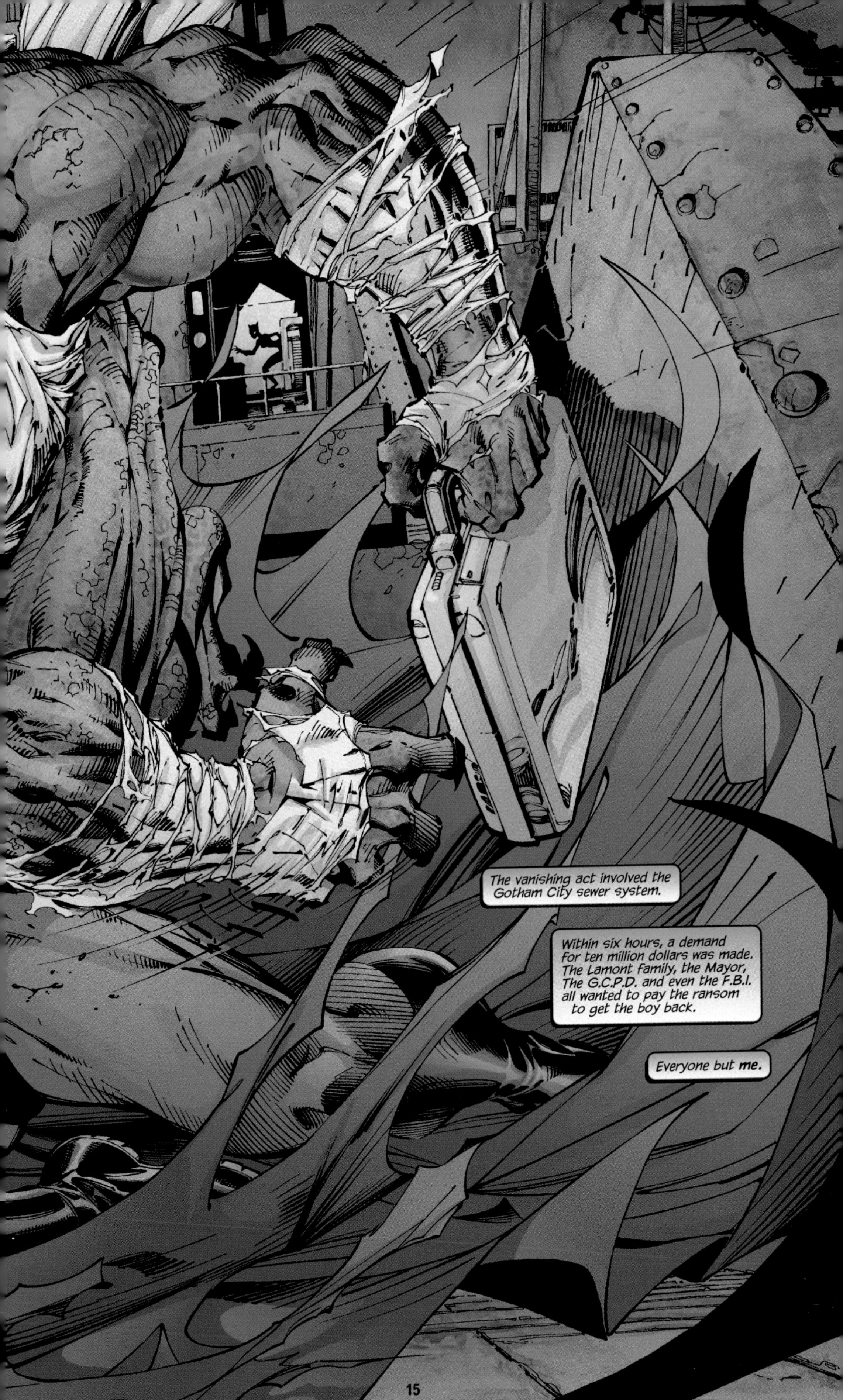
The vanishing act involved the Gotham City sewer system.
Within six hours, a demand for ten million dollars was made. The Lamont family, the Mayor, The G.C.P.D. and even the F.B.I. all wanted to pay the ransom to get the boy back.
Everyone but **me.**

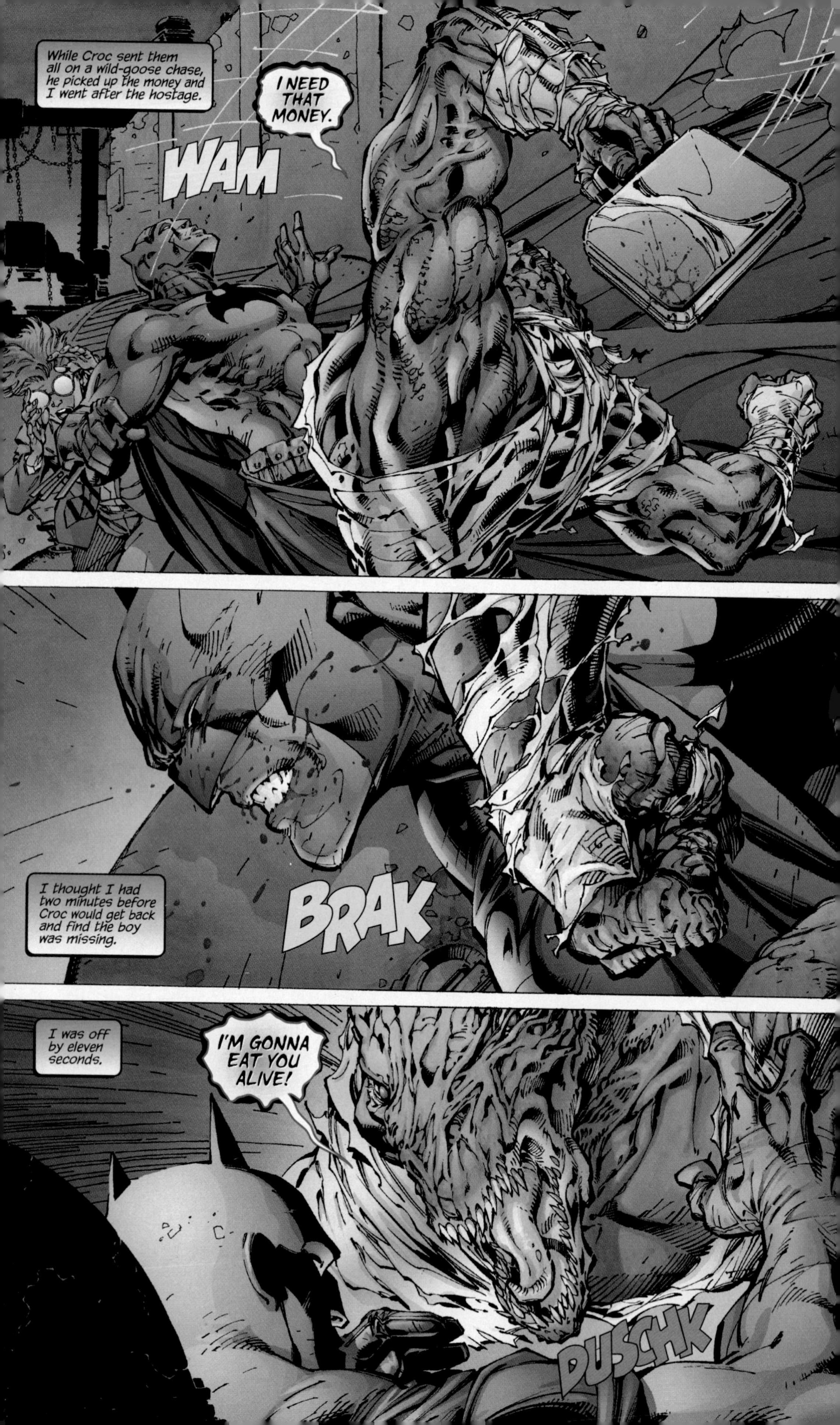

While Croc sent them all on a wild-goose chase, he picked up the money and I went after the hostage.
I NEED THAT MONEY.
WAM
I thought I had two minutes before Croc would get back and find the boy was missing.
BRAK
I was off by eleven seconds.
I'M GONNA EAT YOU ALIVE!
DUSCHK

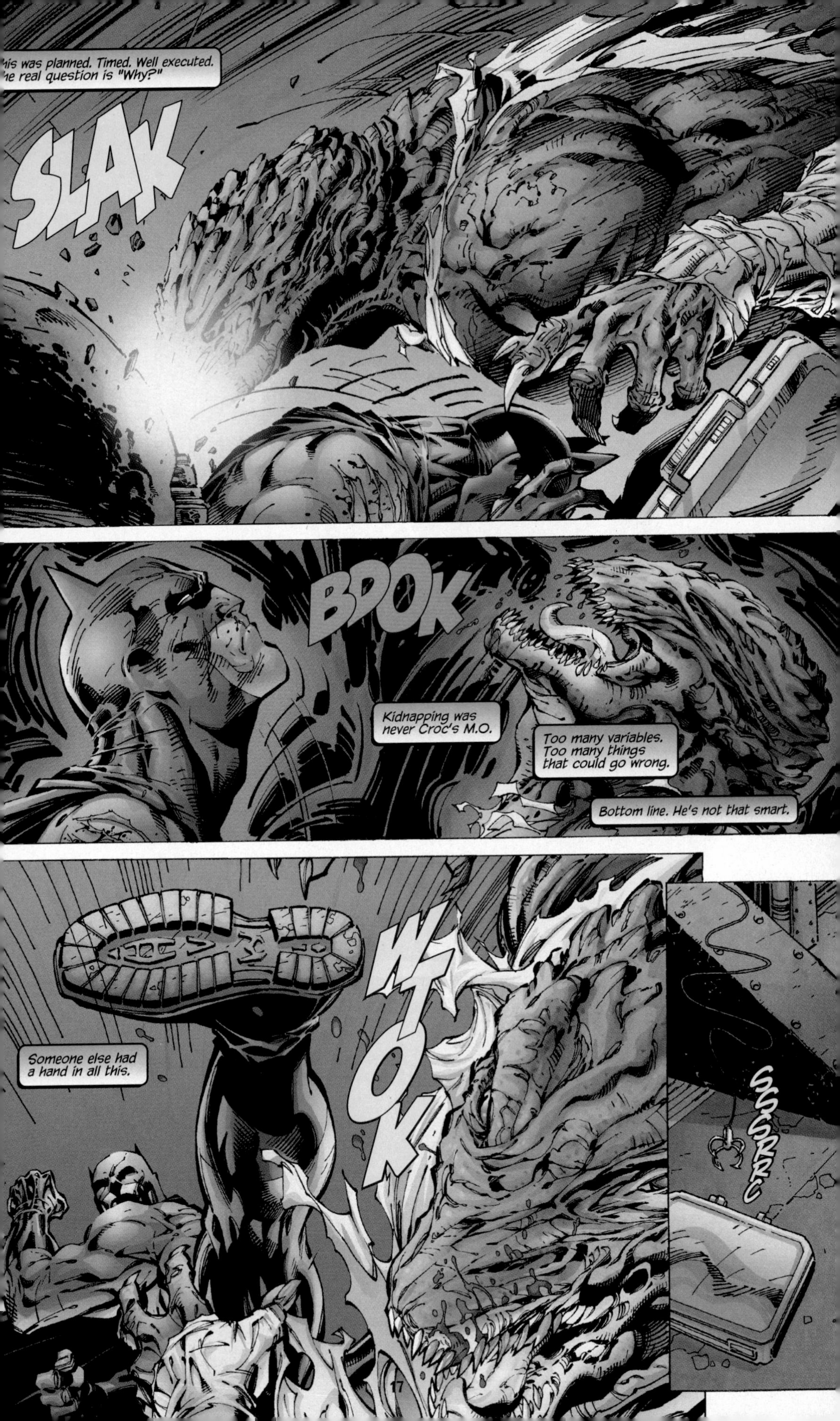
his was planned. Timed. Well executed.
he real question is "Why?"
SLAK
BDOK
Kidnapping was never Croc's M.O.
Too many variables. Too many things that could go wrong.
Bottom line. He's not that smart.
WTOK
Someone else had a hand in all this.
SCGRRRC

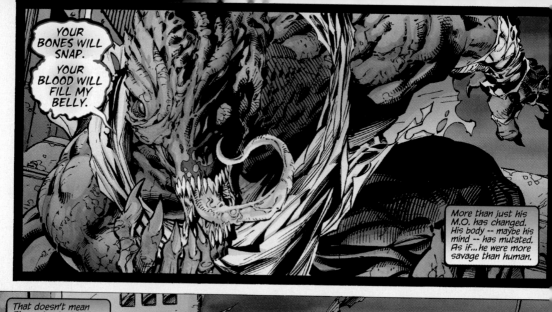

YOUR BONES WILL SNAP. YOUR BLOOD WILL FILL MY BELLY.

More than just his M.O. has changed. His body -- maybe his mind -- has mutated. As if...he were more savage than human.

That doesn't mean I'm going to let him beat the pulp out of me.

RARRR

KRACSH

What Croc has in strength and speed, he lacks in other areas.

And a vulnerability to hypersonics.

FAP

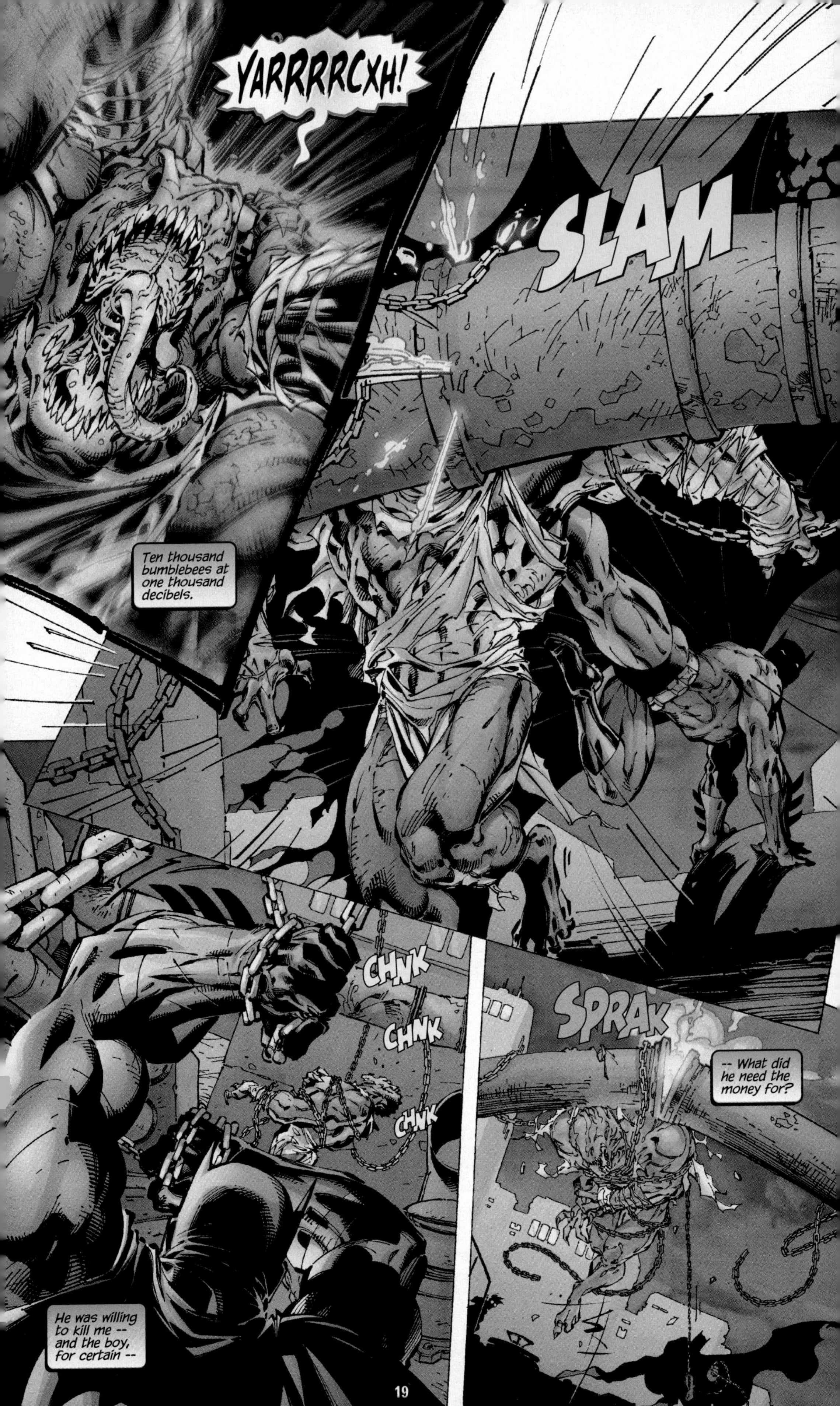
YARRRRCXH!
SLAM
Ten thousand bumblebees at one thousand decibels.
He was willing to kill me -- and the boy, for certain --
CHNK
CHNK
CHNK
SPRAK
-- What did he need the money for?

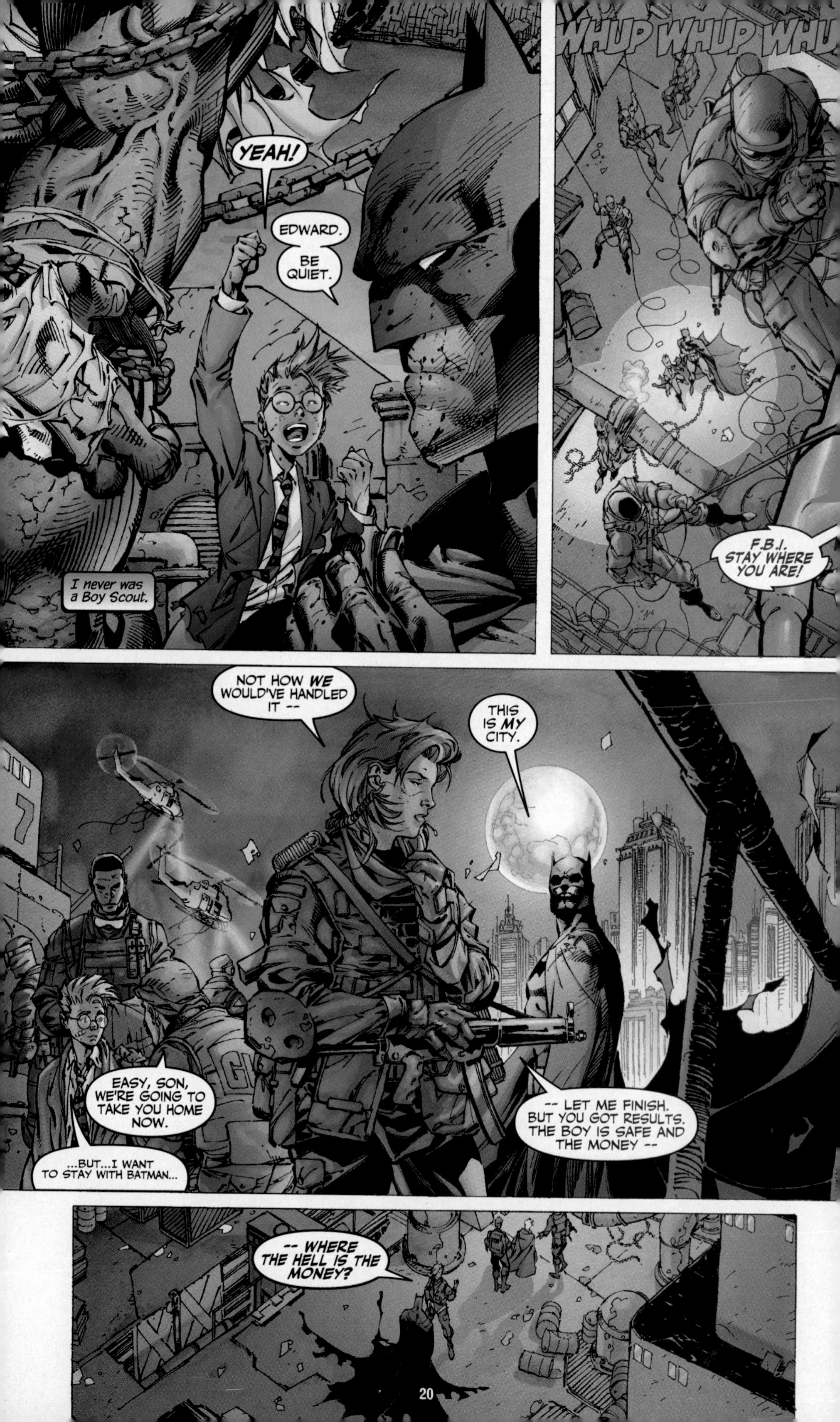

YEAH!
EDWARD.
BE QUIET.
I never was a Boy Scout.
WHUP WHUP WHU
F.B.I. STAY WHERE YOU ARE!
NOT HOW WE WOULD'VE HANDLED IT --
THIS IS MY CITY.
-- LET ME FINISH. BUT YOU GOT RESULTS. THE BOY IS SAFE AND THE MONEY --
EASY, SON, WE'RE GOING TO TAKE YOU HOME NOW.
...BUT...I WANT TO STAY WITH BATMAN...
-- WHERE THE HELL IS THE MONEY?

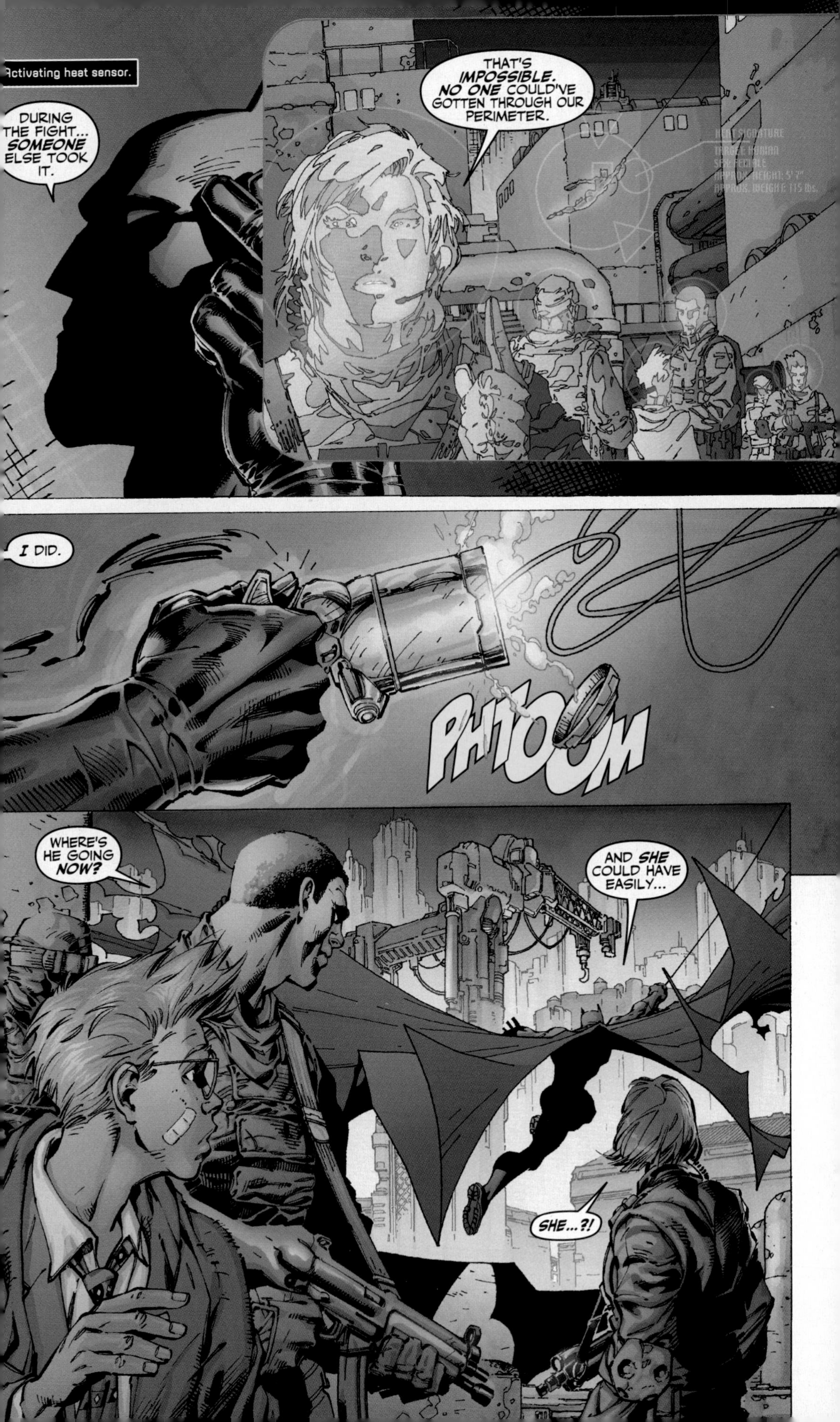
Activating heat sensor.
DURING THE FIGHT... SOMEONE ELSE TOOK IT.
THAT'S IMPOSSIBLE. NO ONE COULD'VE GOTTEN THROUGH OUR PERIMETER.
I DID.
PHTOOM
WHERE'S HE GOING NOW?
AND SHE COULD HAVE EASILY...
SHE...?!

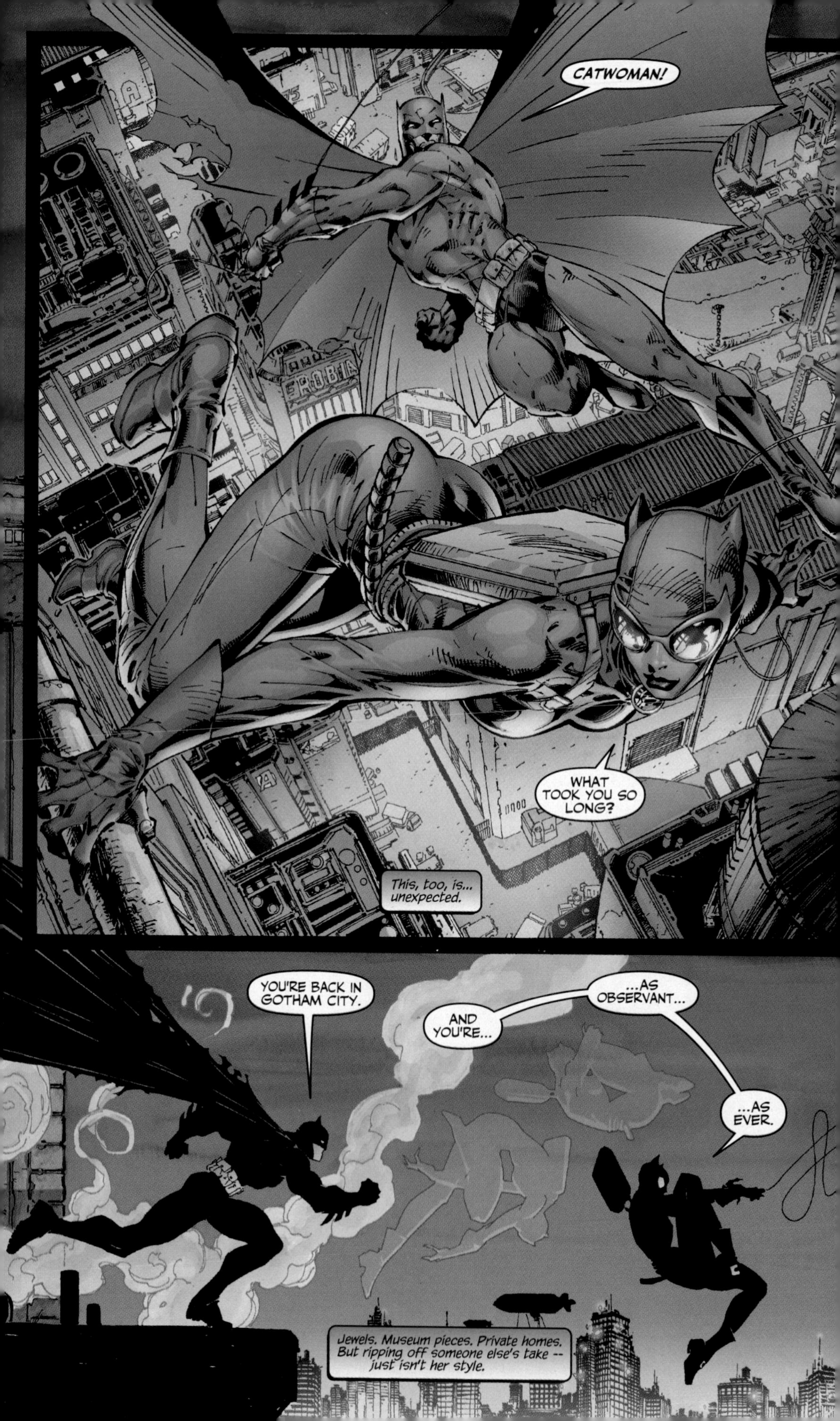
CATWOMAN!
WHAT TOOK YOU SO LONG?
This, too, is... unexpected.
YOU'RE BACK IN GOTHAM CITY.
AND YOU'RE...
...AS OBSERVANT...
...AS EVER.
Jewels. Museum pieces. Private homes. But ripping off someone else's take -- just isn't her style.

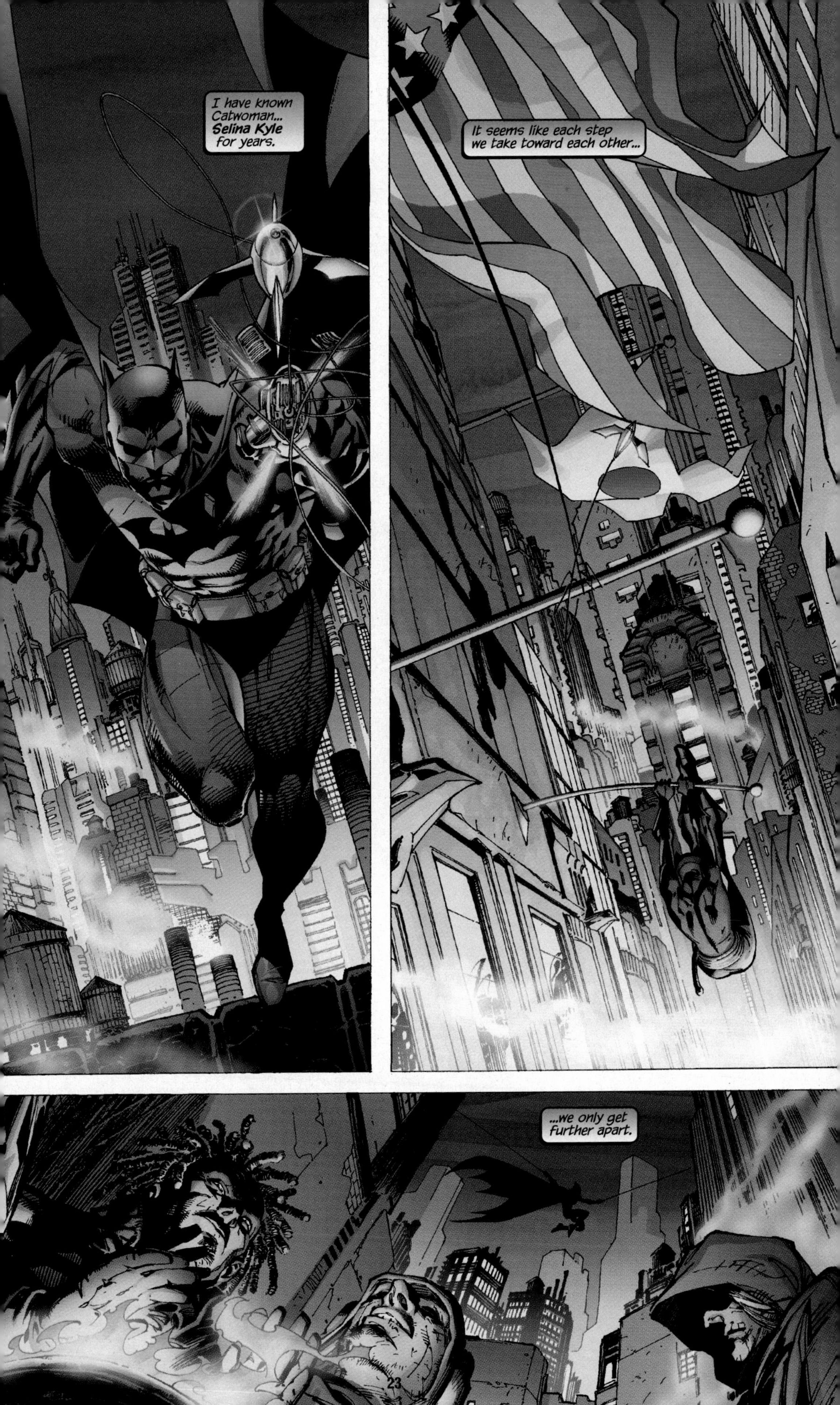
I have known Catwoman... Selina Kyle for years.
It seems like each step we take toward each other...
...we only get further apart.

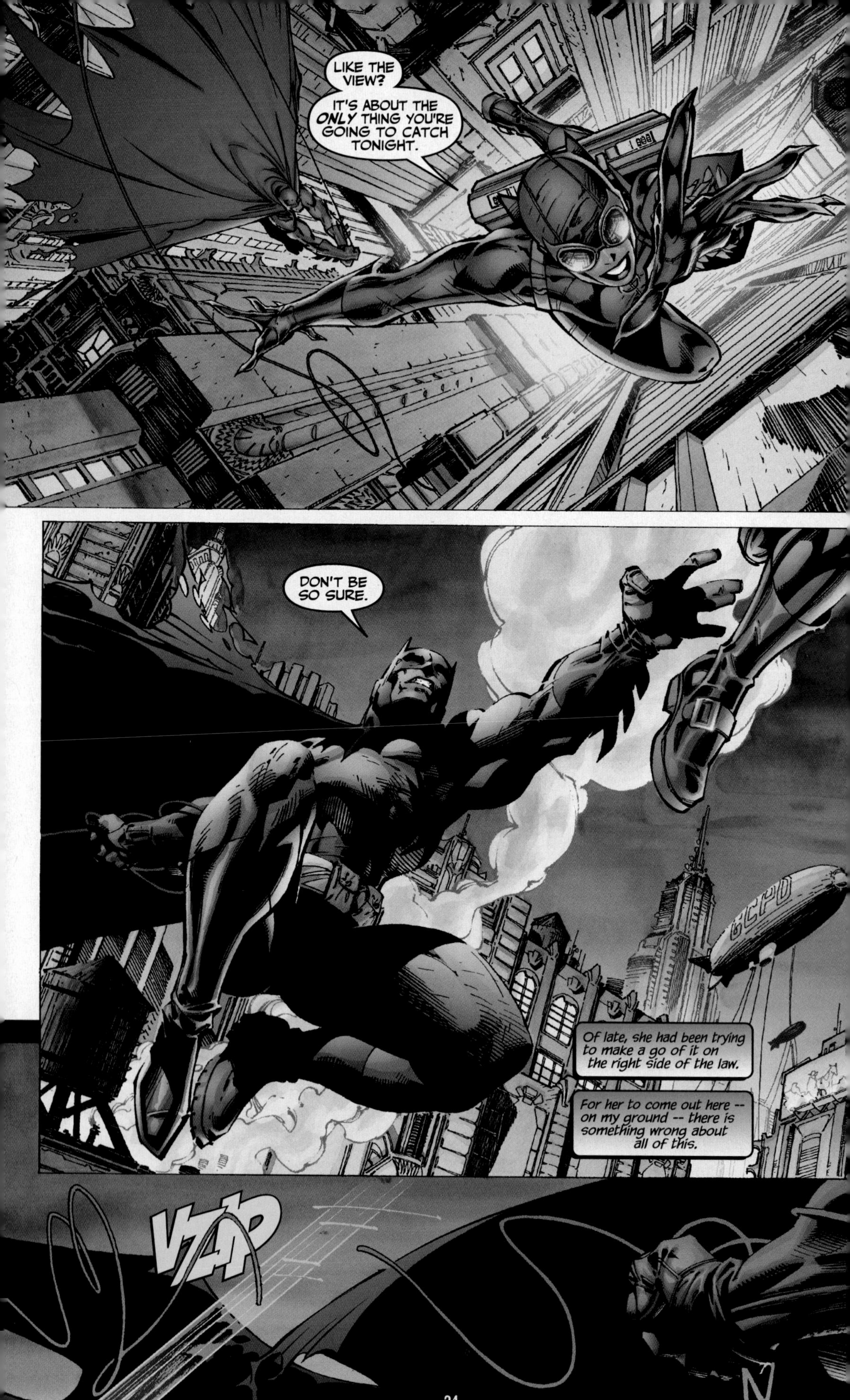
LIKE THE VIEW?
IT'S ABOUT THE ONLY THING YOU'RE GOING TO CATCH TONIGHT.
DON'T BE SO SURE.
Of late, she had been trying to make a go of it on the right side of the law.
For her to come out here -- on my ground -- there is something wrong about all of this.
VZZIP

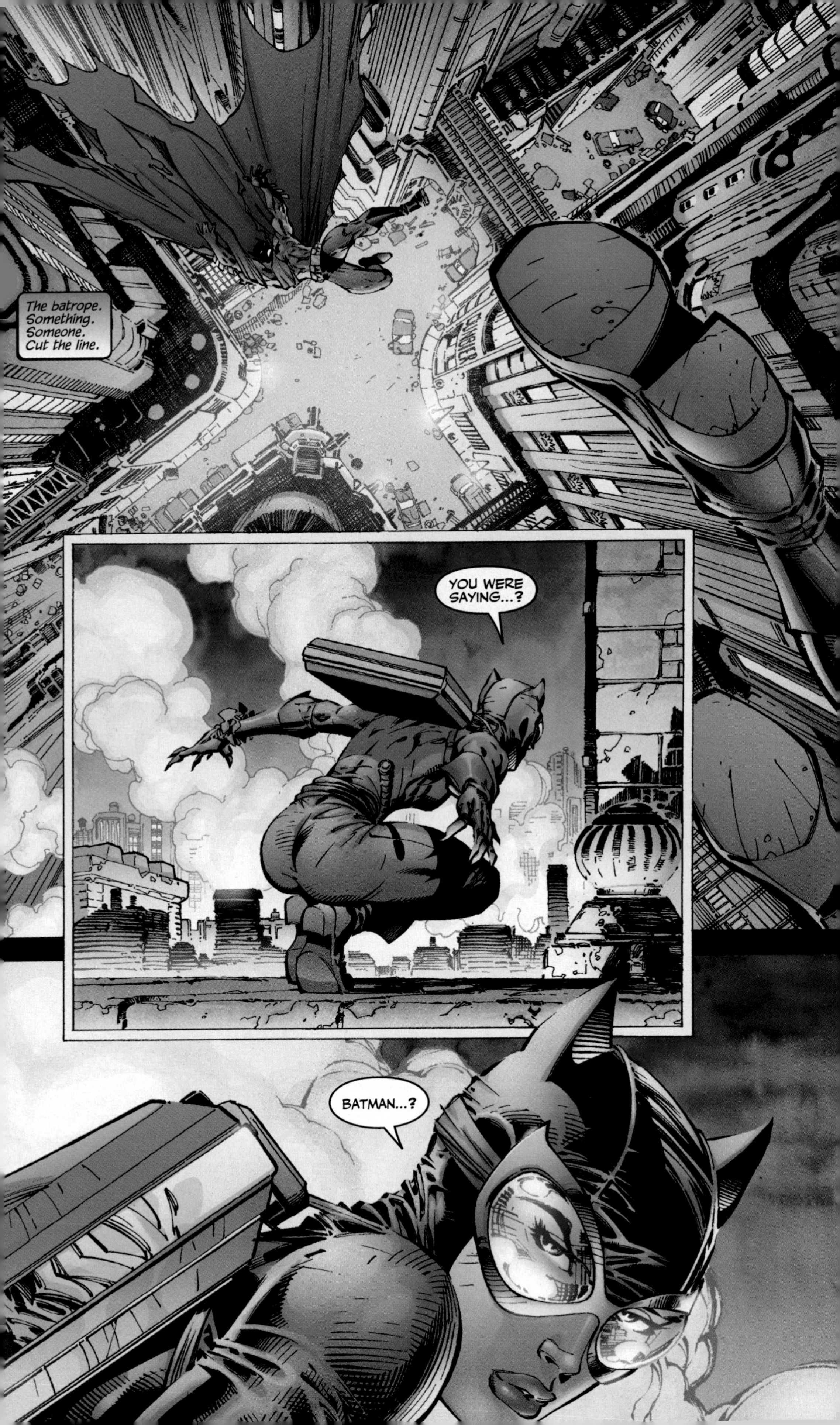
The batrope. Something. Someone. Cut the line.
YOU WERE SAYING...?
BATMAN...?

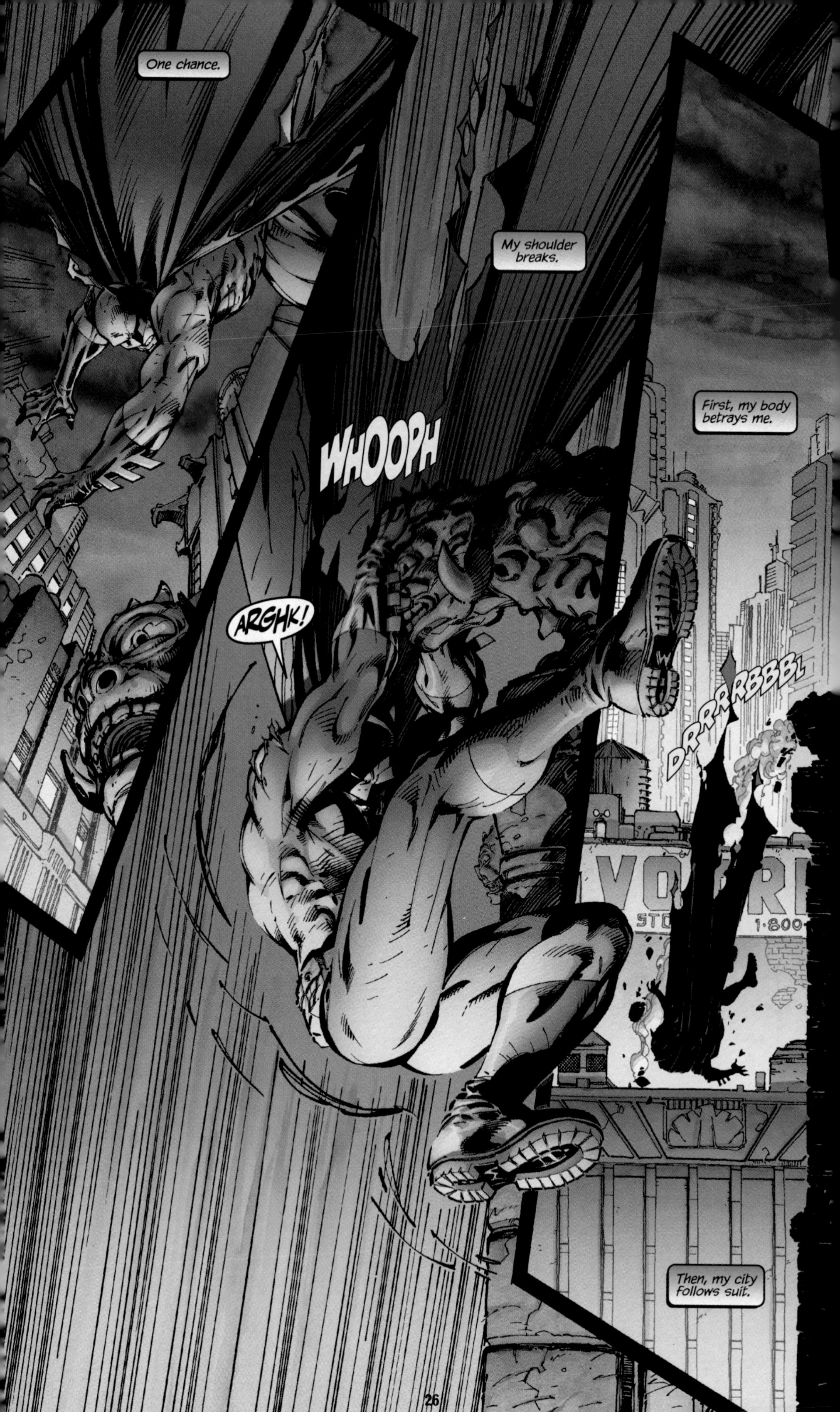
One chance.
My shoulder breaks.
WHOOPH
ARGHK!
First, my body betrays me.
DRRRRRBBBL
Then, my city follows suit.

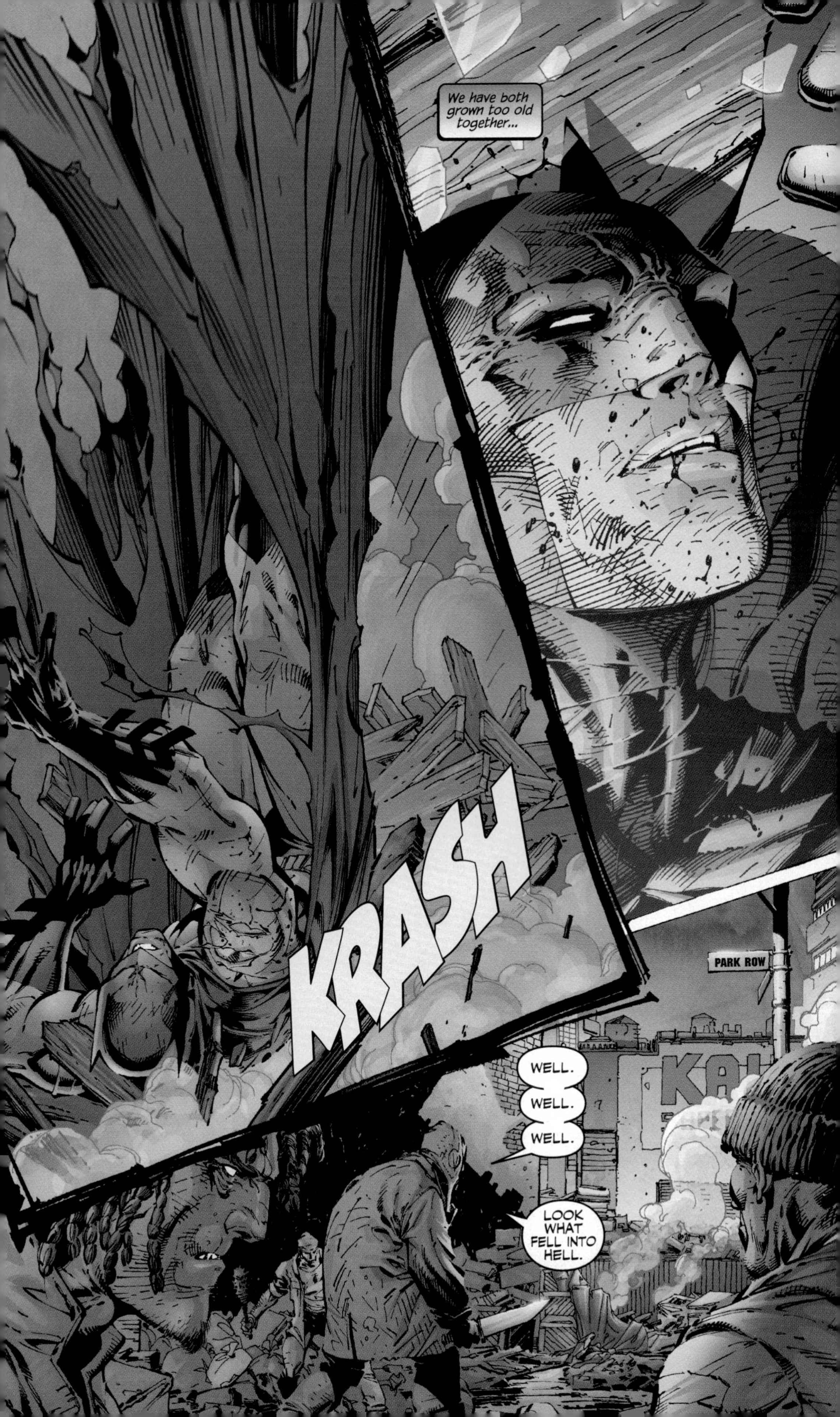
We have both grown too old together...
KRASH
PARK ROW
WELL.
WELL.
WELL.
LOOK WHAT FELL INTO HELL.

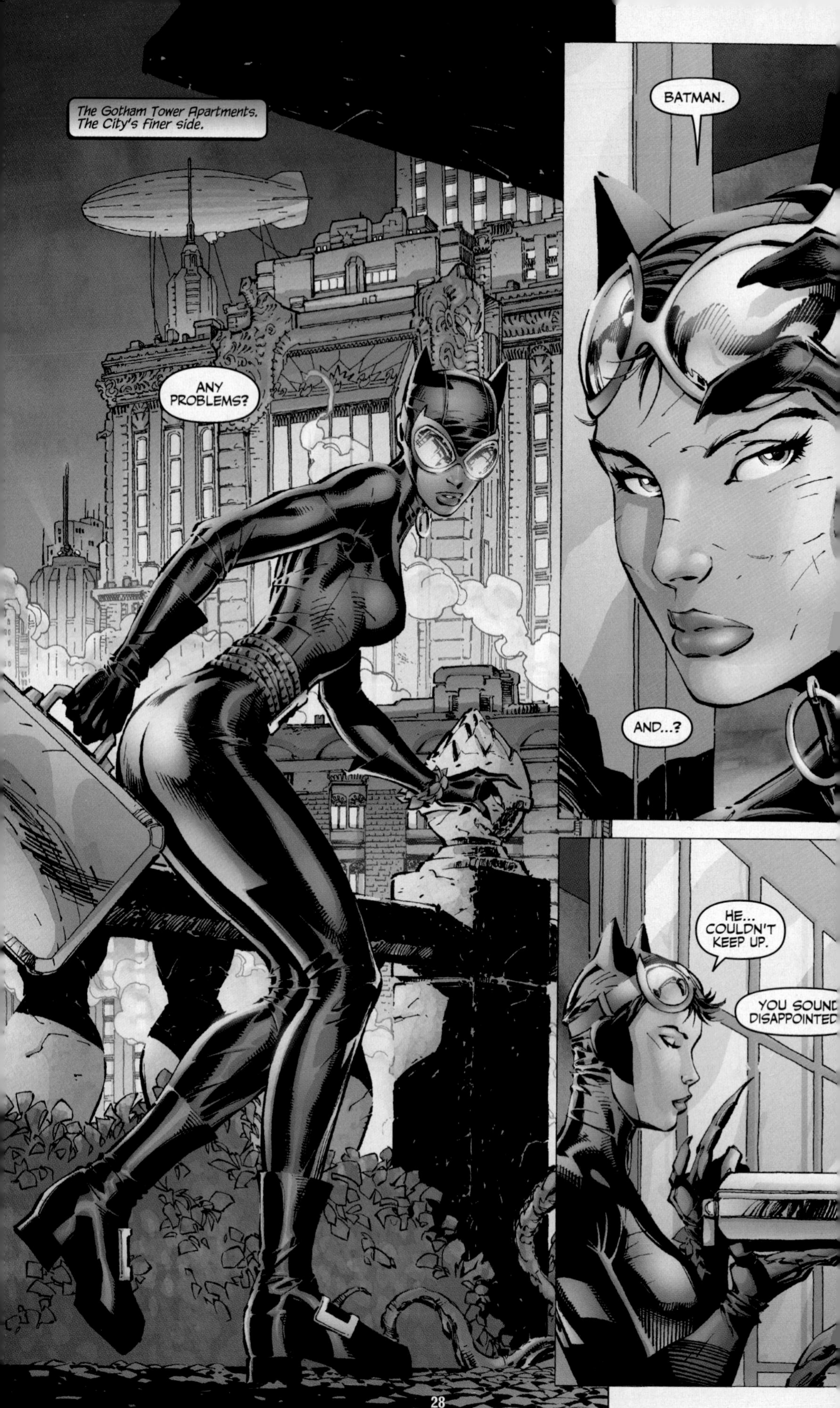
The Gotham Tower Apartments.
The City's finer side.
ANY PROBLEMS?
BATMAN.
AND...?
HE... COULDN'T KEEP UP.
YOU SOUND DISAPPOINTED

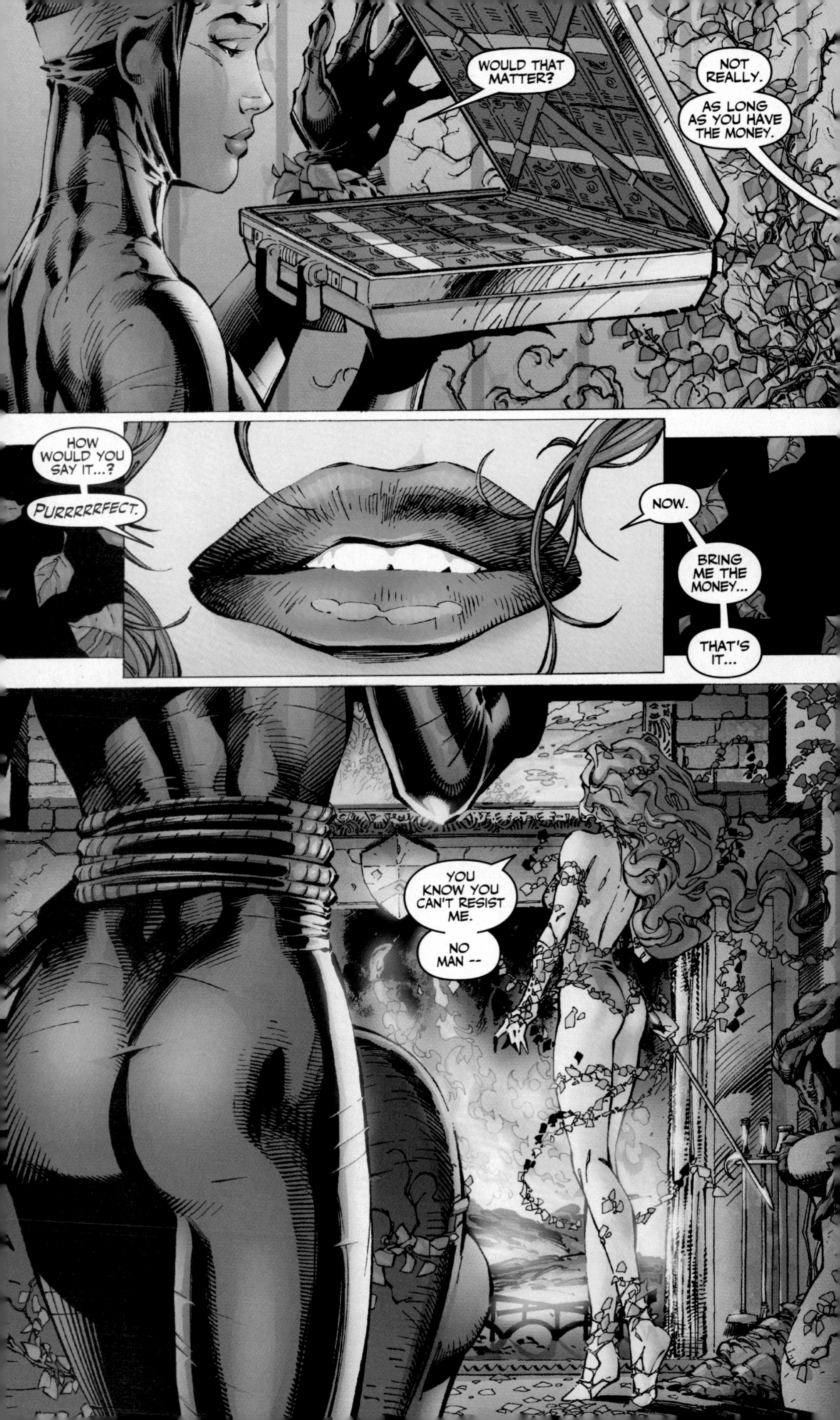
WOULD THAT MATTER?
NOT REALLY.
AS LONG AS YOU HAVE THE MONEY.
HOW WOULD YOU SAY IT...?
PURRRRRRFECT.
NOW.
BRING ME THE MONEY...
THAT'S IT...
YOU KNOW YOU CAN'T RESIST ME.
NO MAN --

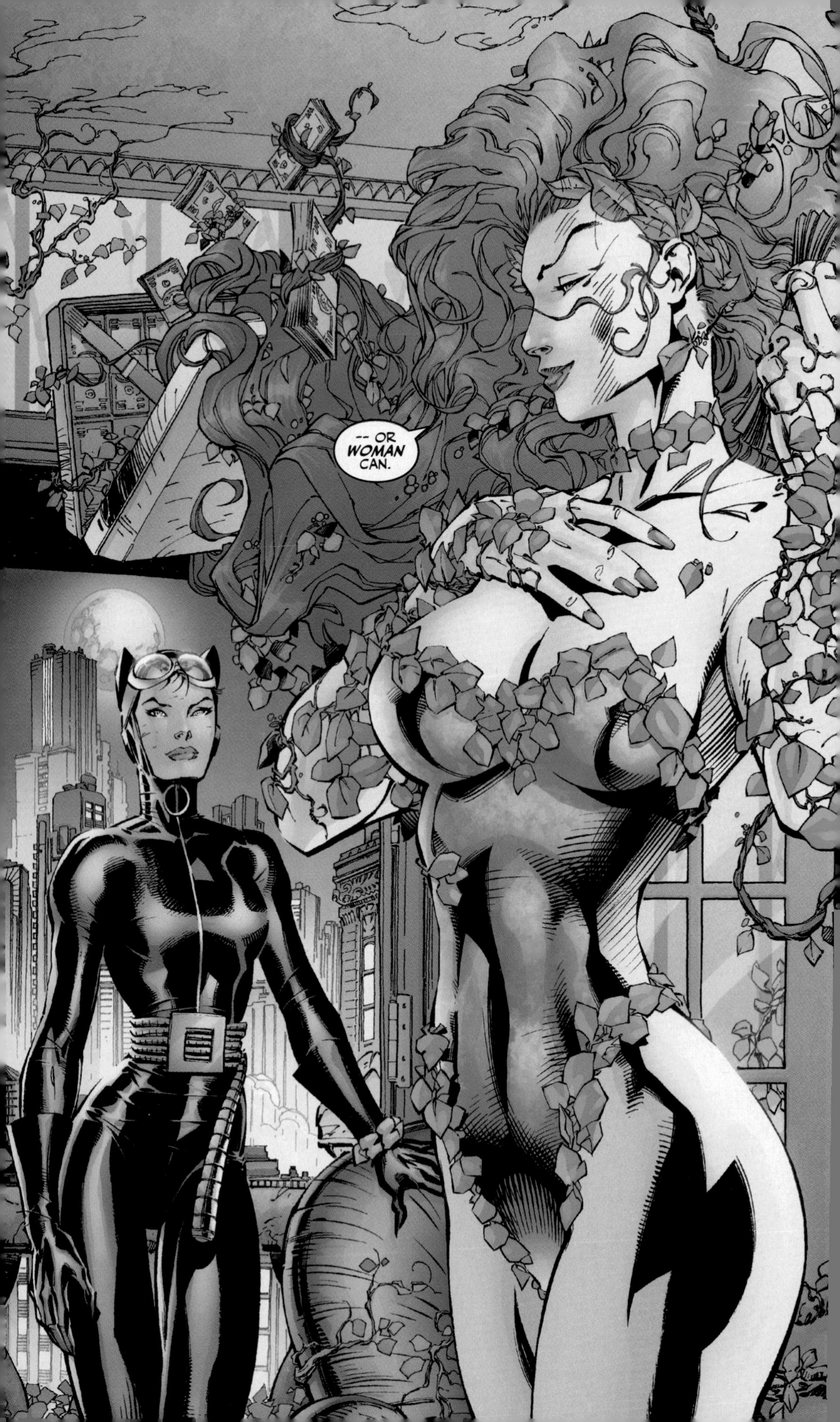
-- OR WOMAN CAN.

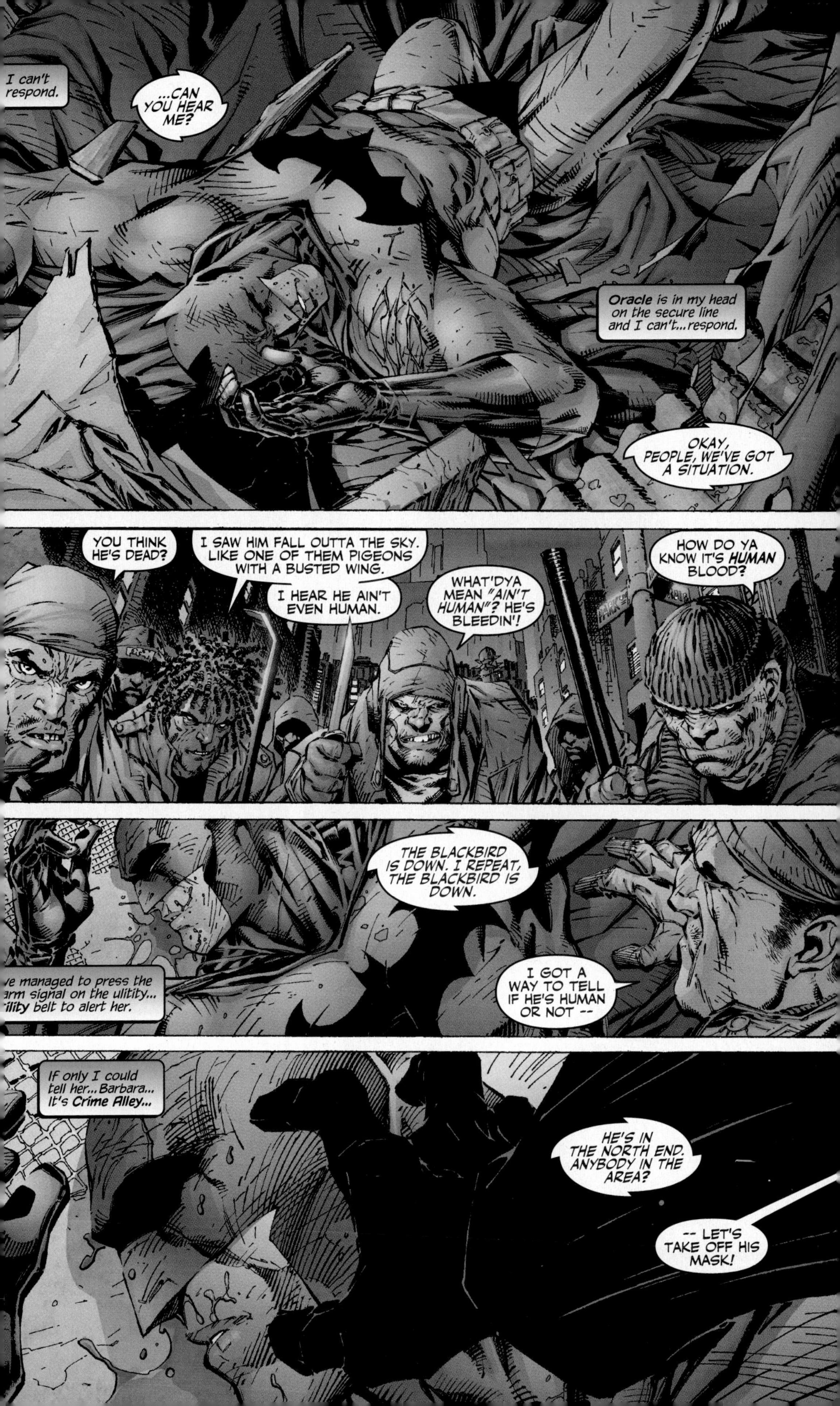
I can't respond.
...CAN YOU HEAR ME?
Oracle is in my head on the secure line and I can't...respond.
OKAY, PEOPLE, WE'VE GOT A SITUATION.
YOU THINK HE'S DEAD?
I SAW HIM FALL OUTTA THE SKY. LIKE ONE OF THEM PIGEONS WITH A BUSTED WING.
I HEAR HE AIN'T EVEN HUMAN.
WHAT'DYA MEAN "AIN'T HUMAN"? HE'S BLEEDIN'!
HOW DO YA KNOW IT'S HUMAN BLOOD?
THE BLACKBIRD IS DOWN. I REPEAT, THE BLACKBIRD IS DOWN.
ve managed to press the arm signal on the ulitity... tility belt to alert her.
I GOT A WAY TO TELL IF HE'S HUMAN OR NOT --
If only I could tell her... Barbara... It's Crime Alley...
HE'S IN THE NORTH END. ANYBODY IN THE AREA?
-- LET'S TAKE OFF HIS MASK!

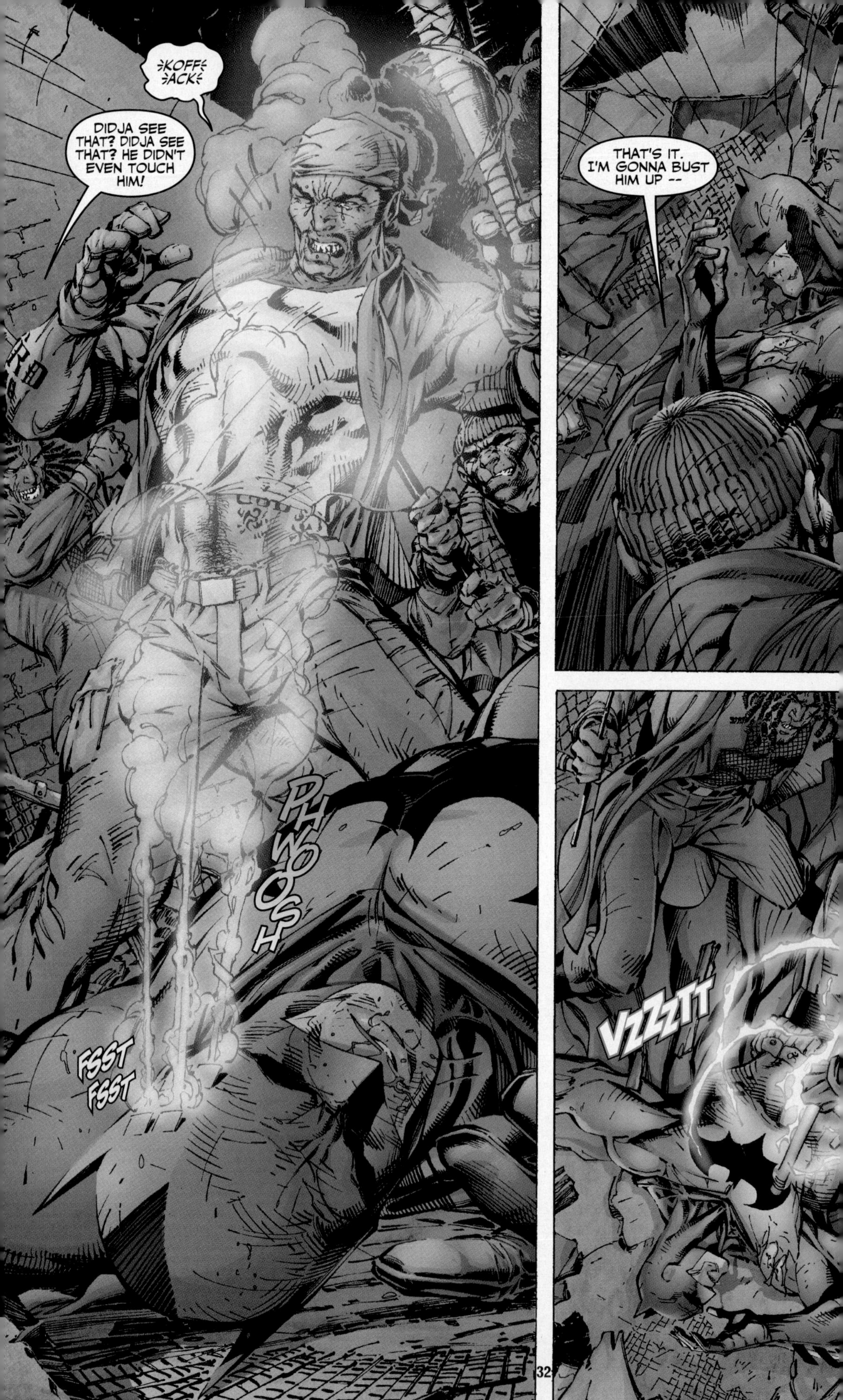
KOFF ACK
DIDJA SEE THAT? DIDJA SEE THAT? HE DIDN'T EVEN TOUCH HIM!
PHWOOSH
FSST FSST
THAT'S IT. I'M GONNA BUST HIM UP --
VZZZTT

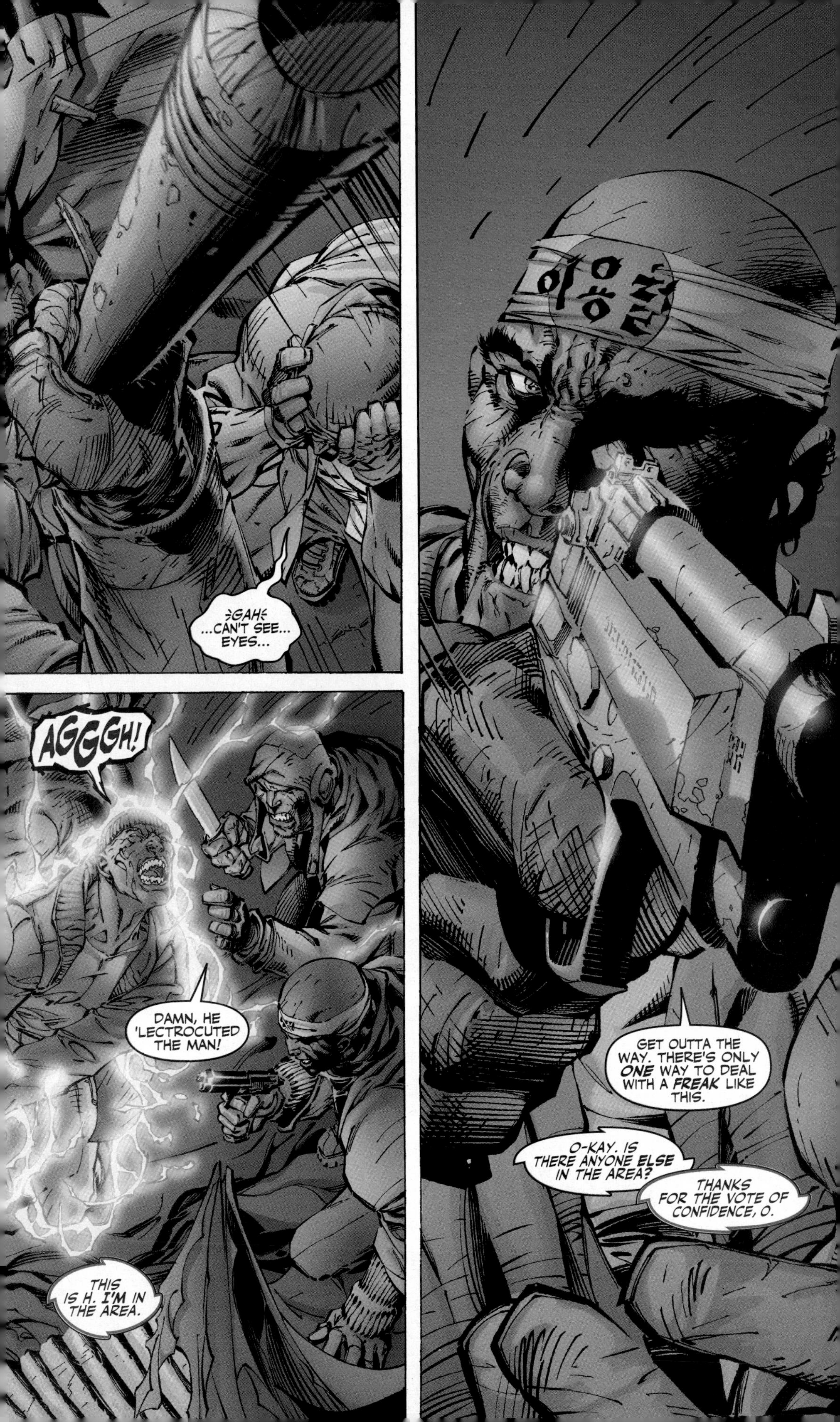

≻GAH≺ ...CAN'T SEE... EYES...
AGGGH!
DAMN, HE 'LECTROCUTED THE MAN!
THIS IS H. I'M IN THE AREA.
GET OUTTA THE WAY. THERE'S ONLY ONE WAY TO DEAL WITH A FREAK LIKE THIS.
O-KAY. IS THERE ANYONE ELSE IN THE AREA?
THANKS FOR THE VOTE OF CONFIDENCE, O.

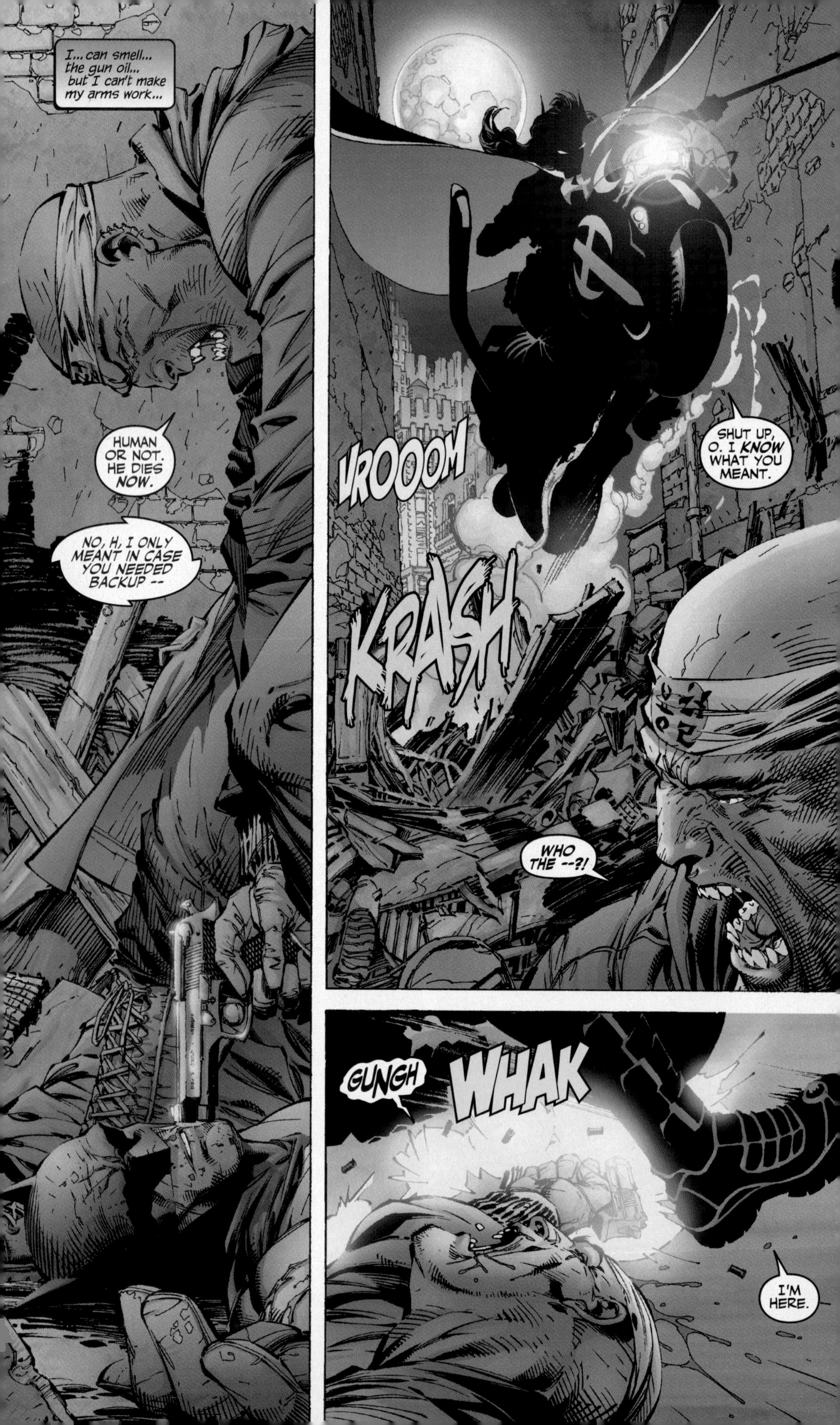
I... can smell... the gun oil... but I can't make my arms work...
HUMAN OR NOT. HE DIES NOW.
NO, H, I ONLY MEANT IN CASE YOU NEEDED BACKUP --
VROOOM
SHUT UP, O. I KNOW WHAT YOU MEANT.
KRASH
WHO THE --?!
GUNGH
WHAK
I'M HERE.

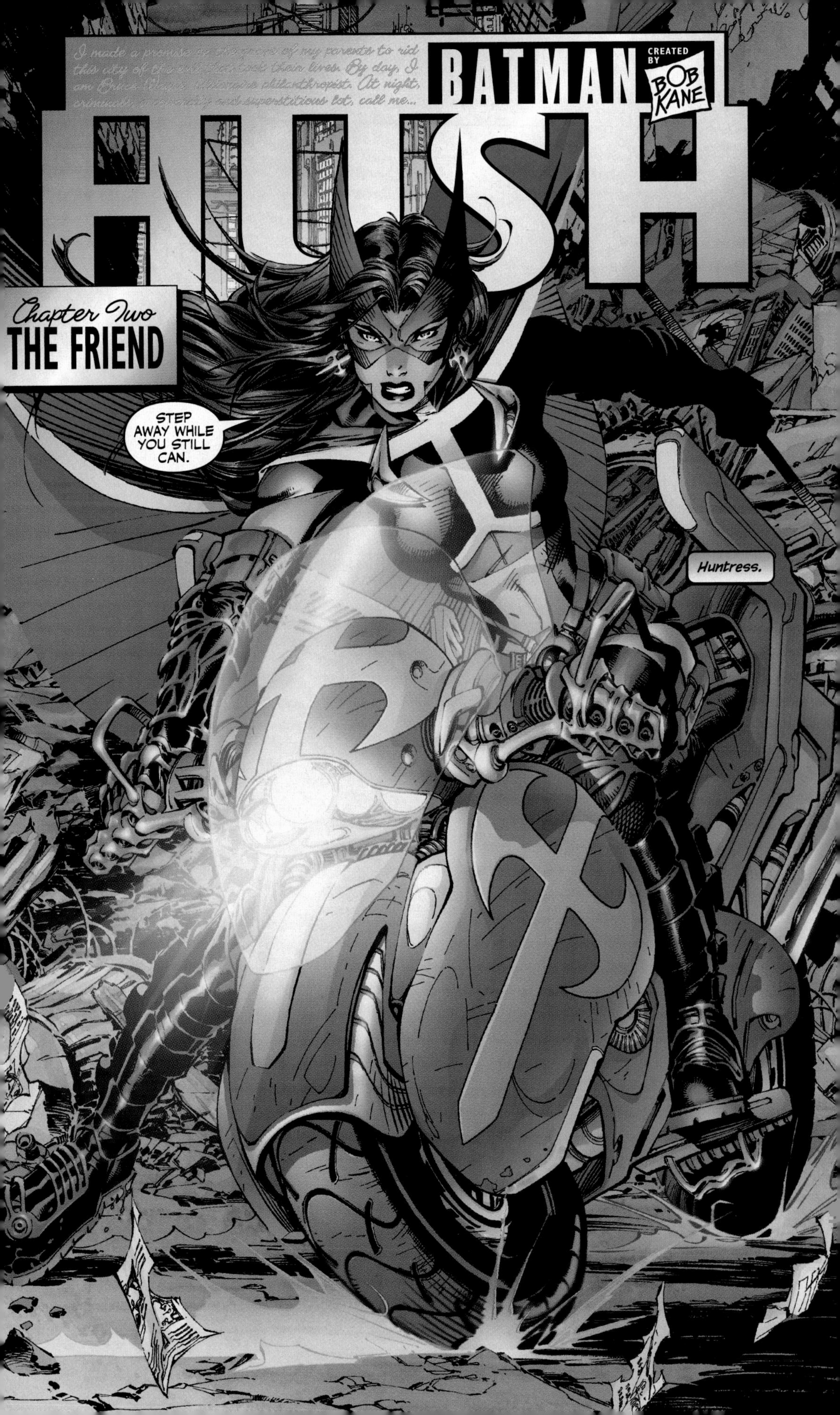
I made a promise on the grave of my parents to rid this city of the evil that took their lives. By day, I am Bruce Wayne, billionaire philanthropist. At night, criminals, a cowardly and superstitious lot, call me...
BATMAN
CREATED BY BOB KANE
HUSH
Chapter Two
THE FRIEND
STEP AWAY WHILE YOU STILL CAN.
Huntress.

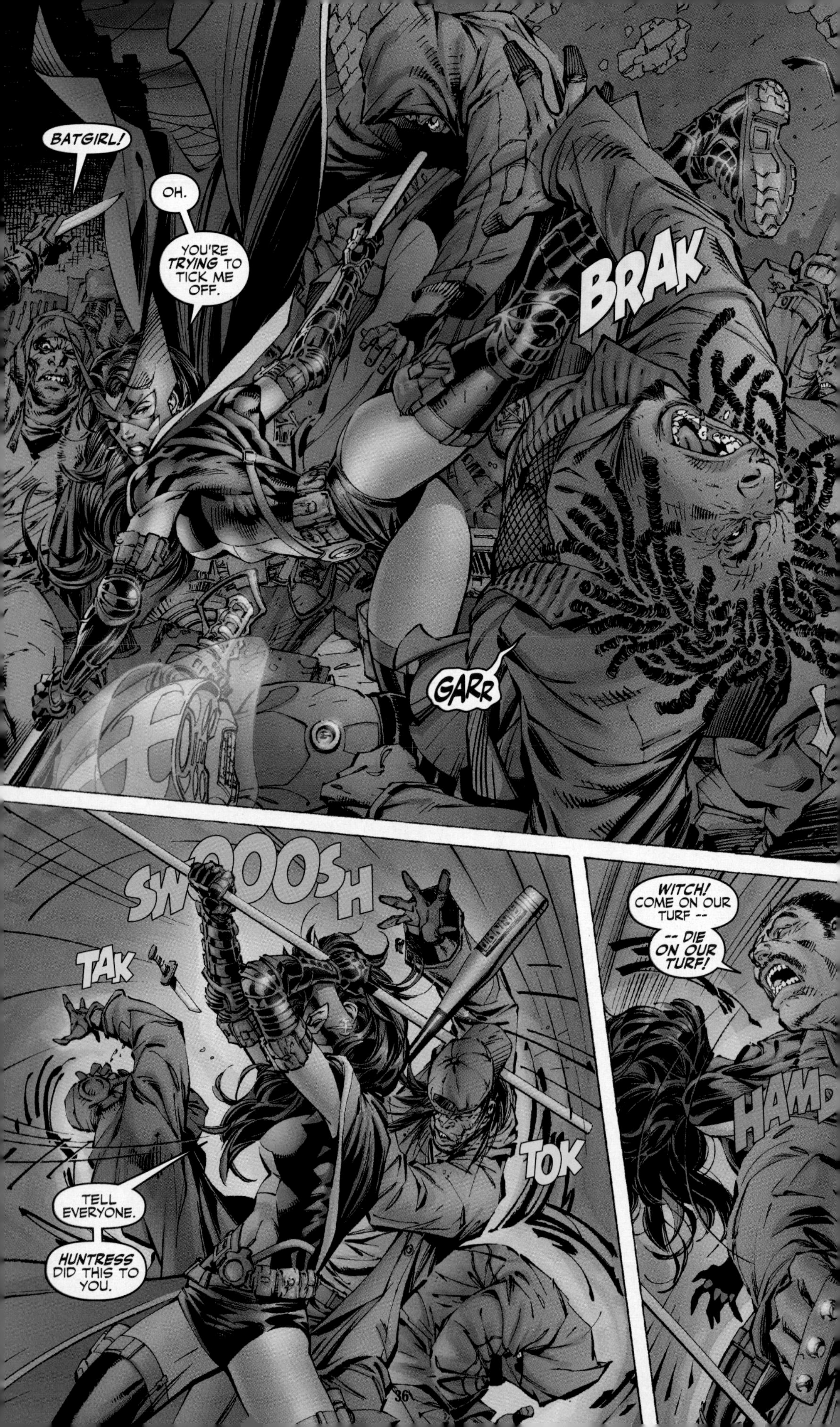
BATGIRL!
OH.
YOU'RE TRYING TO TICK ME OFF.
BRAK
GARR
SWOOOSH
TAK
TOK
TELL EVERYONE.
HUNTRESS DID THIS TO YOU.
WITCH! COME ON OUR TURF --
-- DIE ON OUR TURF!
HAMP

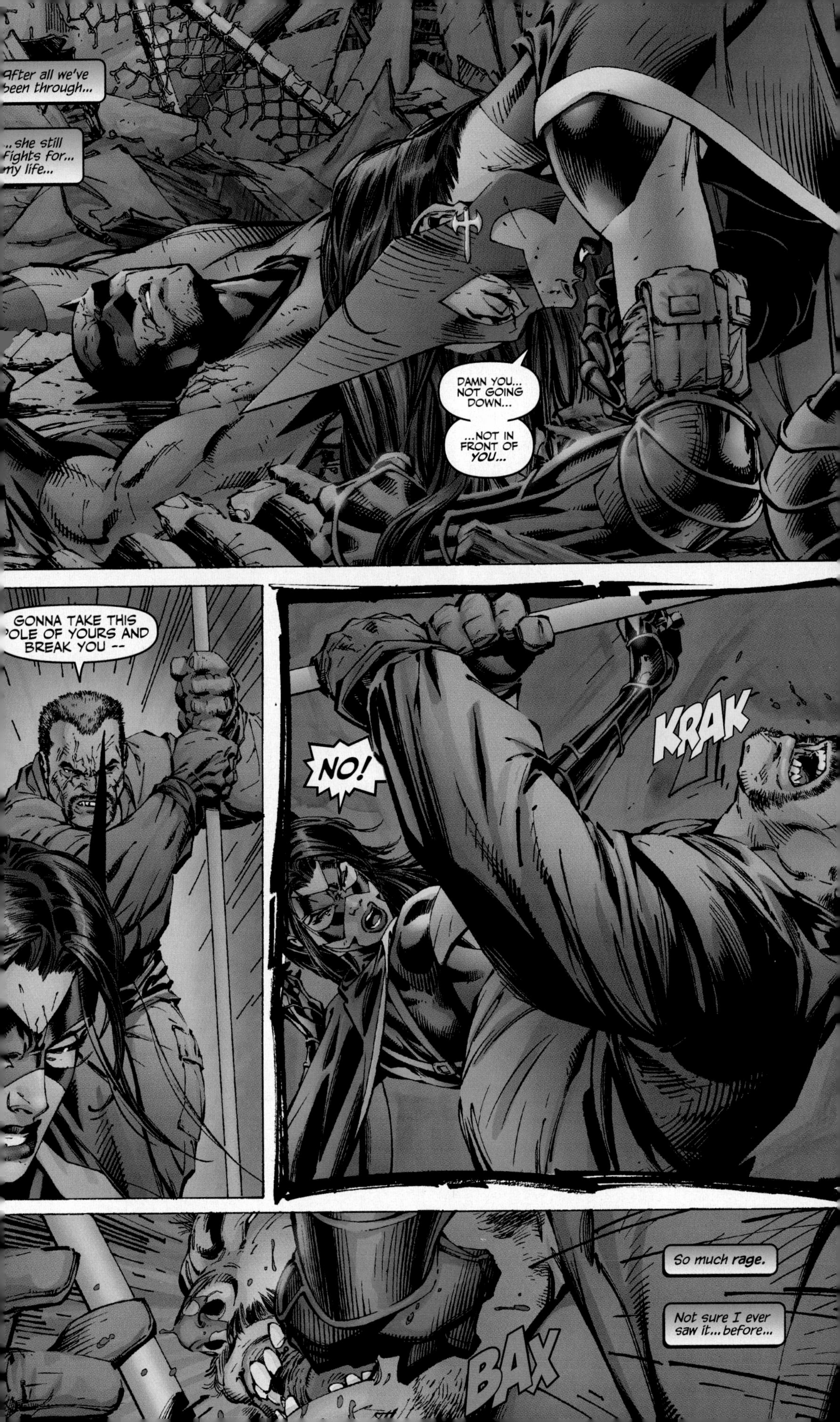
After all we've been through...
...she still fights for... my life...
DAMN YOU... NOT GOING DOWN...
...NOT IN FRONT OF YOU...
GONNA TAKE THIS POLE OF YOURS AND BREAK YOU --
NO!
KRAK
So much rage.
Not sure I ever saw it... before...
BAX

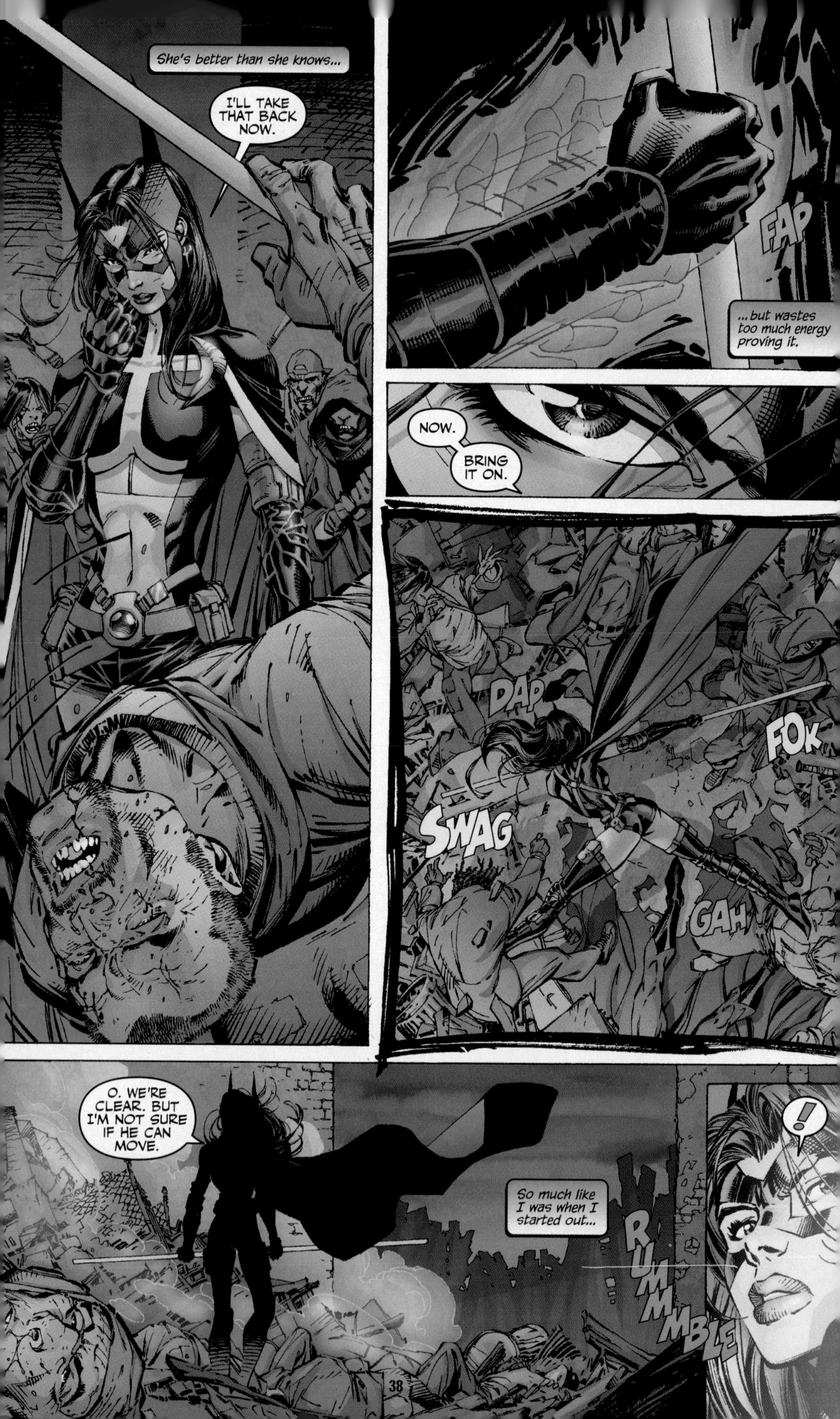

She's better than she knows...
I'LL TAKE THAT BACK NOW.
FAP
...but wastes too much energy proving it.
NOW.
BRING IT ON.
DAP
FOk
SWAG
GAH
O. WE'RE CLEAR. BUT I'M NOT SURE IF HE CAN MOVE.
So much like I was when I started out...
RUMMMBLE
!

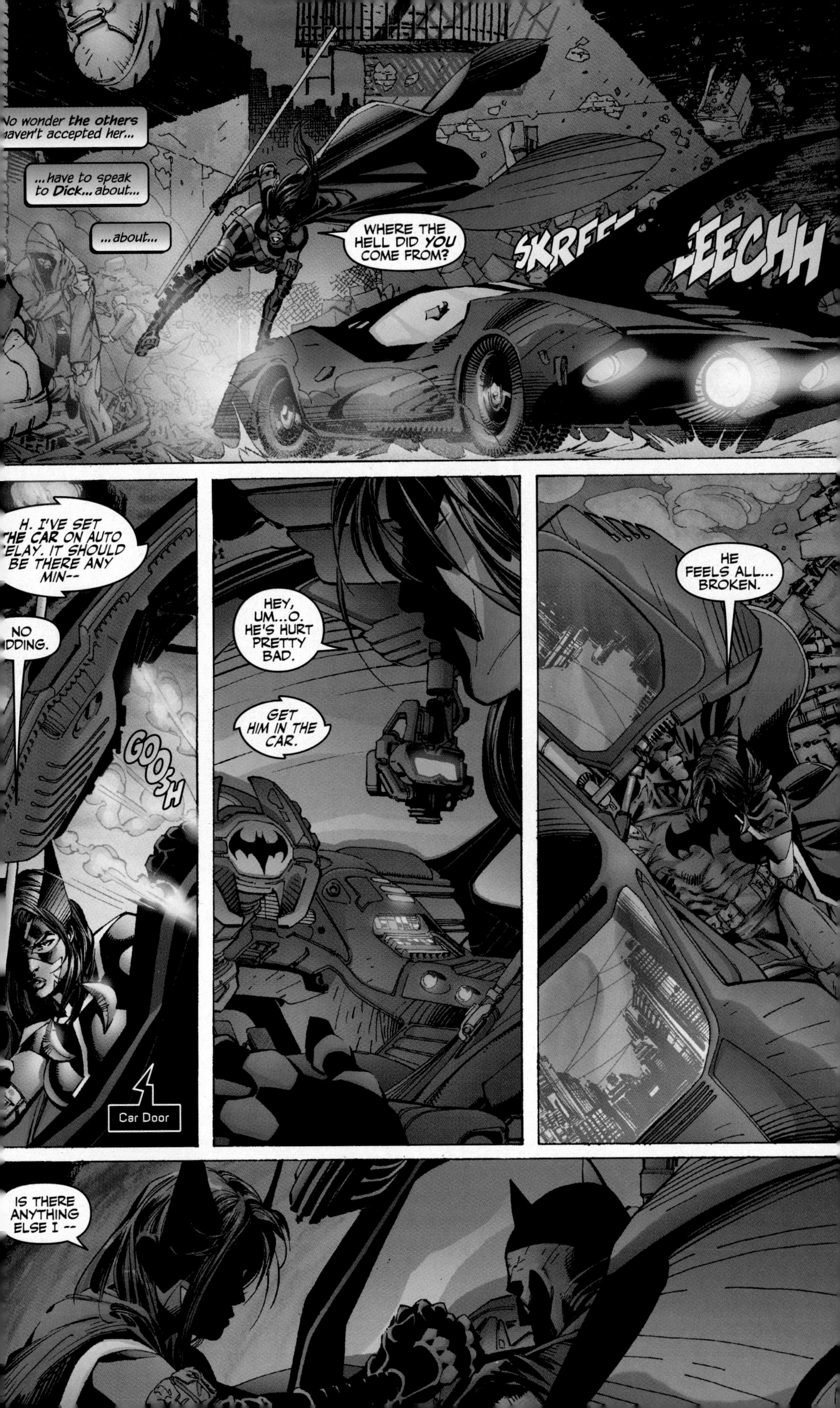

No wonder the others haven't accepted her...
...have to speak to Dick... about...
...about...
WHERE THE HELL DID YOU COME FROM?
SKREE--
--EECHH
H. I'VE SET THE CAR ON AUTO RELAY. IT SHOULD BE THERE ANY MIN--
NO KIDDING.
GOO'H
Car Door
HEY, UM...O. HE'S HURT PRETTY BAD.
GET HIM IN THE CAR.
HE FEELS ALL... BROKEN.
IS THERE ANYTHING ELSE I --

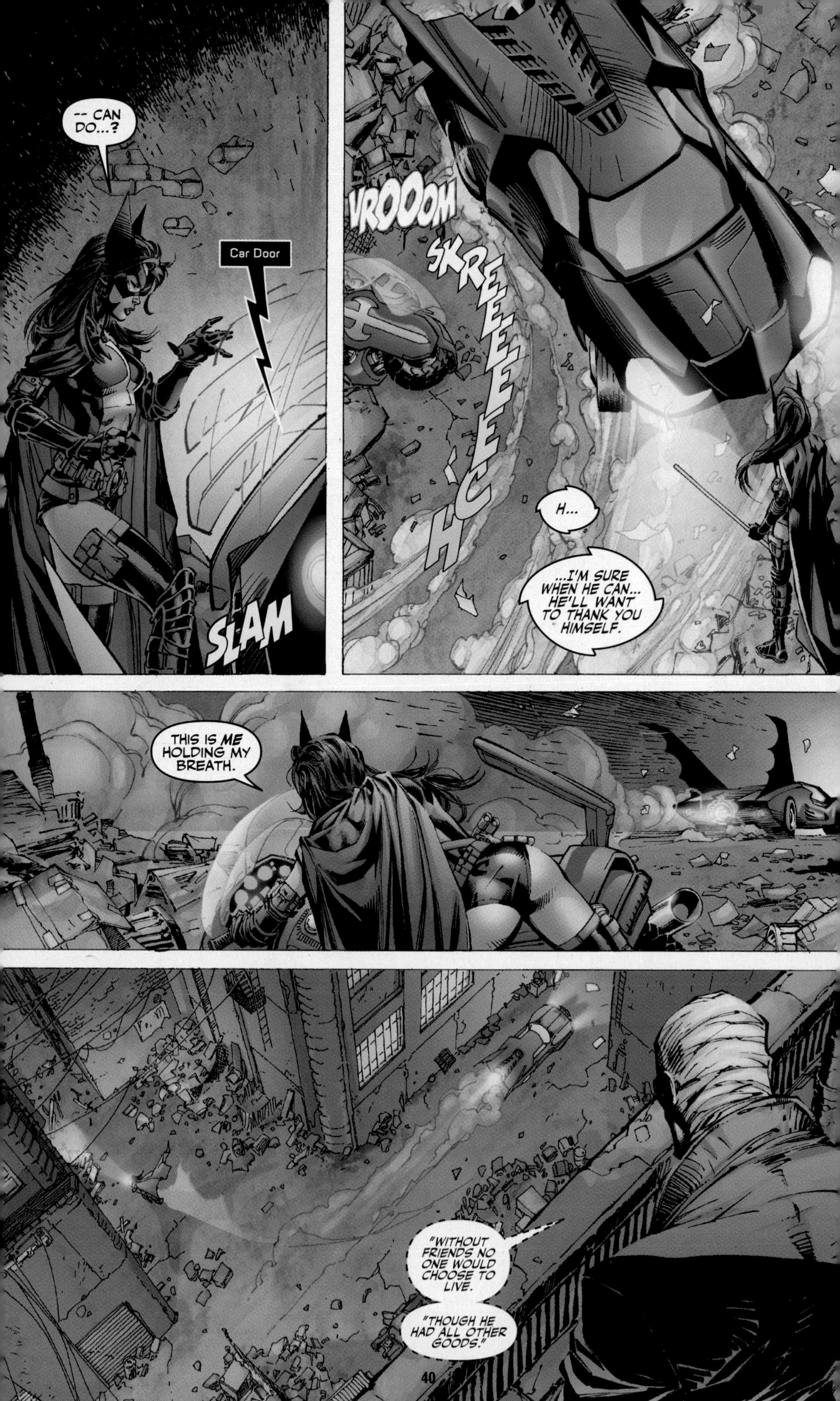
-- CAN DO...?
Car Door
SLAM
VROOOM
SKREEEEEECHH
H...
...I'M SURE WHEN HE CAN... HE'LL WANT TO THANK YOU HIMSELF.
THIS IS ME HOLDING MY BREATH.
"WITHOUT FRIENDS NO ONE WOULD CHOOSE TO LIVE.
"THOUGH HE HAD ALL OTHER GOODS."

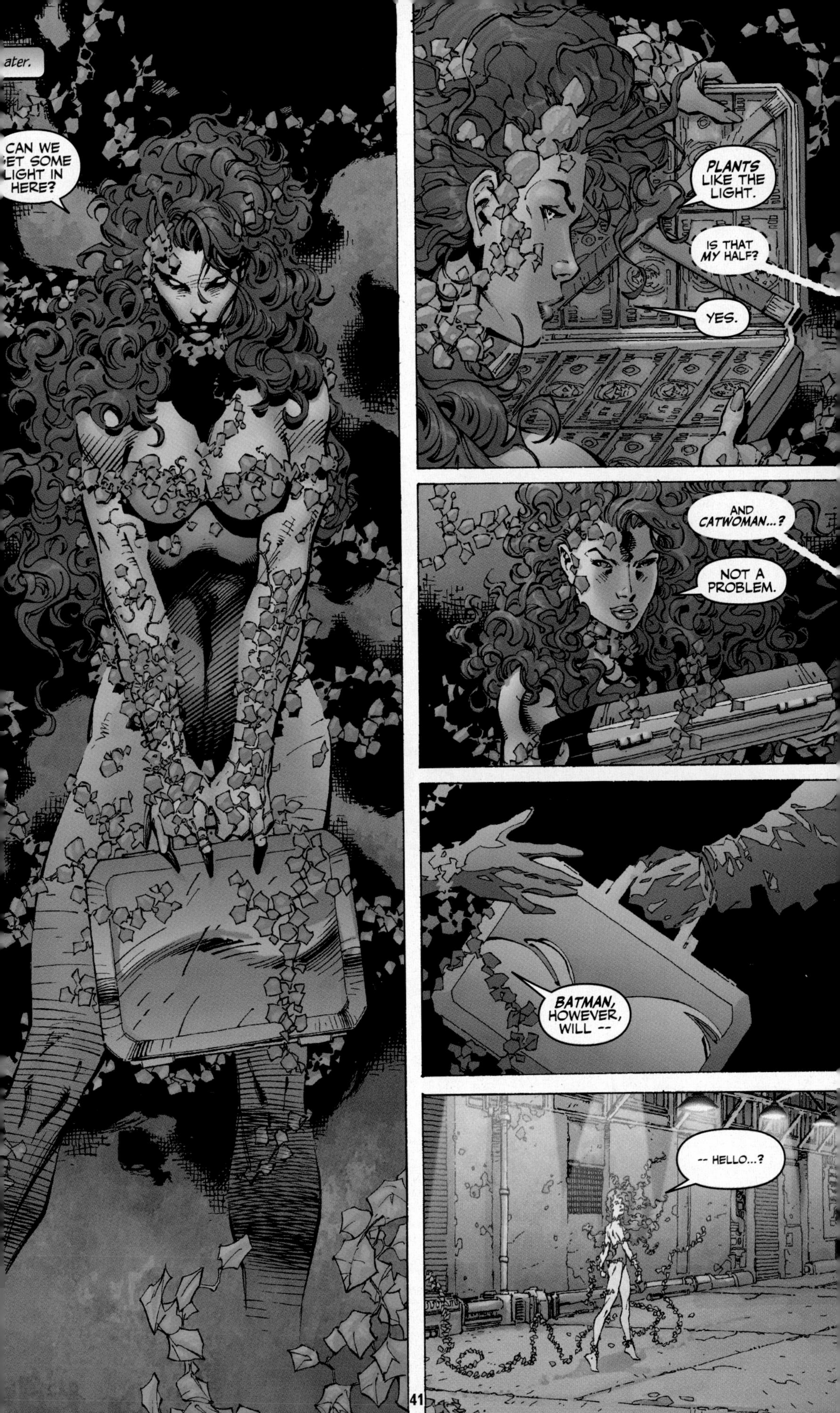

ater.
CAN WE GET SOME LIGHT IN HERE?
PLANTS LIKE THE LIGHT.
IS THAT MY HALF?
YES.
AND CATWOMAN...?
NOT A PROBLEM.
BATMAN, HOWEVER, WILL --
-- HELLO...?

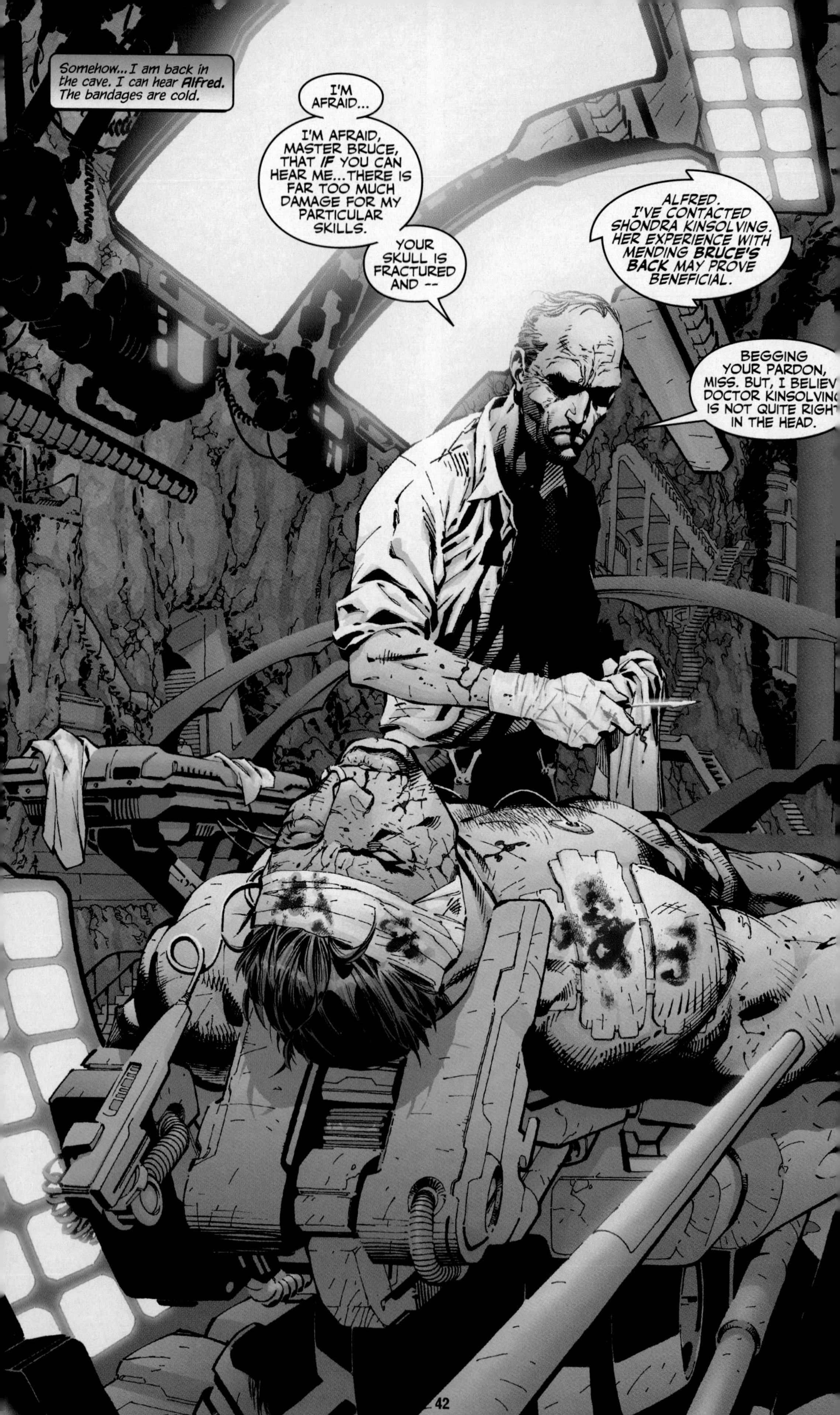
Somehow... I am back in the cave. I can hear Alfred. The bandages are cold.
I'M AFRAID...
I'M AFRAID, MASTER BRUCE, THAT IF YOU CAN HEAR ME...THERE IS FAR TOO MUCH DAMAGE FOR MY PARTICULAR SKILLS.
YOUR SKULL IS FRACTURED AND --
ALFRED. I'VE CONTACTED SHONDRA KINSOLVING. HER EXPERIENCE WITH MENDING BRUCE'S BACK MAY PROVE BENEFICIAL.
BEGGING YOUR PARDON, MISS. BUT, I BELIEV DOCTOR KINSOLVING IS NOT QUITE RIGHT IN THE HEAD.

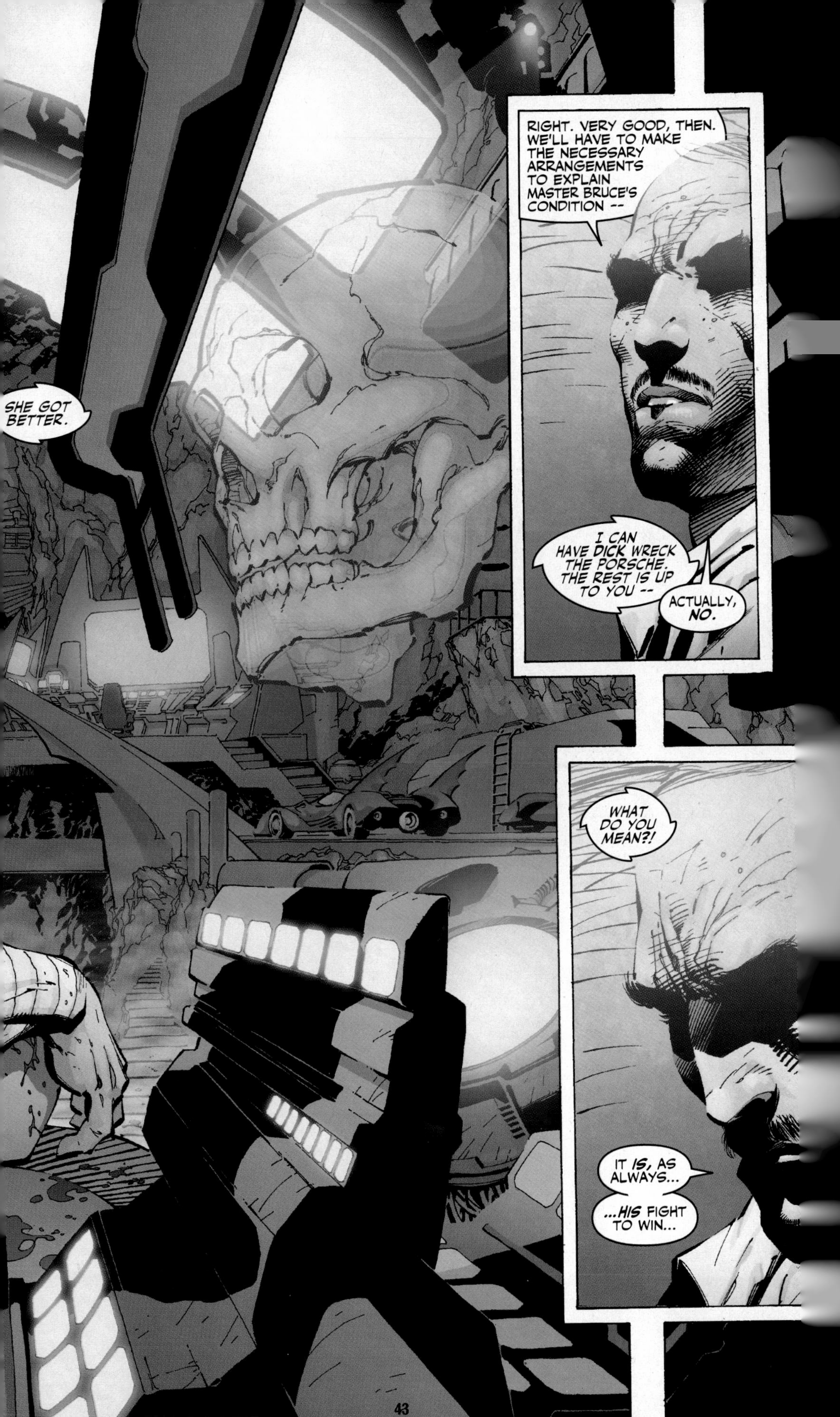
SHE GOT BETTER.
RIGHT. VERY GOOD, THEN. WE'LL HAVE TO MAKE THE NECESSARY ARRANGEMENTS TO EXPLAIN MASTER BRUCE'S CONDITION --
I CAN HAVE DICK WRECK THE PORSCHE. THE REST IS UP TO YOU --
ACTUALLY, NO.
WHAT DO YOU MEAN?!
IT IS, AS ALWAYS...
...HIS FIGHT TO WIN...

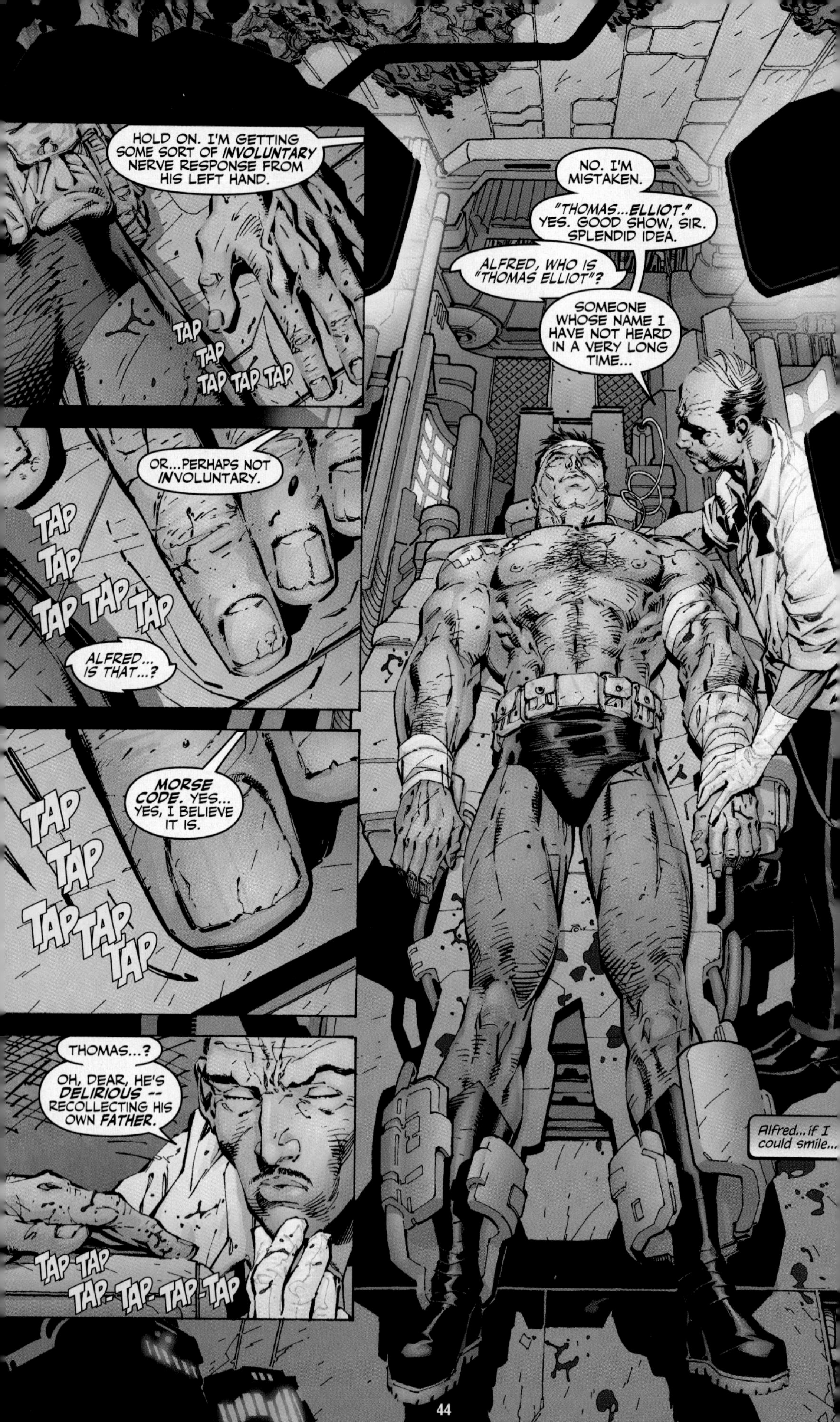
HOLD ON. I'M GETTING SOME SORT OF INVOLUNTARY NERVE RESPONSE FROM HIS LEFT HAND.
TAP TAP TAP TAP TAP
OR...PERHAPS NOT INVOLUNTARY.
TAP TAP TAP TAP TAP
ALFRED... IS THAT...?
MORSE CODE. YES... YES, I BELIEVE IT IS.
TAP TAP TAP TAP TAP
THOMAS...?
OH, DEAR, HE'S DELIRIOUS -- RECOLLECTING HIS OWN FATHER.
TAP TAP TAP- TAP- TAP- TAP
NO. I'M MISTAKEN.
"THOMAS...ELLIOT." YES. GOOD SHOW, SIR. SPLENDID IDEA.
ALFRED, WHO IS "THOMAS ELLIOT"?
SOMEONE WHOSE NAME I HAVE NOT HEARD IN A VERY LONG TIME...
Alfred...if I could smile...

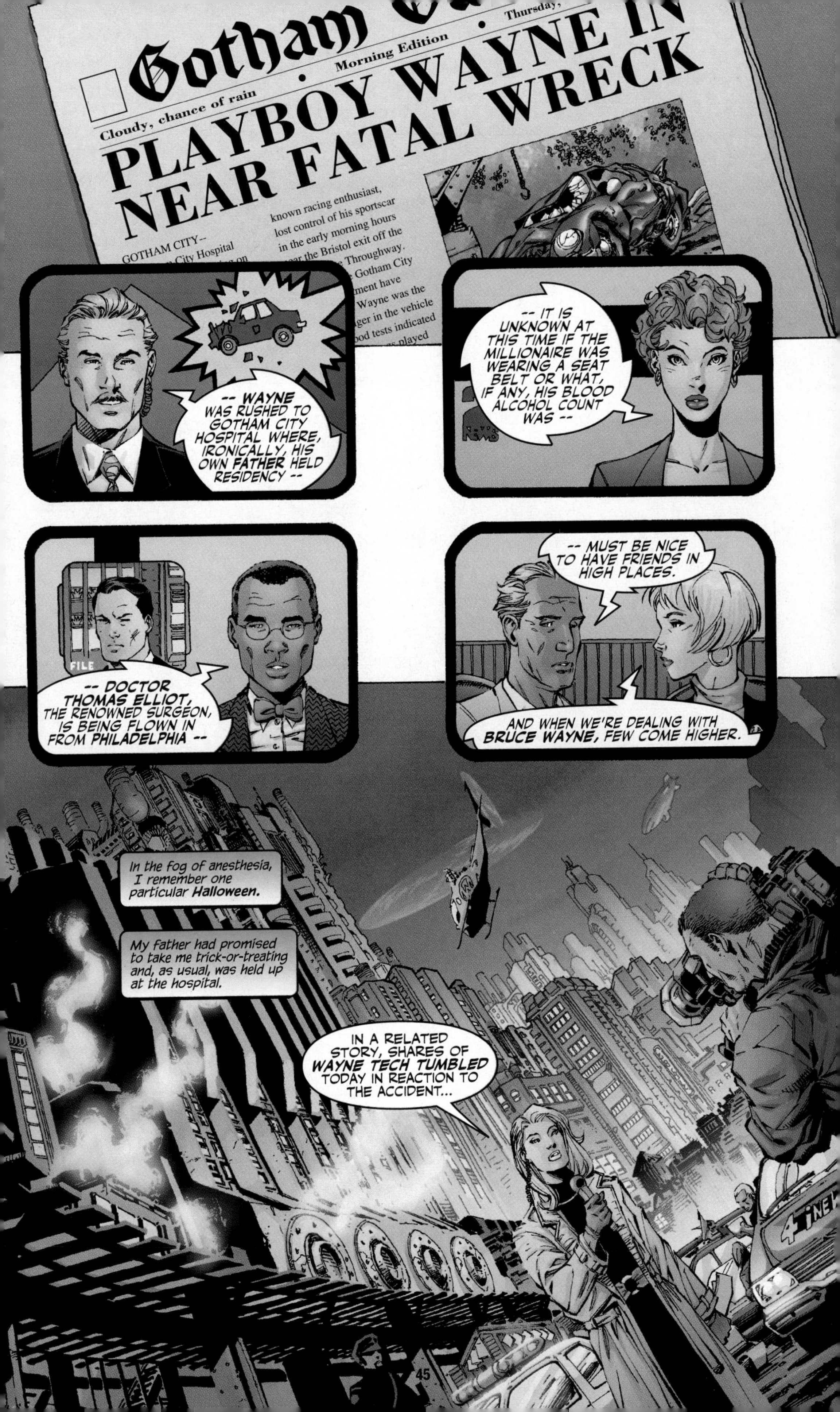
Gotham
Morning Edition
Thursday,
Cloudy, chance of rain
PLAYBOY WAYNE IN NEAR FATAL WRECK
GOTHAM CITY--
known racing enthusiast, lost control of his sportscar in the early morning hours near the Bristol exit off the Throughway.
-- WAYNE WAS RUSHED TO GOTHAM CITY HOSPITAL WHERE, IRONICALLY, HIS OWN FATHER HELD RESIDENCY --
-- IT IS UNKNOWN AT THIS TIME IF THE MILLIONAIRE WAS WEARING A SEAT BELT OR WHAT, IF ANY, HIS BLOOD ALCOHOL COUNT WAS --
FILE
-- DOCTOR THOMAS ELLIOT, THE RENOWNED SURGEON, IS BEING FLOWN IN FROM PHILADELPHIA --
-- MUST BE NICE TO HAVE FRIENDS IN HIGH PLACES.
AND WHEN WE'RE DEALING WITH BRUCE WAYNE, FEW COME HIGHER.
In the fog of anesthesia, I remember one particular Halloween.
My father had promised to take me trick-or-treating and, as usual, was held up at the hospital.
IN A RELATED STORY, SHARES OF WAYNE TECH TUMBLED TODAY IN REACTION TO THE ACCIDENT...

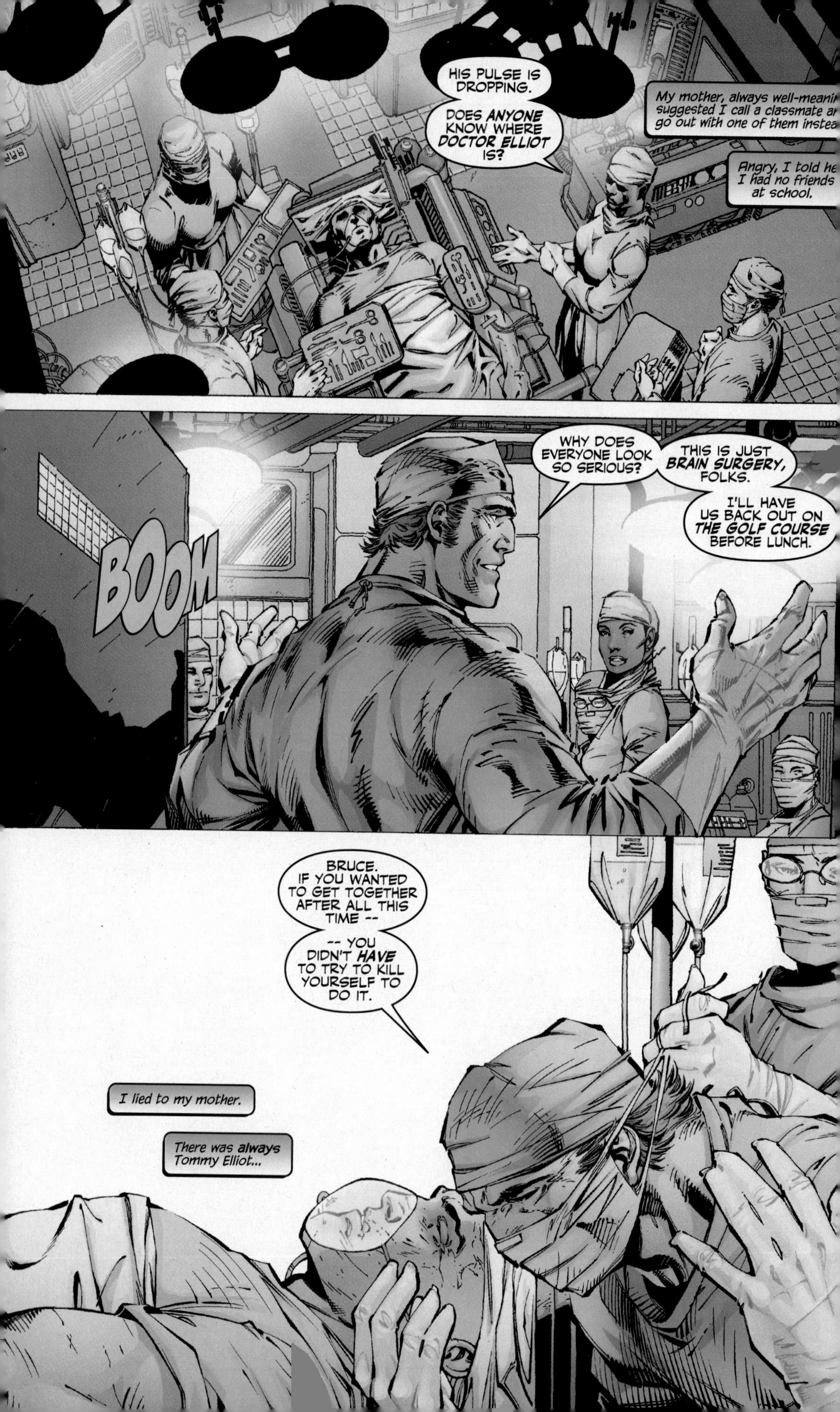
HIS PULSE IS DROPPING.
DOES ANYONE KNOW WHERE DOCTOR ELLIOT IS?
My mother, always well-meani suggested I call a classmate a go out with one of them instea
Angry, I told he I had no friends at school.
BOOM
WHY DOES EVERYONE LOOK SO SERIOUS?
THIS IS JUST BRAIN SURGERY, FOLKS.
I'LL HAVE US BACK OUT ON THE GOLF COURSE BEFORE LUNCH.
BRUCE. IF YOU WANTED TO GET TOGETHER AFTER ALL THIS TIME --
-- YOU DIDN'T HAVE TO TRY TO KILL YOURSELF TO DO IT.
I lied to my mother.
There was always Tommy Elliot...

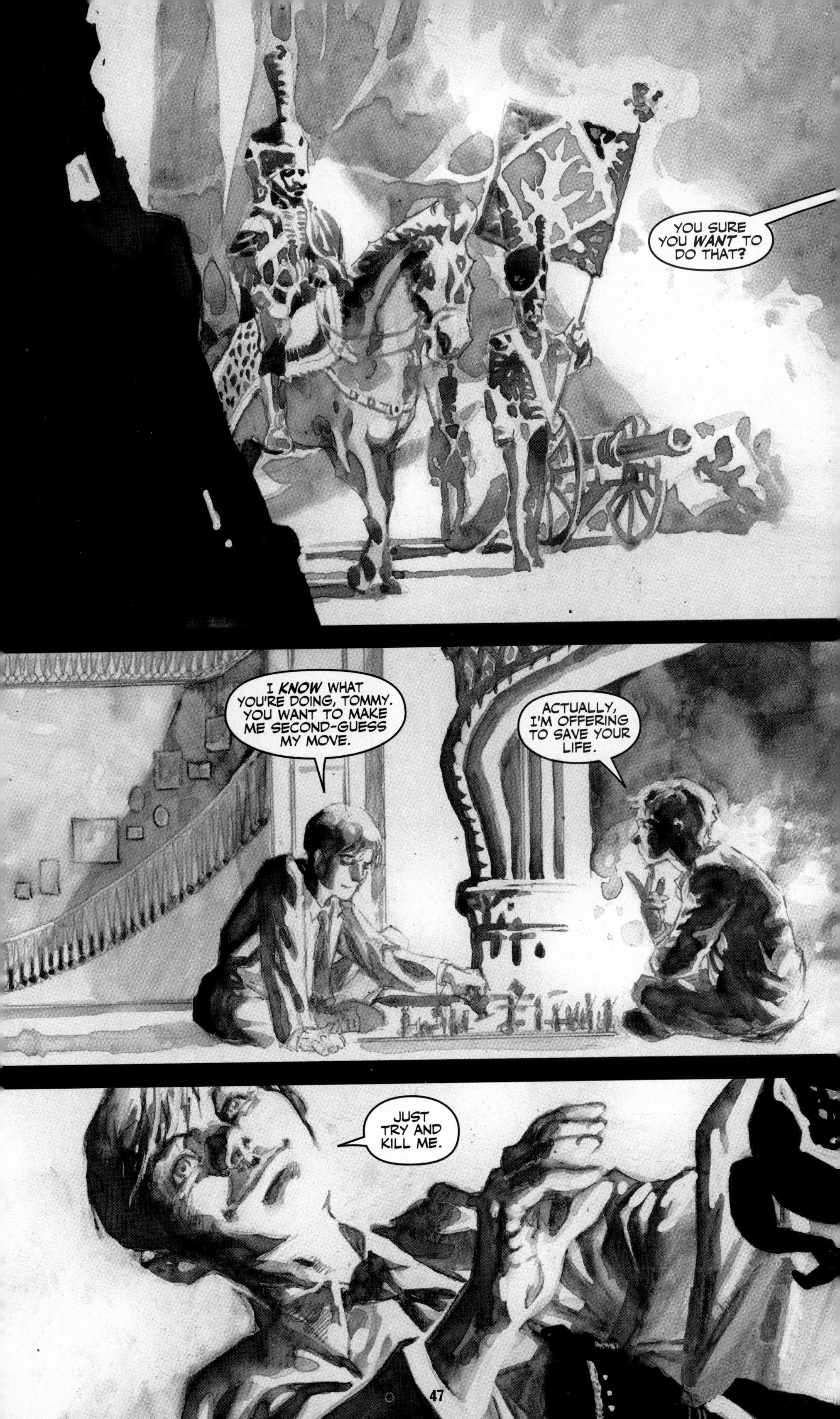
YOU SURE YOU *WANT* TO DO THAT?
I *KNOW* WHAT YOU'RE DOING, TOMMY. YOU WANT TO MAKE ME SECOND-GUESS MY MOVE.
ACTUALLY, I'M OFFERING TO SAVE YOUR LIFE.
JUST TRY AND KILL ME.

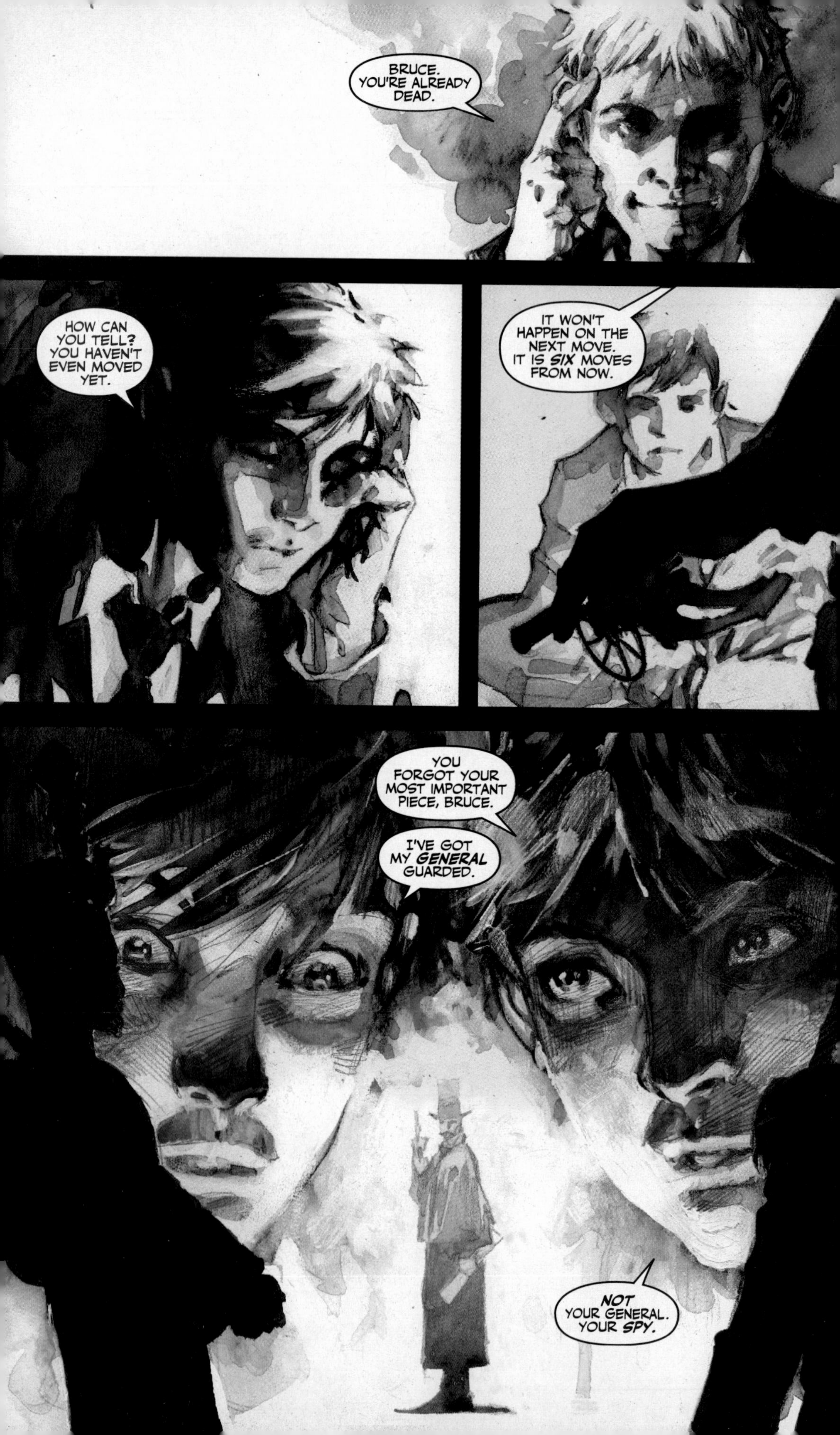
BRUCE. YOU'RE ALREADY DEAD.
HOW CAN YOU TELL? YOU HAVEN'T EVEN MOVED YET.
IT WON'T HAPPEN ON THE NEXT MOVE. IT IS SIX MOVES FROM NOW.
YOU FORGOT YOUR MOST IMPORTANT PIECE, BRUCE.
I'VE GOT MY GENERAL GUARDED.
NOT YOUR GENERAL. YOUR SPY.

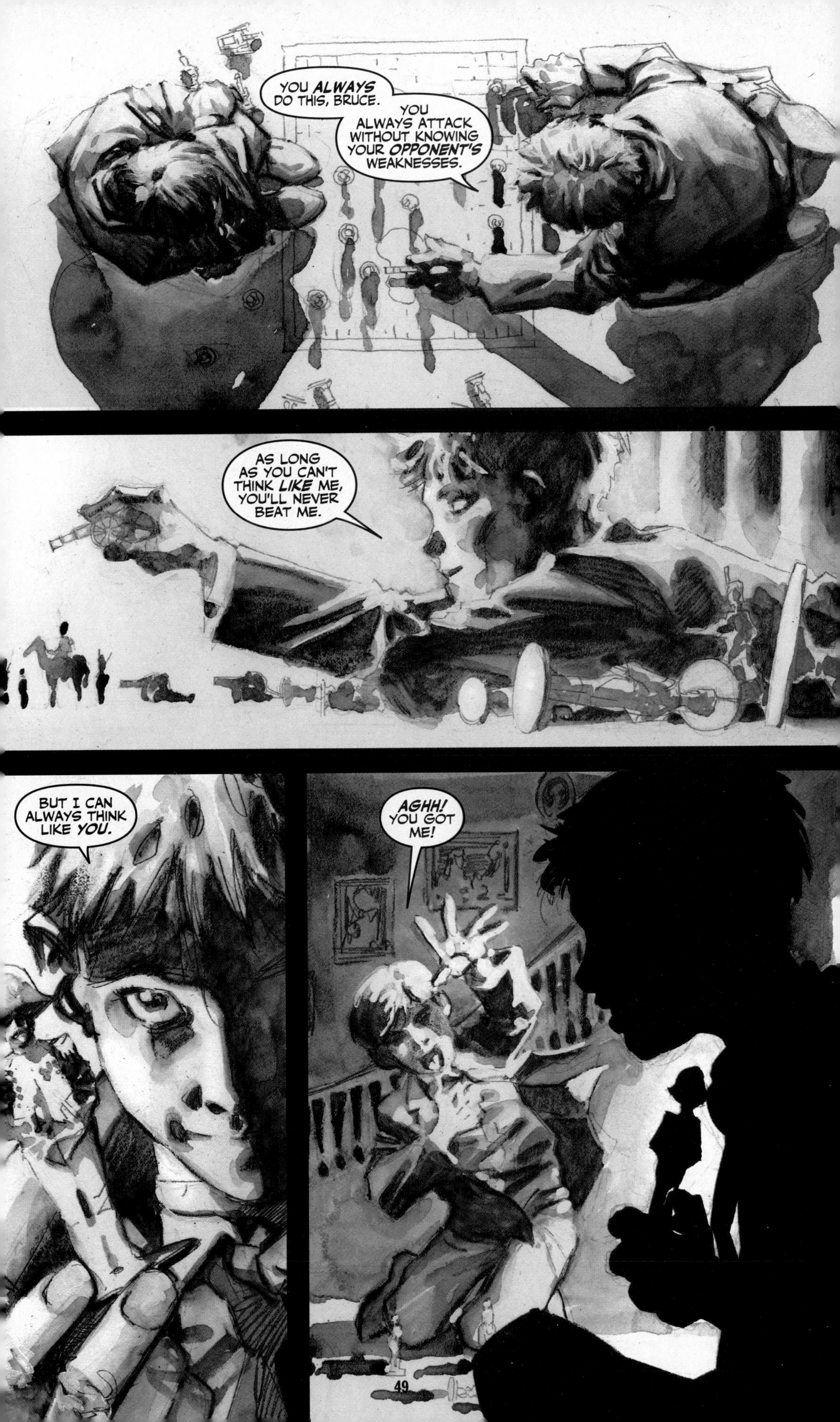
YOU *ALWAYS* DO THIS, BRUCE.
YOU ALWAYS ATTACK WITHOUT KNOWING YOUR *OPPONENT'S* WEAKNESSES.
AS LONG AS YOU CAN'T THINK *LIKE* ME, YOU'LL NEVER BEAT ME.
BUT I CAN ALWAYS THINK LIKE *YOU*.
AGHH! YOU GOT ME!

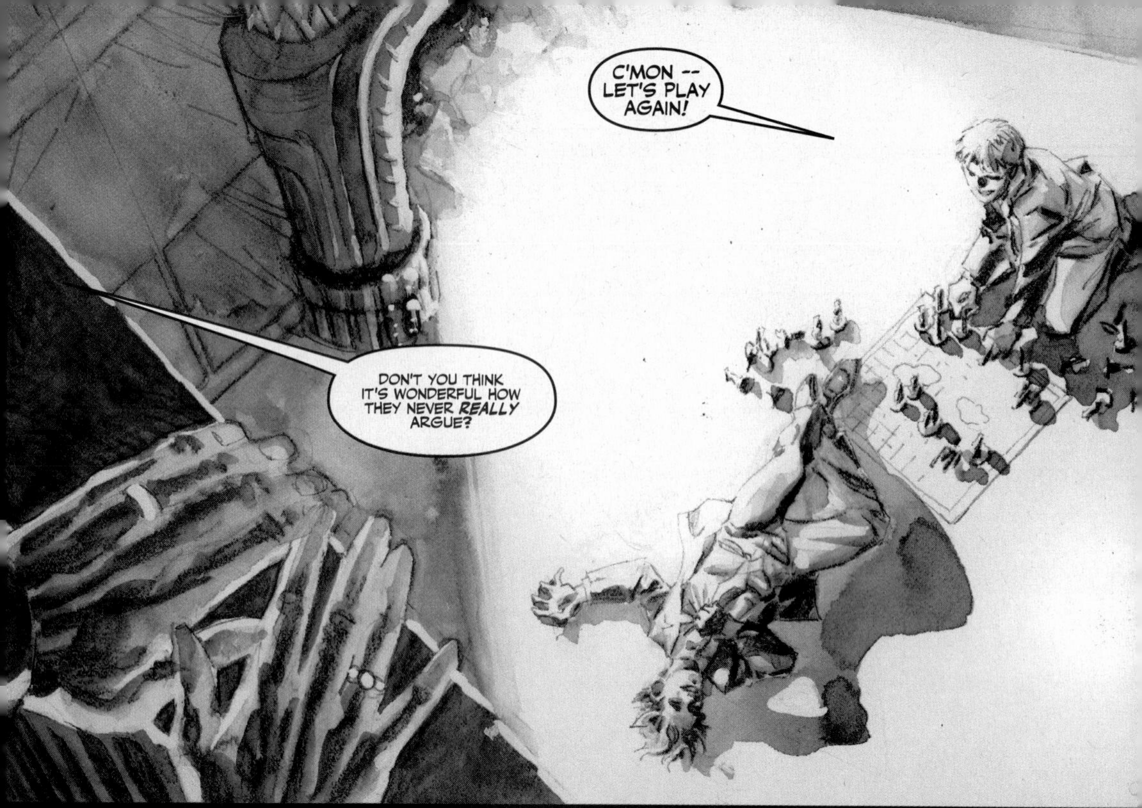
C'MON -- LET'S PLAY AGAIN!
DON'T YOU THINK IT'S WONDERFUL HOW THEY NEVER REALLY ARGUE?

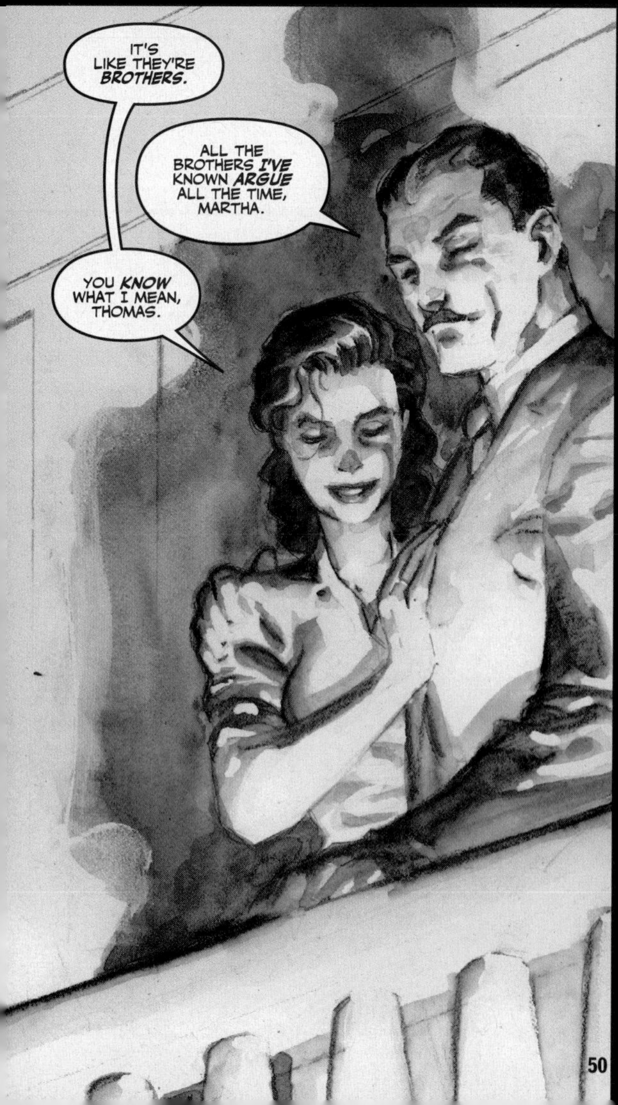
IT'S LIKE THEY'RE BROTHERS.
ALL THE BROTHERS I'VE KNOWN ARGUE ALL THE TIME, MARTHA.
YOU KNOW WHAT I MEAN, THOMAS.

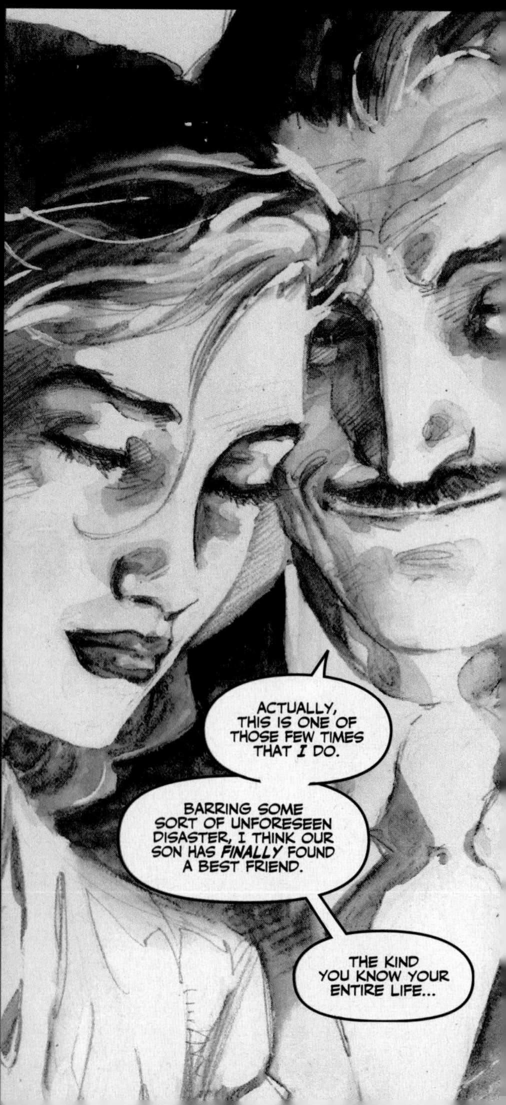
ACTUALLY, THIS IS ONE OF THOSE FEW TIMES THAT I DO.
BARRING SOME SORT OF UNFORESEEN DISASTER, I THINK OUR SON HAS FINALLY FOUND A BEST FRIEND.
THE KIND YOU KNOW YOUR ENTIRE LIFE...

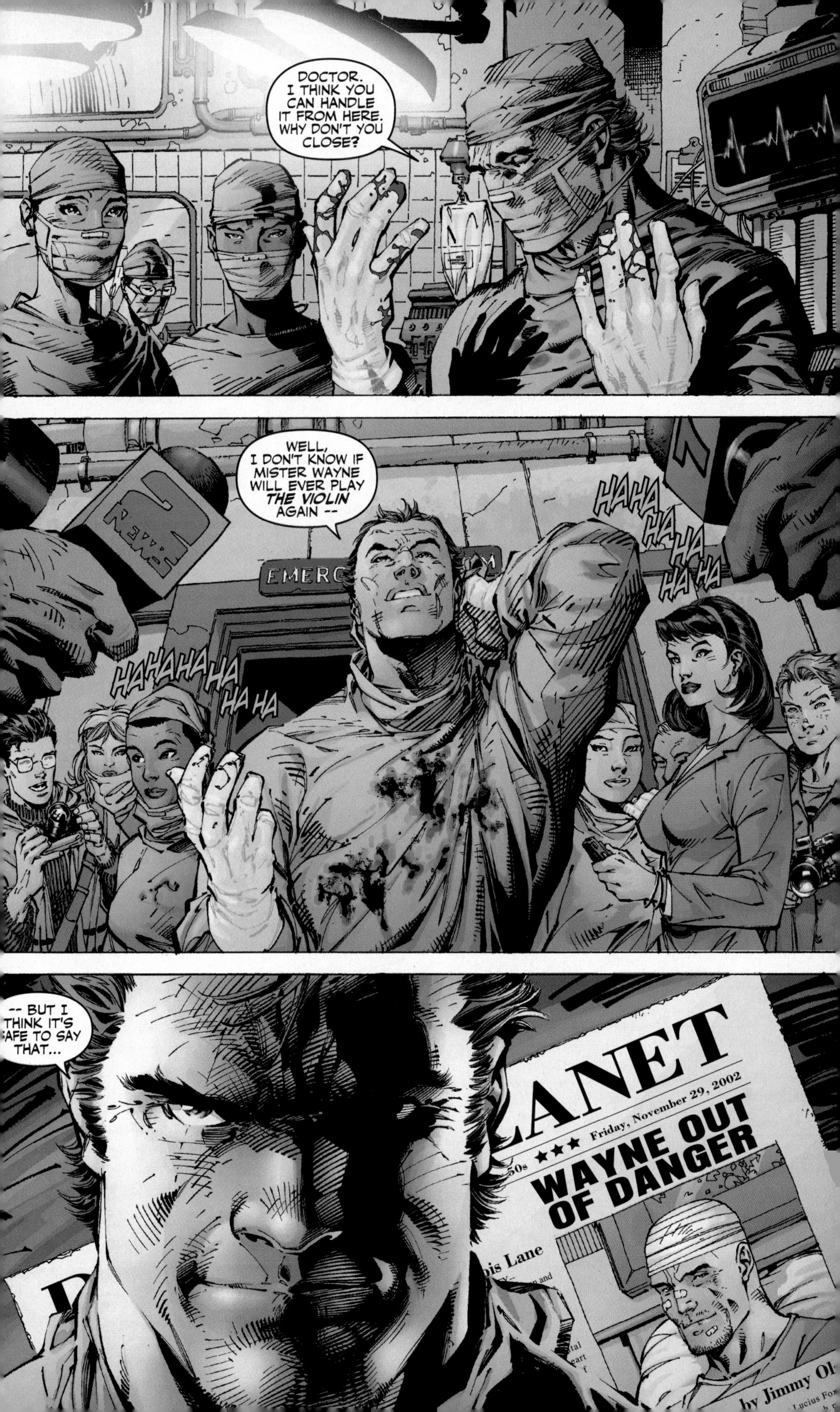
DOCTOR. I THINK YOU CAN HANDLE IT FROM HERE. WHY DON'T YOU CLOSE?
WELL, I DON'T KNOW IF MISTER WAYNE WILL EVER PLAY *THE VIOLIN* AGAIN --
NEWS
EMERG
HAHA HA HA HA HA
HAHAHAHA HA HA
-- BUT I THINK IT'S AFE TO SAY THAT...
LANET
Friday, November 29, 2002
WAYNE OUT OF DANGER
ois Lane
by Jimmy Ol

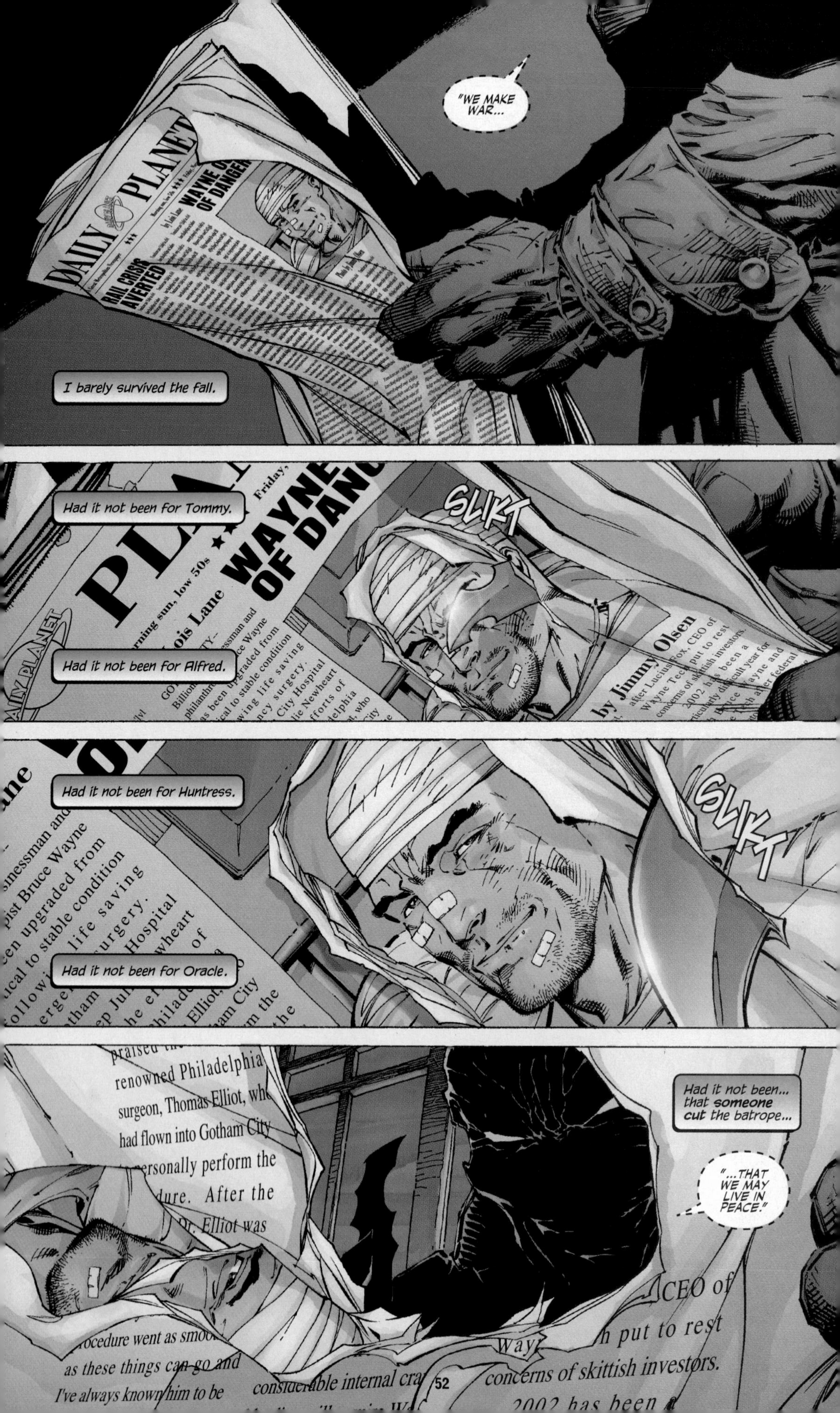
"WE MAKE WAR...
DAILY PLANET
RAIL CRISIS AVERTED
I barely survived the fall.
Had it not been for Tommy.
SLIKT
Had it not been for Alfred.
Had it not been for Huntress.
SLIKT
Had it not been for Oracle.
Had it not been... that **someone cut** the batrope...
"...THAT WE MAY LIVE IN PEACE."

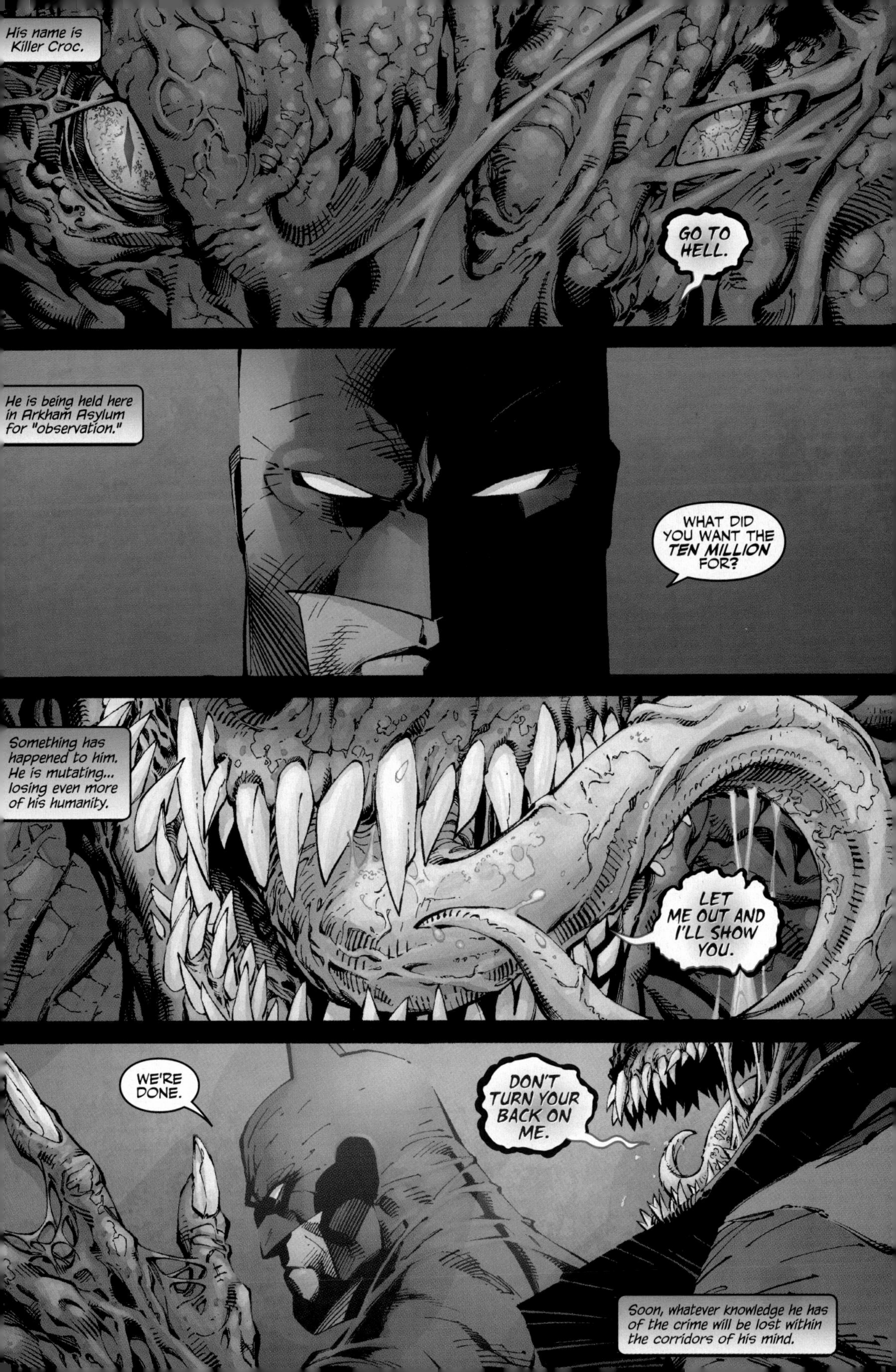
His name is Killer Croc.
GO TO HELL.
He is being held here in Arkham Asylum for "observation."
WHAT DID YOU WANT THE TEN MILLION FOR?
Something has happened to him. He is mutating... losing even more of his humanity.
LET ME OUT AND I'LL SHOW YOU.
WE'RE DONE.
DON'T TURN YOUR BACK ON ME.
Soon, whatever knowledge he has of the crime will be lost within the corridors of his mind.

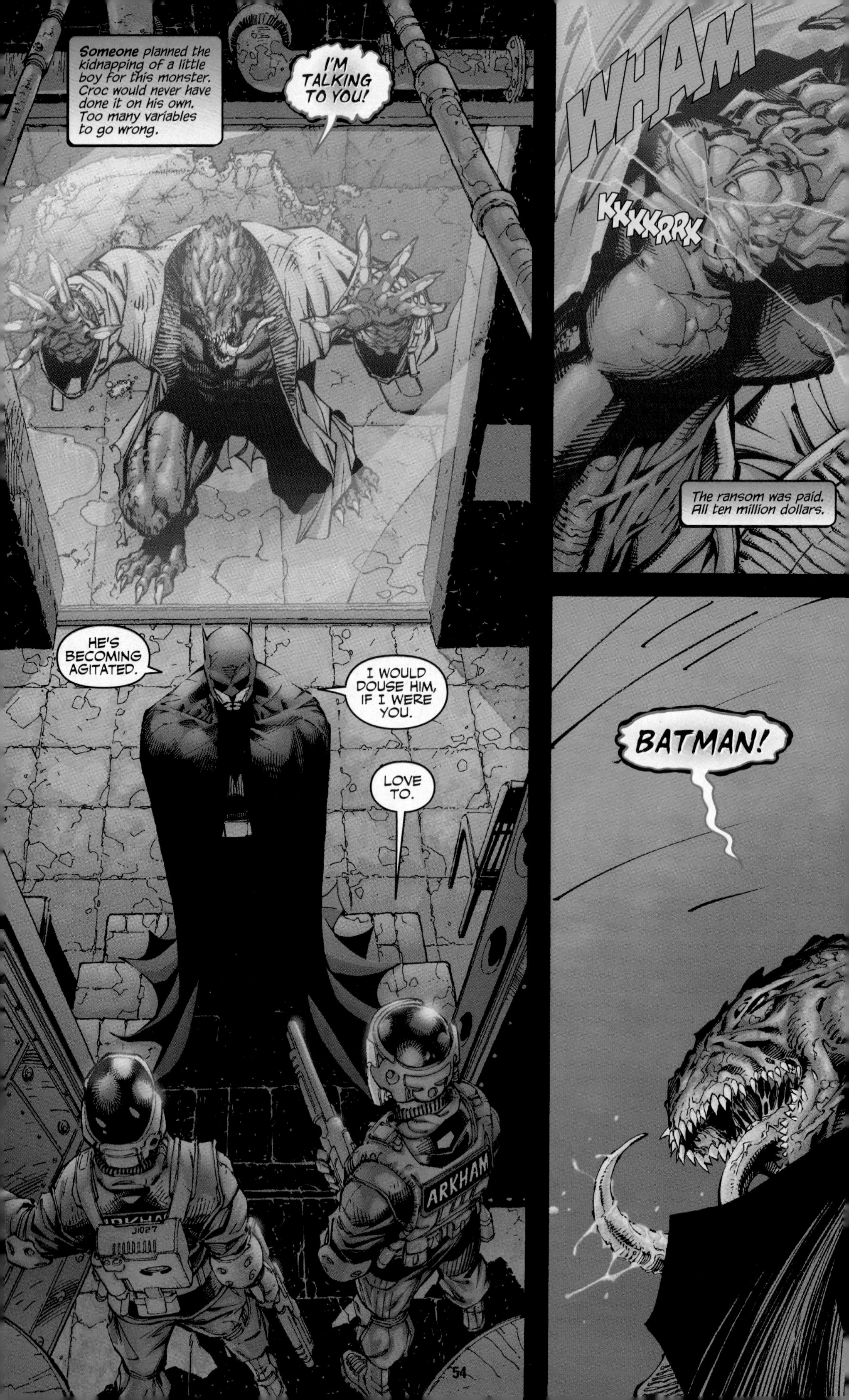
Someone planned the kidnapping of a little boy for this monster. Croc would never have done it on his own. Too many variables to go wrong.
I'M TALKING TO YOU!
HE'S BECOMING AGITATED.
I WOULD DOUSE HIM, IF I WERE YOU.
LOVE TO.
ARKHAM
WHAM
KXXXRRK
The ransom was paid. All ten million dollars.
BATMAN!

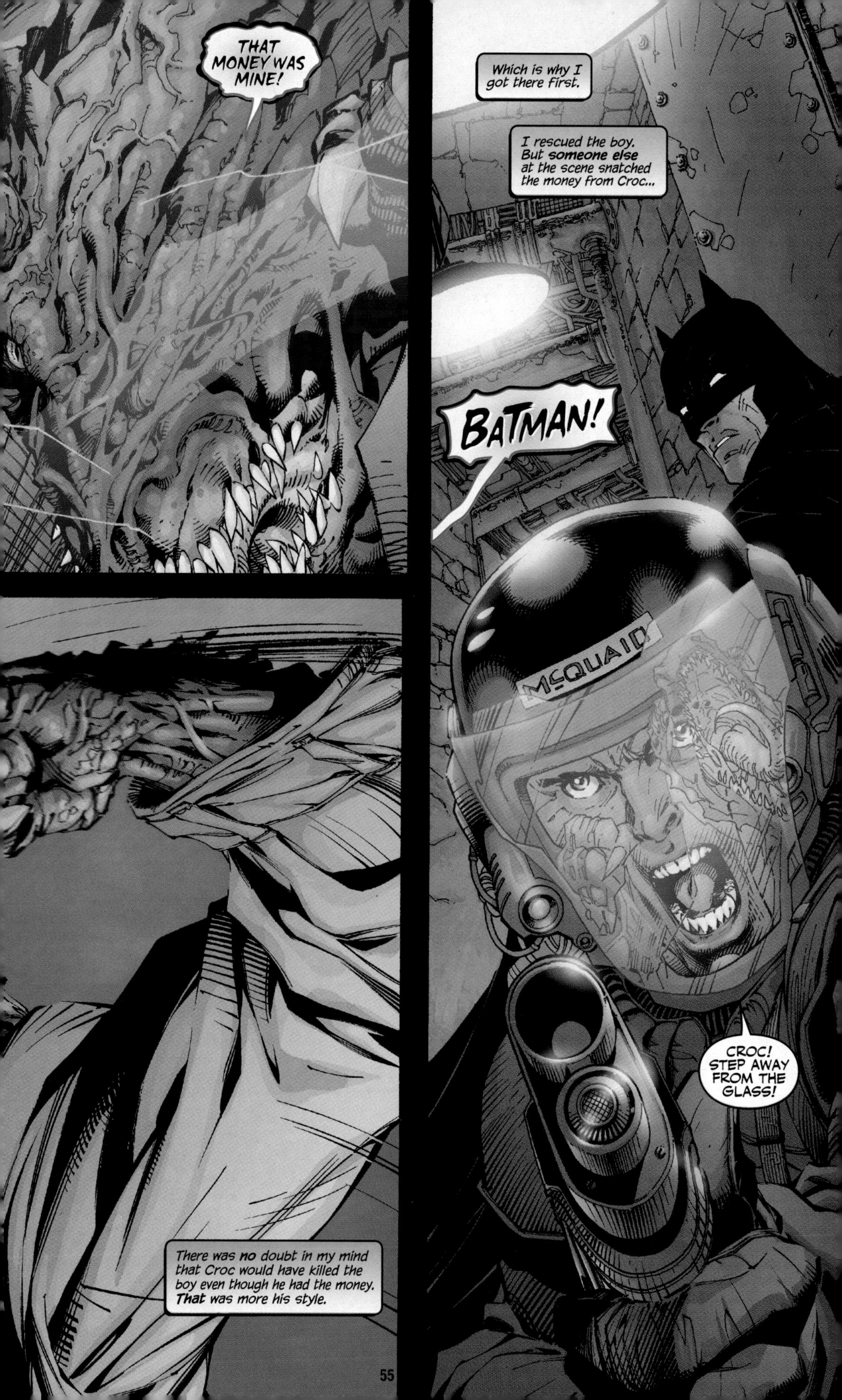
THAT MONEY WAS MINE!
Which is why I got there first.
I rescued the boy. But **someone else** at the scene snatched the money from Croc...
There was **no** doubt in my mind that Croc would have killed the boy even though he had the money. ***That*** was more his style.
BATMAN!
McQUAID
CROC! STEP AWAY FROM THE GLASS!

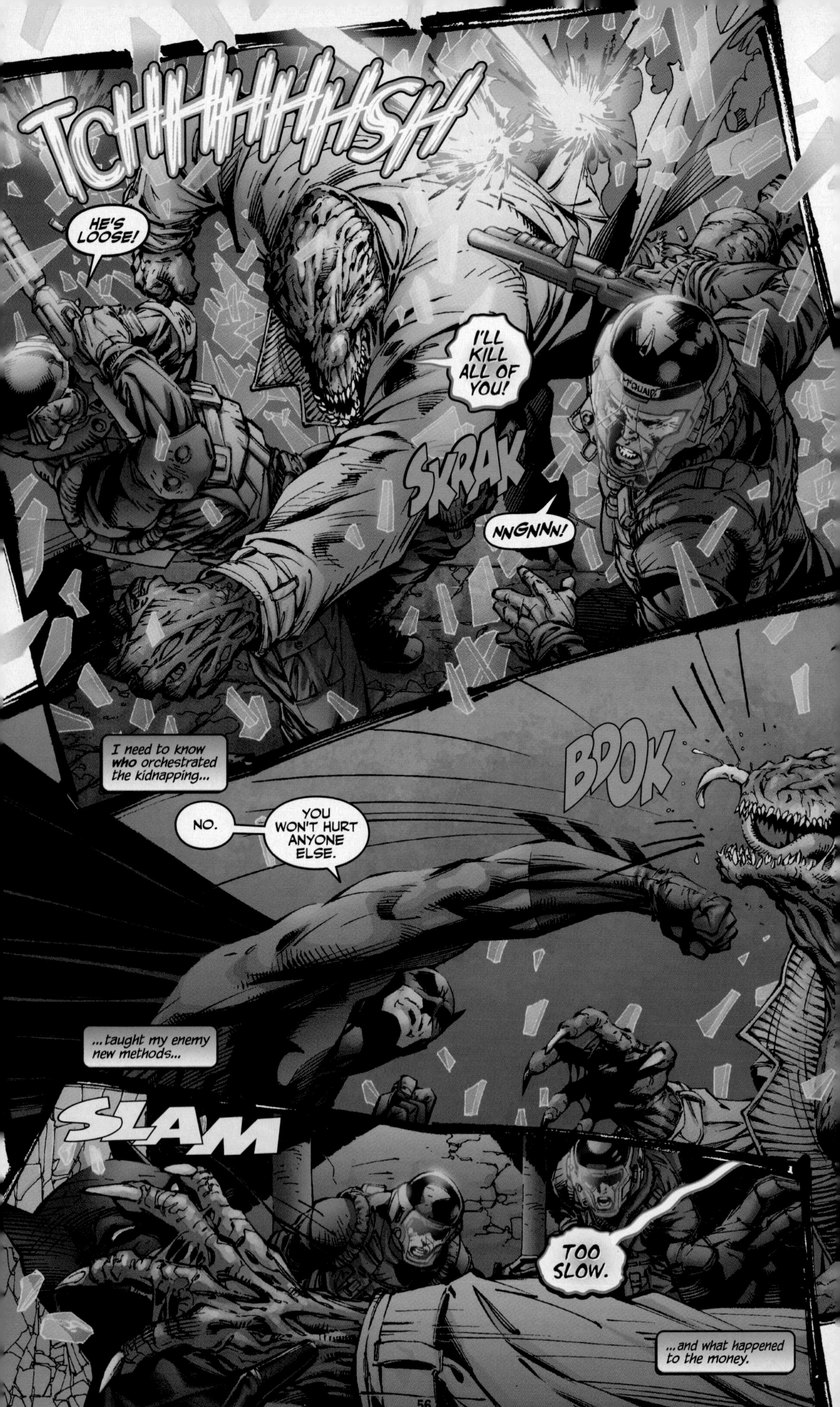
TCHHHHHHSH
HE'S LOOSE!
I'LL KILL ALL OF YOU!
SKRAK
NNGNNN!
I need to know **who** orchestrated the kidnapping...
BDOK
NO.
YOU WON'T HURT ANYONE ELSE.
...taught my enemy new methods...
SLAM
TOO SLOW.
...and what happened to the money.

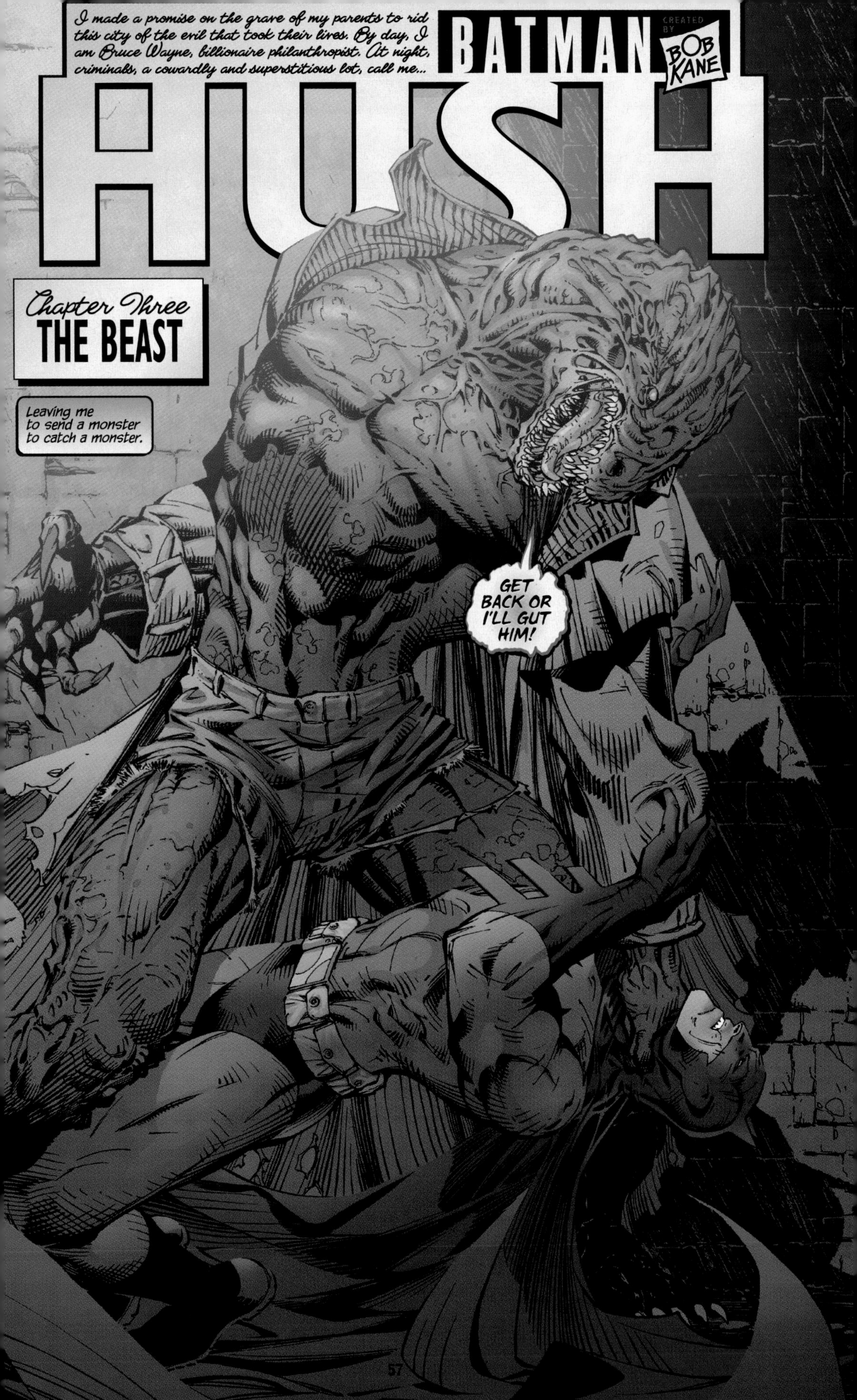
I made a promise on the grave of my parents to rid this city of the evil that took their lives. By day, I am Bruce Wayne, billionaire philanthropist. At night, criminals, a cowardly and superstitious lot, call me...
BATMAN
CREATED BY BOB KANE
HUSH
Chapter Three
THE BEAST
Leaving me to send a monster to catch a monster.
GET BACK OR I'LL GUT HIM!

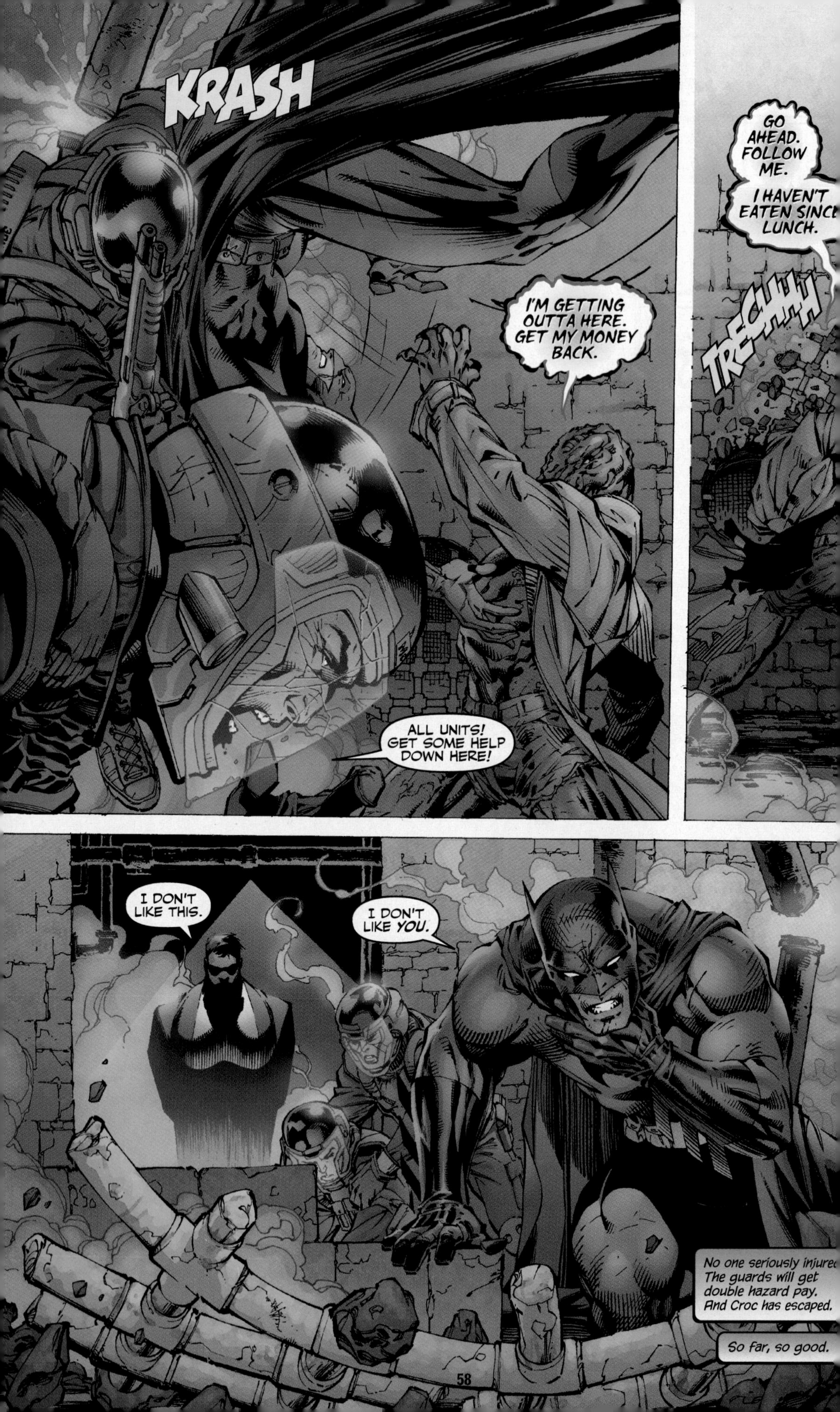
KRASH
I'M GETTING OUTTA HERE. GET MY MONEY BACK.
ALL UNITS! GET SOME HELP DOWN HERE!
GO AHEAD. FOLLOW ME.
I HAVEN'T EATEN SINCE LUNCH.
TRECHHHH
I DON'T LIKE THIS.
I DON'T LIKE *YOU*.
No one seriously injured. The guards will get double hazard pay. And Croc has escaped.
So far, so good.

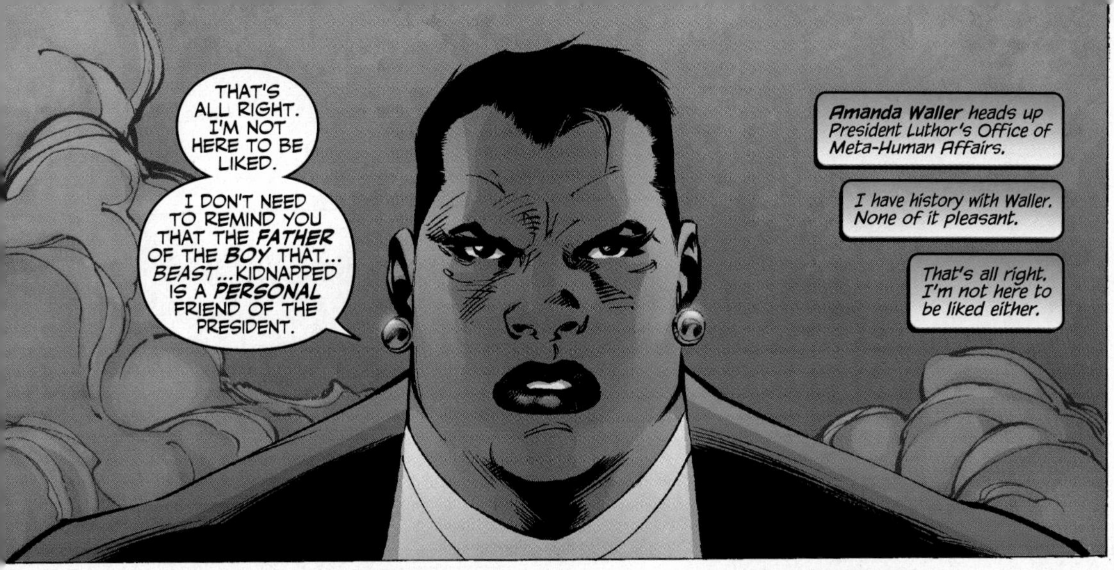
THAT'S ALL RIGHT. I'M NOT HERE TO BE LIKED.
I DON'T NEED TO REMIND YOU THAT THE FATHER OF THE BOY THAT... BEAST...KIDNAPPED IS A PERSONAL FRIEND OF THE PRESIDENT.
Amanda Waller heads up President Luthor's Office of Meta-Human Affairs.
I have history with Waller. None of it pleasant.
That's all right. I'm not here to be liked either.

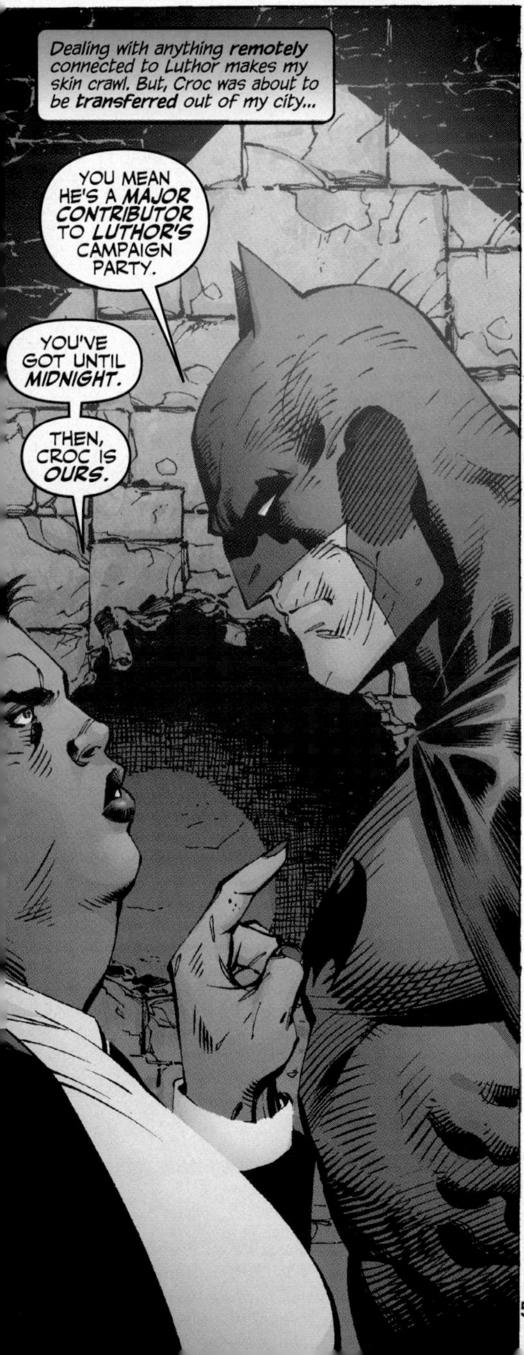
Dealing with anything remotely connected to Luthor makes my skin crawl. But, Croc was about to be transferred out of my city...
YOU MEAN HE'S A MAJOR CONTRIBUTOR TO LUTHOR'S CAMPAIGN PARTY.
YOU'VE GOT UNTIL MIDNIGHT.
THEN, CROC IS OURS.

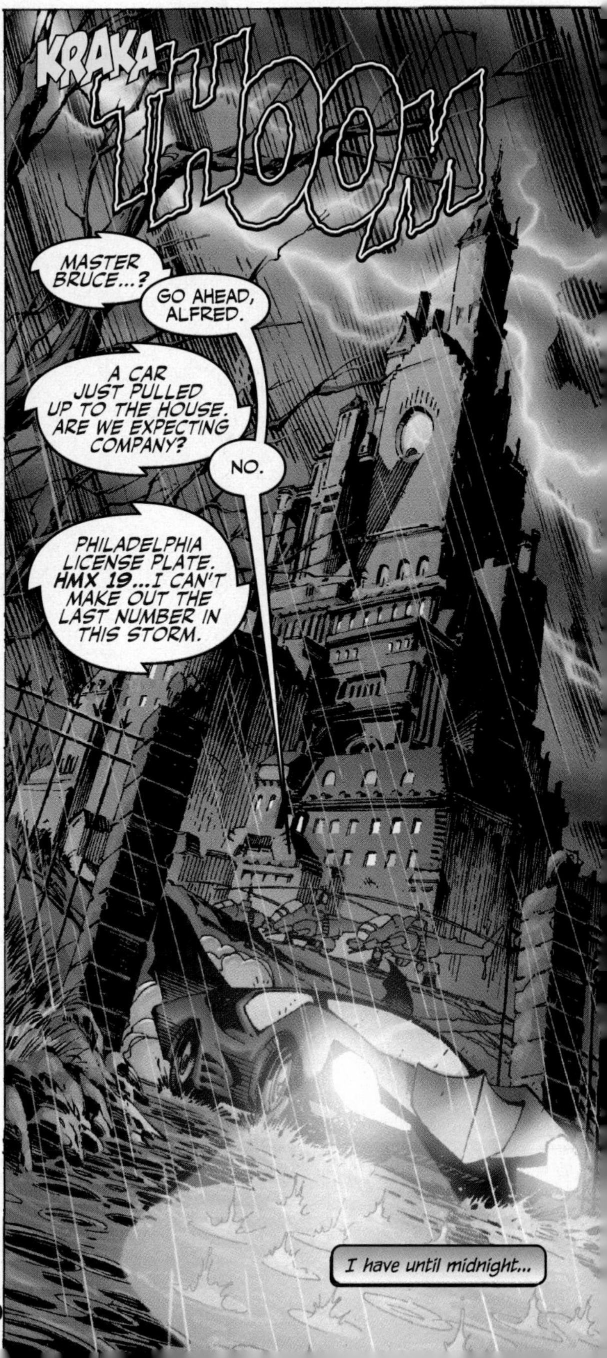
KRAKA THOOM
MASTER BRUCE...?
GO AHEAD, ALFRED.
A CAR JUST PULLED UP TO THE HOUSE. ARE WE EXPECTING COMPANY?
NO.
PHILADELPHIA LICENSE PLATE. HMX 19...I CAN'T MAKE OUT THE LAST NUMBER IN THIS STORM.
I have until midnight...

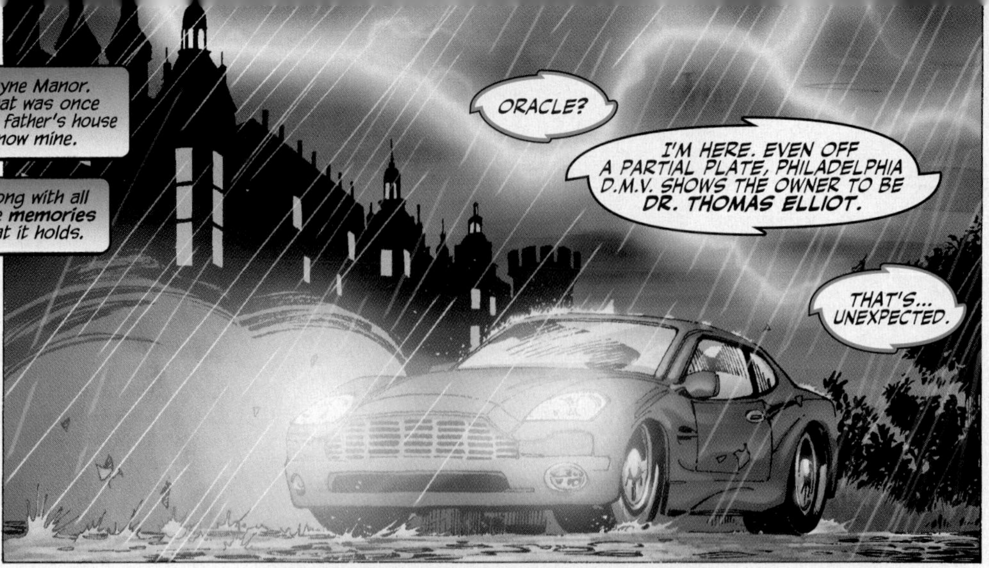
Wayne Manor. What was once my father's house is now mine.
Along with all the **memories** that it holds.
ORACLE?
I'M HERE. EVEN OFF A PARTIAL PLATE, PHILADELPHIA D.M.V. SHOWS THE OWNER TO BE **DR. THOMAS ELLIOT.**
THAT'S... UNEXPECTED.

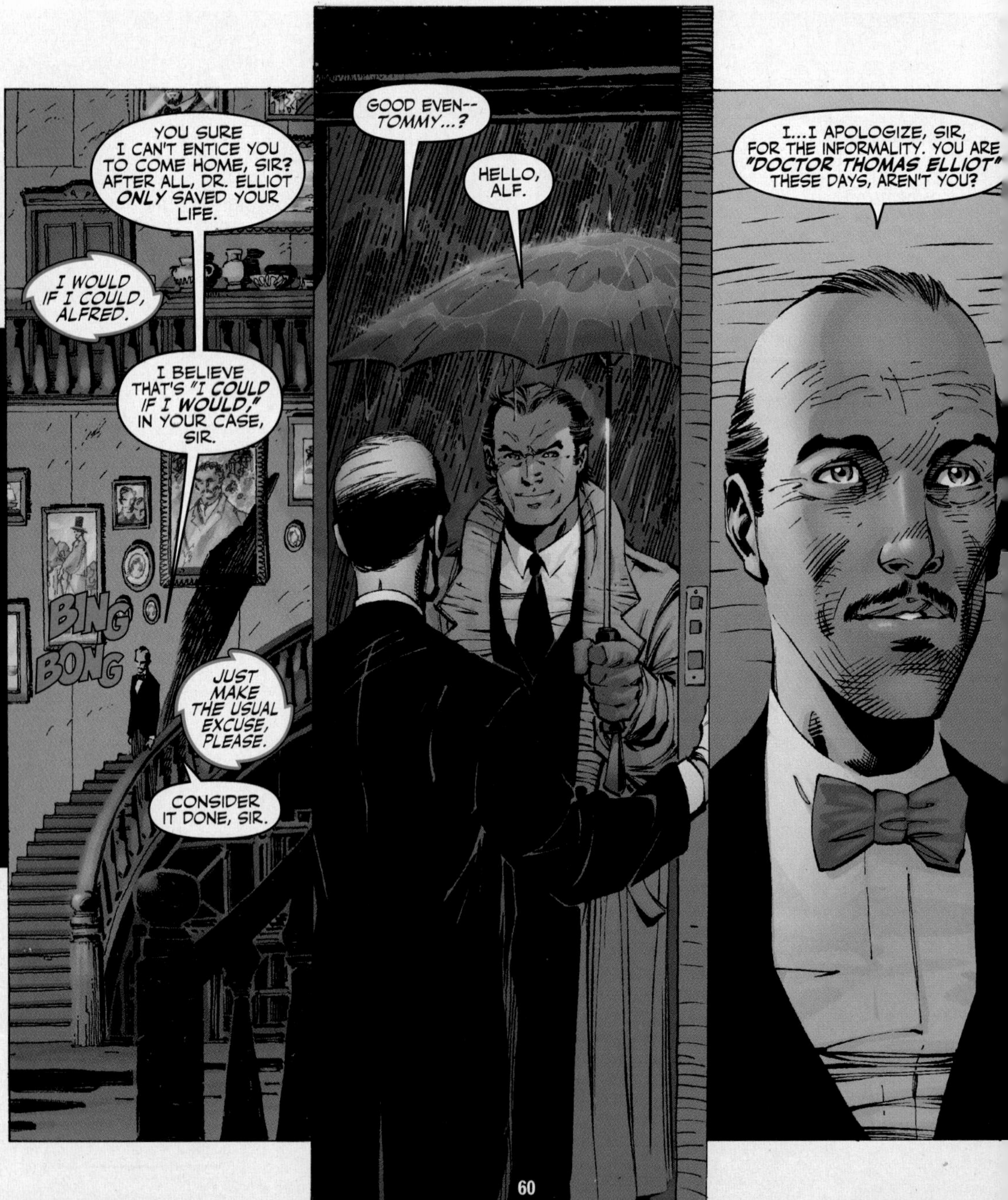
YOU SURE I CAN'T ENTICE YOU TO COME HOME, SIR? AFTER ALL, DR. ELLIOT **ONLY** SAVED YOUR LIFE.
I WOULD IF I COULD, ALFRED.
I BELIEVE THAT'S **"I COULD IF I WOULD,"** IN YOUR CASE, SIR.
BING
BONG
JUST MAKE THE USUAL EXCUSE, PLEASE.
CONSIDER IT DONE, SIR.
GOOD EVEN-- TOMMY...?
HELLO, ALF.
I...I APOLOGIZE, SIR, FOR THE INFORMALITY. YOU ARE **"DOCTOR THOMAS ELLIOT"** THESE DAYS, AREN'T YOU?

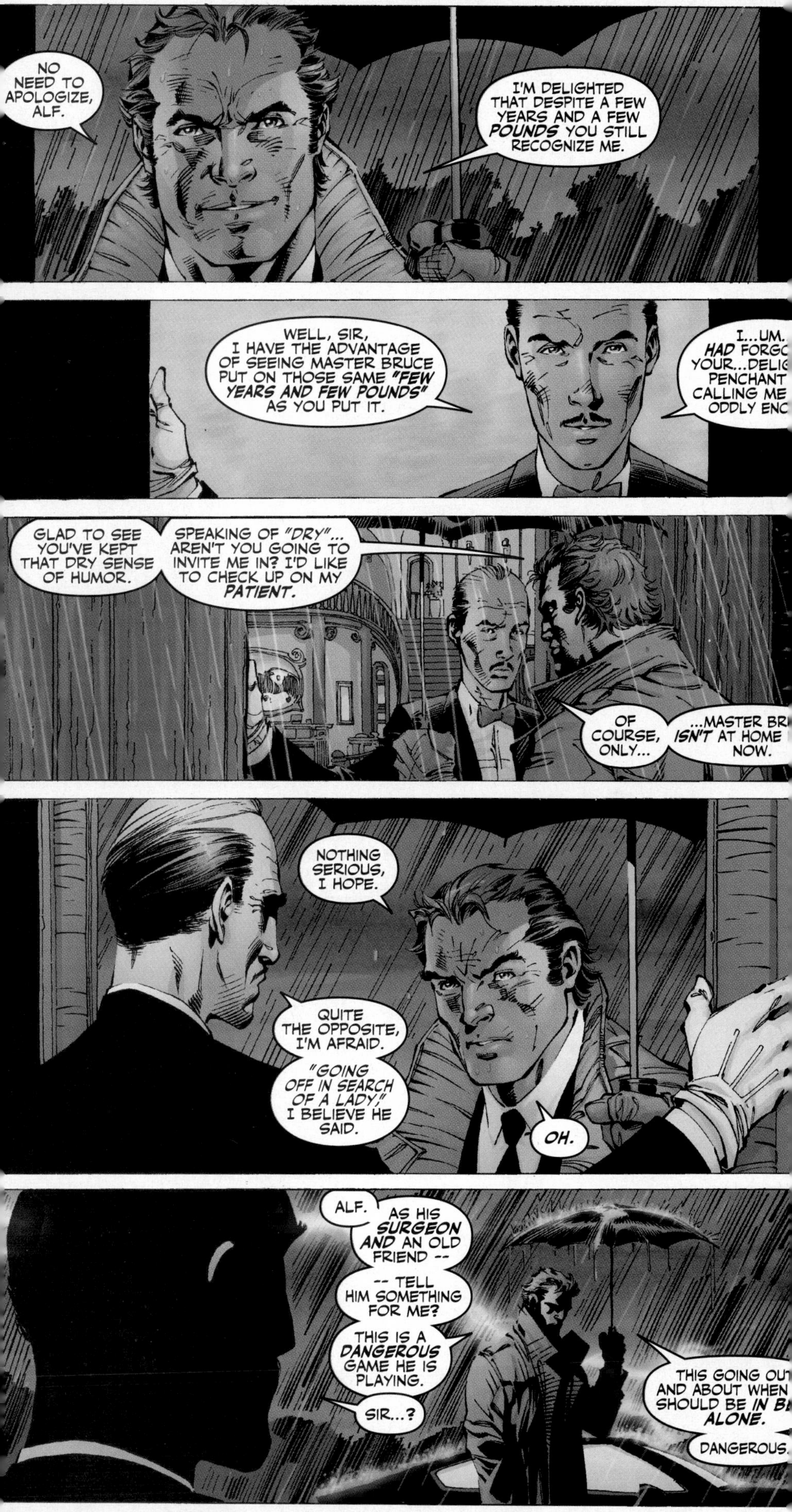
NO NEED TO APOLOGIZE, ALF.
I'M DELIGHTED THAT DESPITE A FEW YEARS AND A FEW POUNDS YOU STILL RECOGNIZE ME.
WELL, SIR, I HAVE THE ADVANTAGE OF SEEING MASTER BRUCE PUT ON THOSE SAME "FEW YEARS AND FEW POUNDS" AS YOU PUT IT.
I...UM. HAD YOUR... PENCHANT CALLING ME ODDLY
GLAD TO SEE YOU'VE KEPT THAT DRY SENSE OF HUMOR.
SPEAKING OF "DRY"... AREN'T YOU GOING TO INVITE ME IN? I'D LIKE TO CHECK UP ON MY PATIENT.
OF COURSE, ONLY...
...MASTER ISN'T AT HOME NOW.
NOTHING SERIOUS, I HOPE.
QUITE THE OPPOSITE, I'M AFRAID.
"GOING OFF IN SEARCH OF A LADY," I BELIEVE HE SAID.
OH.
ALF.
AS HIS SURGEON AND AN OLD FRIEND --
-- TELL HIM SOMETHING FOR ME?
THIS IS A DANGEROUS GAME HE IS PLAYING.
SIR...?
THIS GOING AND ABOUT WHEN SHOULD BE ALONE.
DANGEROUS.

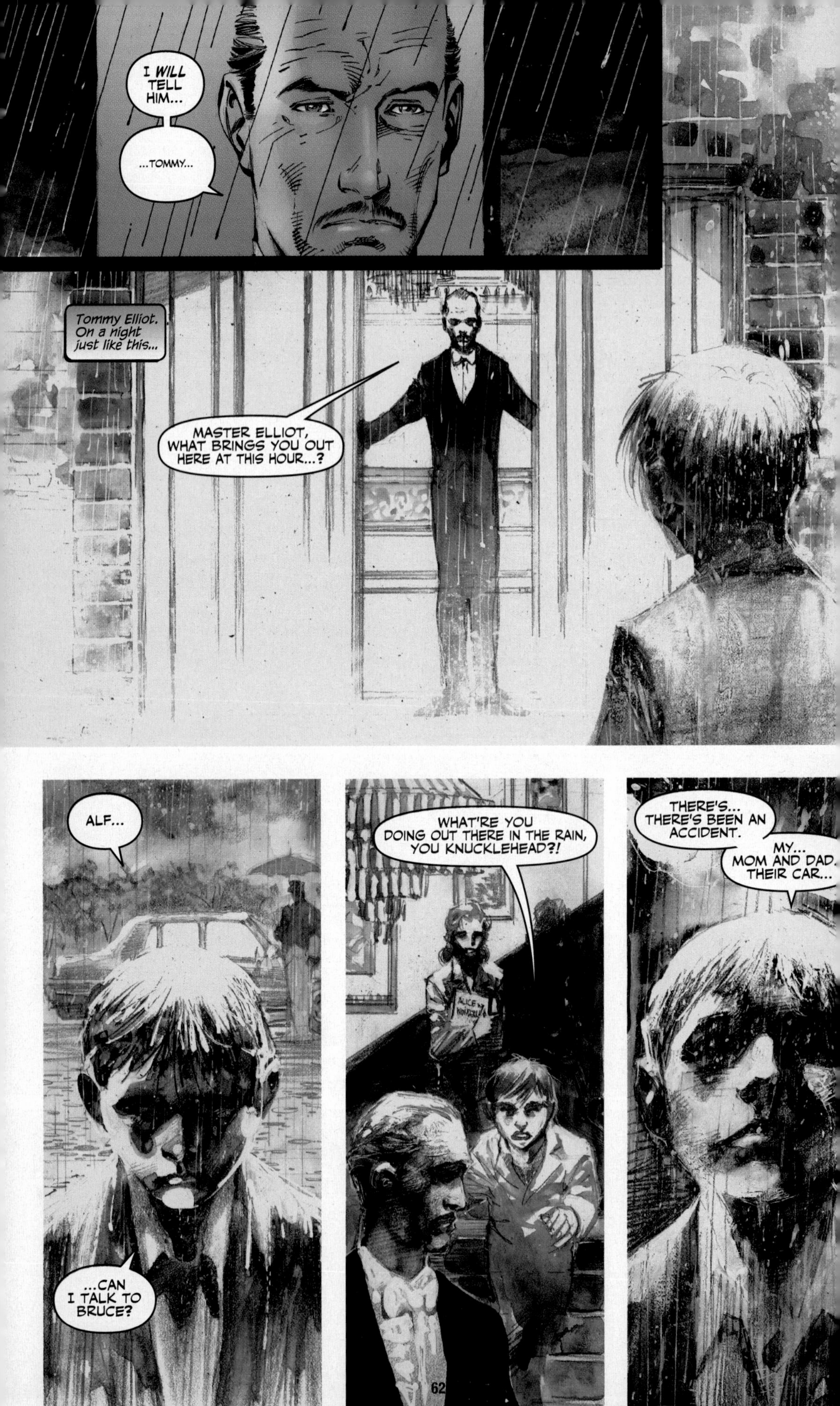
I WILL TELL HIM...
...TOMMY...
Tommy Elliot. On a night just like this...
MASTER ELLIOT, WHAT BRINGS YOU OUT HERE AT THIS HOUR...?
ALF...
...CAN I TALK TO BRUCE?
WHAT'RE YOU DOING OUT THERE IN THE RAIN, YOU KNUCKLEHEAD?!
THERE'S... THERE'S BEEN AN ACCIDENT.
MY... MOM AND DAD. THEIR CAR...

Gotham City Hospital. My father was Head of Trauma Surgery back then.

Hospitals are awful places at night.

Especially for children...

MY DAD IS IN THERE, TOMMY. NOTHING BAD IS GOING TO HAPPEN.

I *TRIED* TO WARN MISTER ELLIOT.

NIGHT LIKE THIS, THE ROADS GET SLIPPERY.

I SHOULD HAVE BEEN DRIVING THEM -- BUT HE *INSISTED* ON GOING OUT ALONE WITH THE MISSUS.

YOU MUSTN'T BLAME YOURSELF, *CLARENCE. ACCIDENTS* WILL HAPPEN.

AND GIVEN THE SITUATION, THEY COULD NOT BE IN BETTER HANDS.

YOU SWEAR...?

STICK A NEEDLE IN MY EYE.

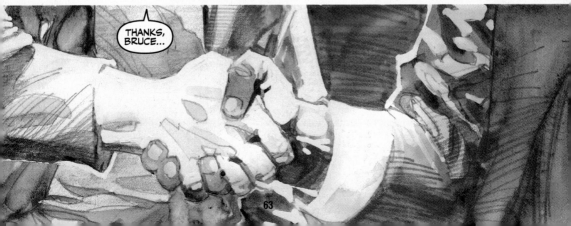

THANKS, BRUCE...

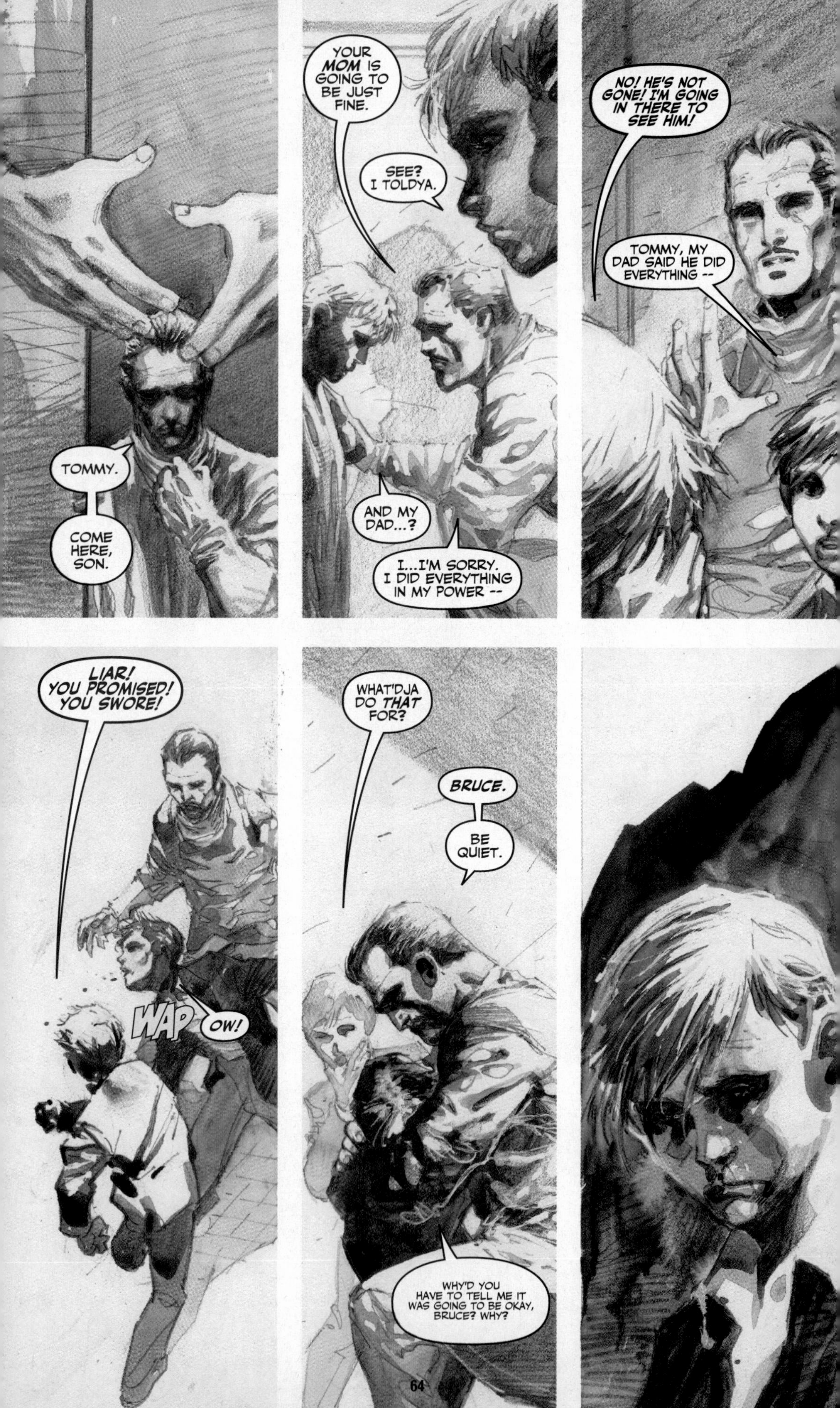
TOMMY.
COME HERE, SON.
YOUR MOM IS GOING TO BE JUST FINE.
SEE? I TOLDYA.
AND MY DAD...?
I...I'M SORRY. I DID EVERYTHING IN MY POWER --
NO! HE'S NOT GONE! I'M GOING IN THERE TO SEE HIM!
TOMMY, MY DAD SAID HE DID EVERYTHING --
LIAR! YOU PROMISED! YOU SWORE!
WAP
OW!
WHAT'DJA DO THAT FOR?
BRUCE.
BE QUIET.
WHY'D YOU HAVE TO TELL ME IT WAS GOING TO BE OKAY, BRUCE? WHY?

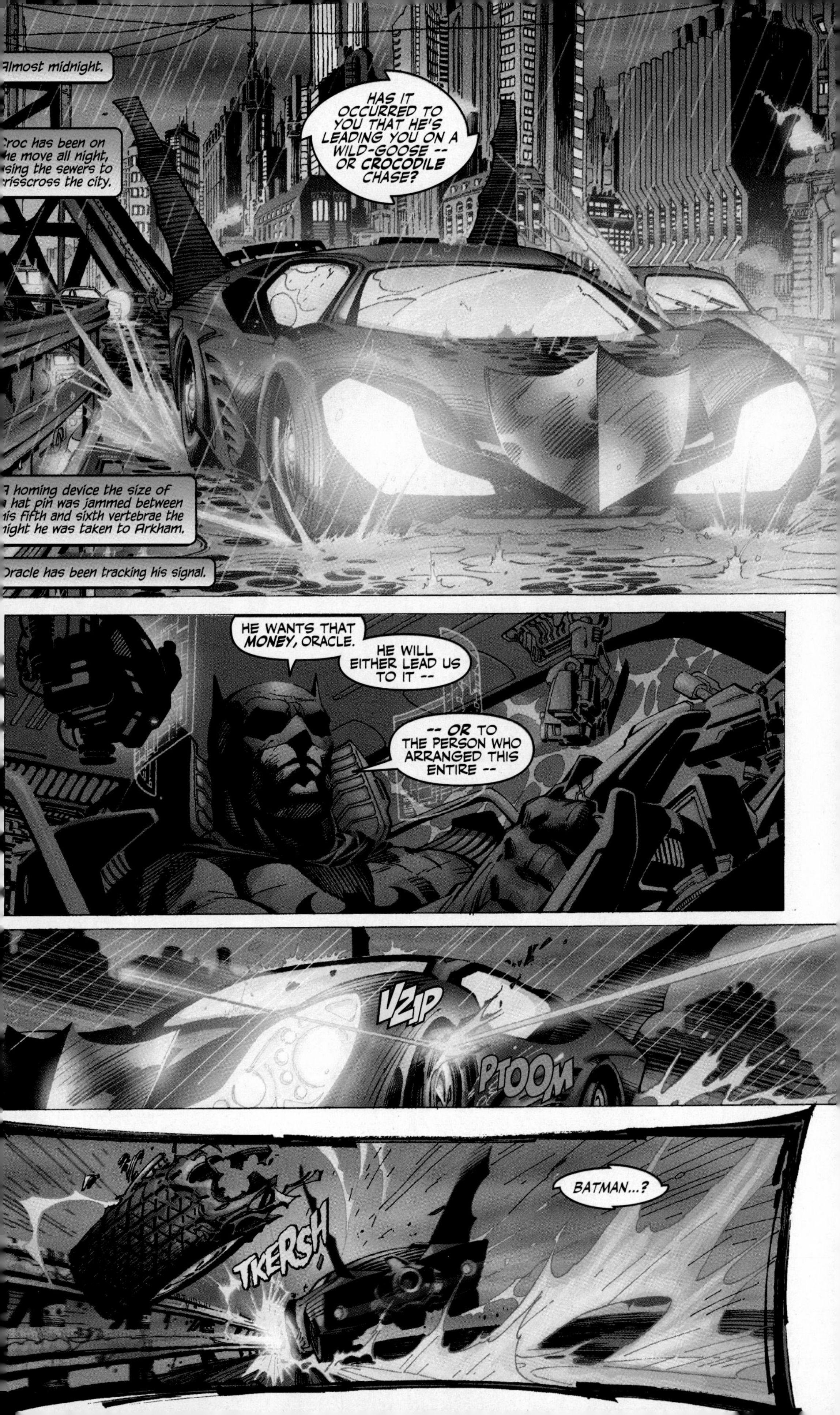
Almost midnight.
HAS IT OCCURRED TO YOU THAT HE'S LEADING YOU ON A WILD-GOOSE -- OR CROCODILE CHASE?
Croc has been on
he move all night,
sing the sewers to
risscross the city.
homing device the size of
hat pin was jammed between
is fifth and sixth vertebrae the
night he was taken to Arkham.
racle has been tracking his signal.
HE WANTS THAT MONEY, ORACLE.
HE WILL EITHER LEAD US TO IT --
-- OR TO THE PERSON WHO ARRANGED THIS ENTIRE --
VZIP
PTOOM
TKERSH
BATMAN...?

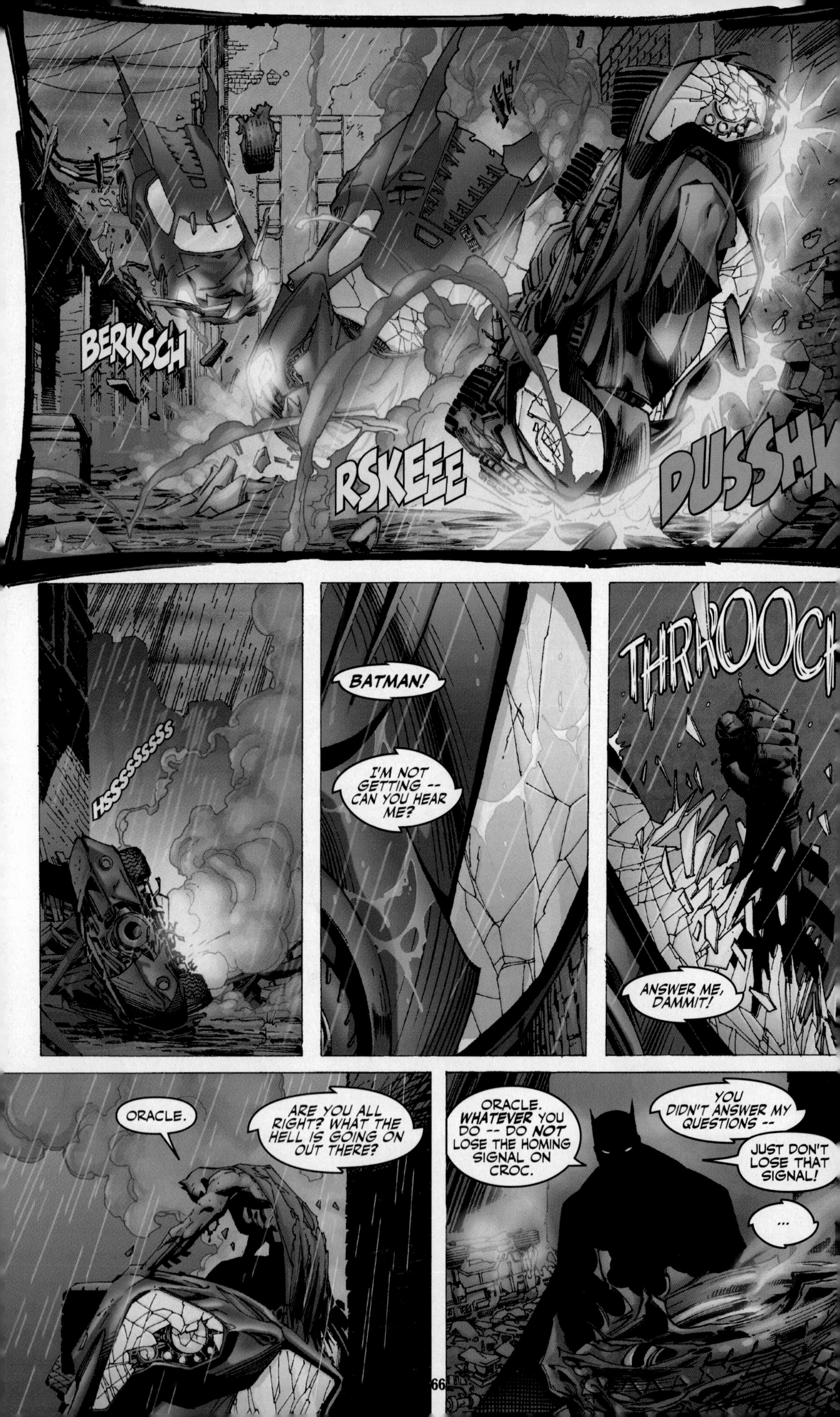
BERKSCH
RSKEEE
DUSSHK
HSSSSSSSSS
BATMAN!
I'M NOT GETTING -- CAN YOU HEAR ME?
THRROOCH
ANSWER ME, DAMMIT!
ORACLE.
ARE YOU ALL RIGHT? WHAT THE HELL IS GOING ON OUT THERE?
ORACLE. WHATEVER YOU DO -- DO NOT LOSE THE HOMING SIGNAL ON CROC.
YOU DIDN'T ANSWER MY QUESTIONS --
JUST DON'T LOSE THAT SIGNAL!
...

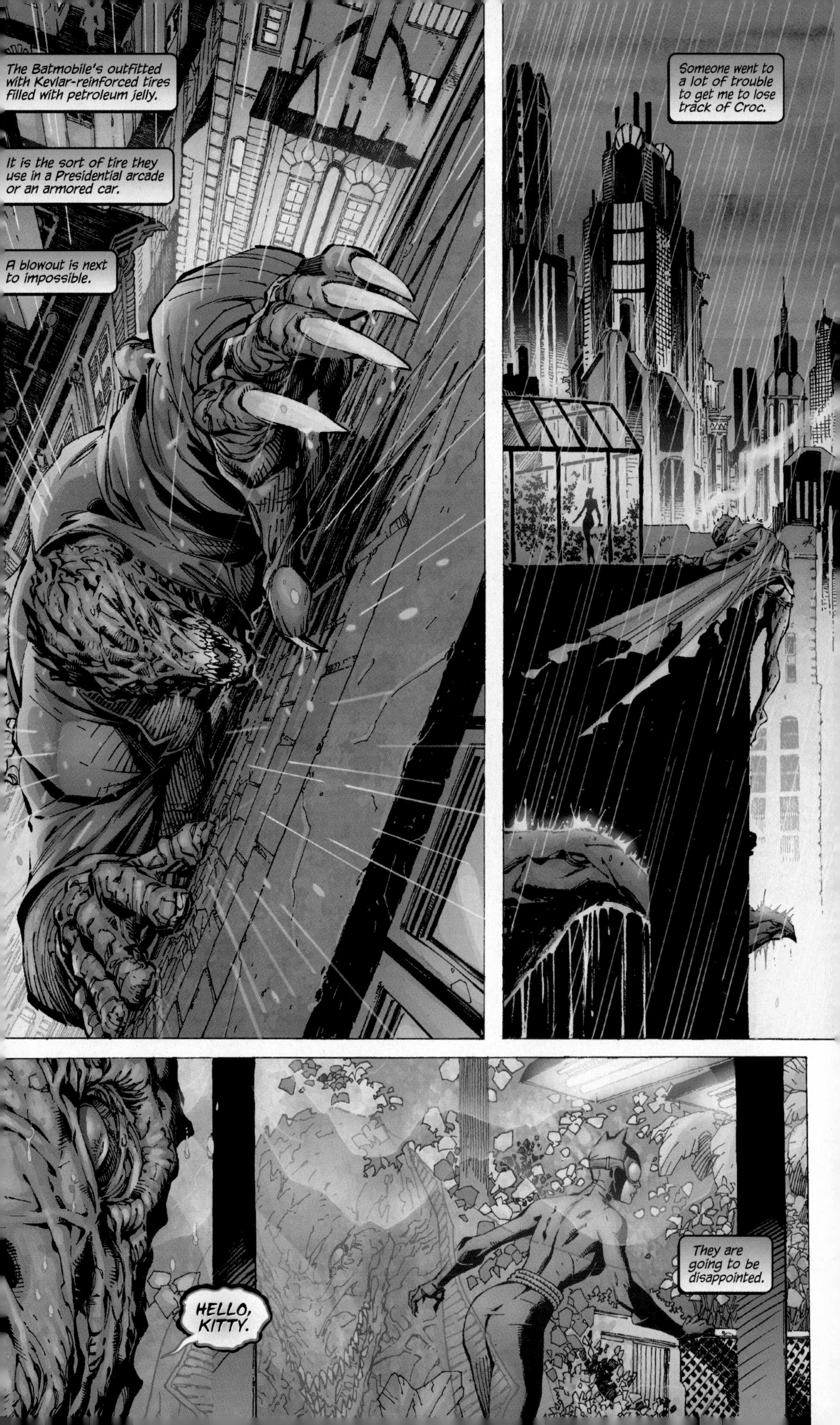

The Batmobile's outfitted with Kevlar-reinforced tires filled with petroleum jelly.
It is the sort of tire they use in a Presidential arcade or an armored car.
A blowout is next to impossible.
Someone went to a lot of trouble to get me to lose track of Croc.
HELLO, KITTY.
They are going to be disappointed.

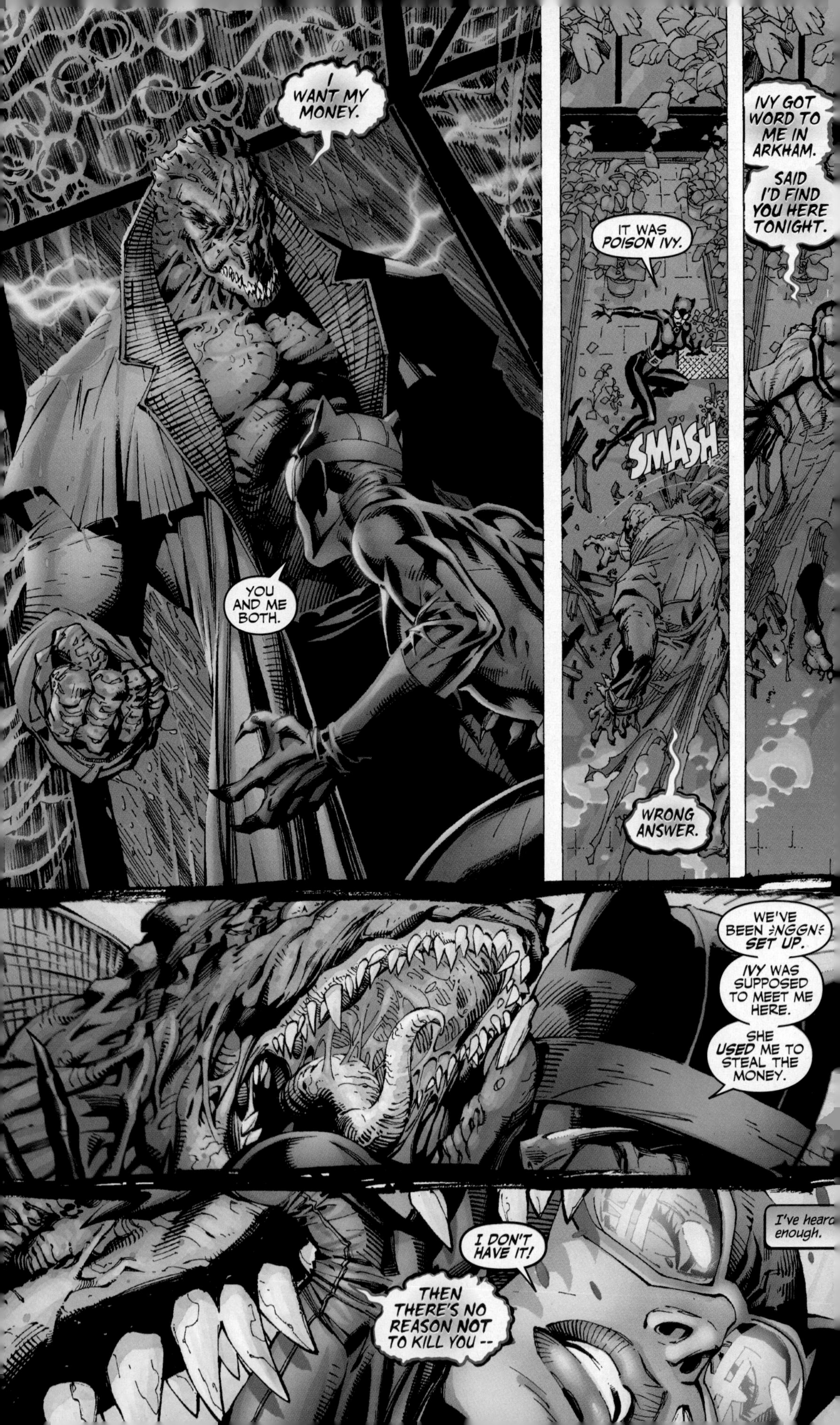
I WANT MY MONEY.
YOU AND ME BOTH.
IT WAS POISON IVY.
SMASH
WRONG ANSWER.
IVY GOT WORD TO ME IN ARKHAM.
SAID I'D FIND YOU HERE TONIGHT.
WE'VE BEEN NGGN SET UP.
IVY WAS SUPPOSED TO MEET ME HERE.
SHE USED ME TO STEAL THE MONEY.
I DON'T HAVE IT!
THEN THERE'S NO REASON NOT TO KILL YOU --
I've heard enough.

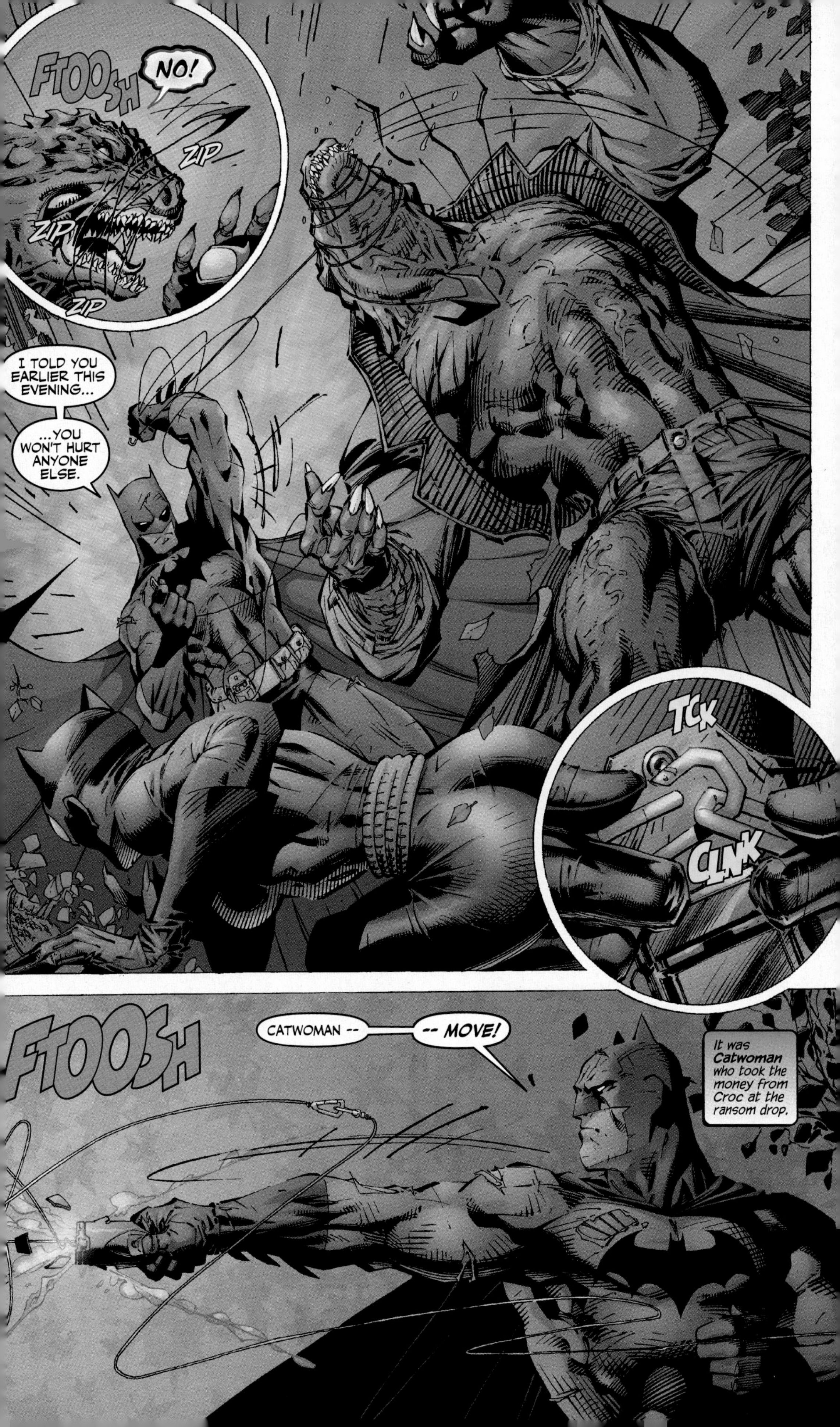
FTOOSH
NO!
ZIP
ZIP
ZIP
I TOLD YOU EARLIER THIS EVENING...
...YOU WON'T HURT ANYONE ELSE.
TCK
CLINK
FTOOSH
CATWOMAN --
-- MOVE!
It was Catwoman who took the money from Croc at the ransom drop.

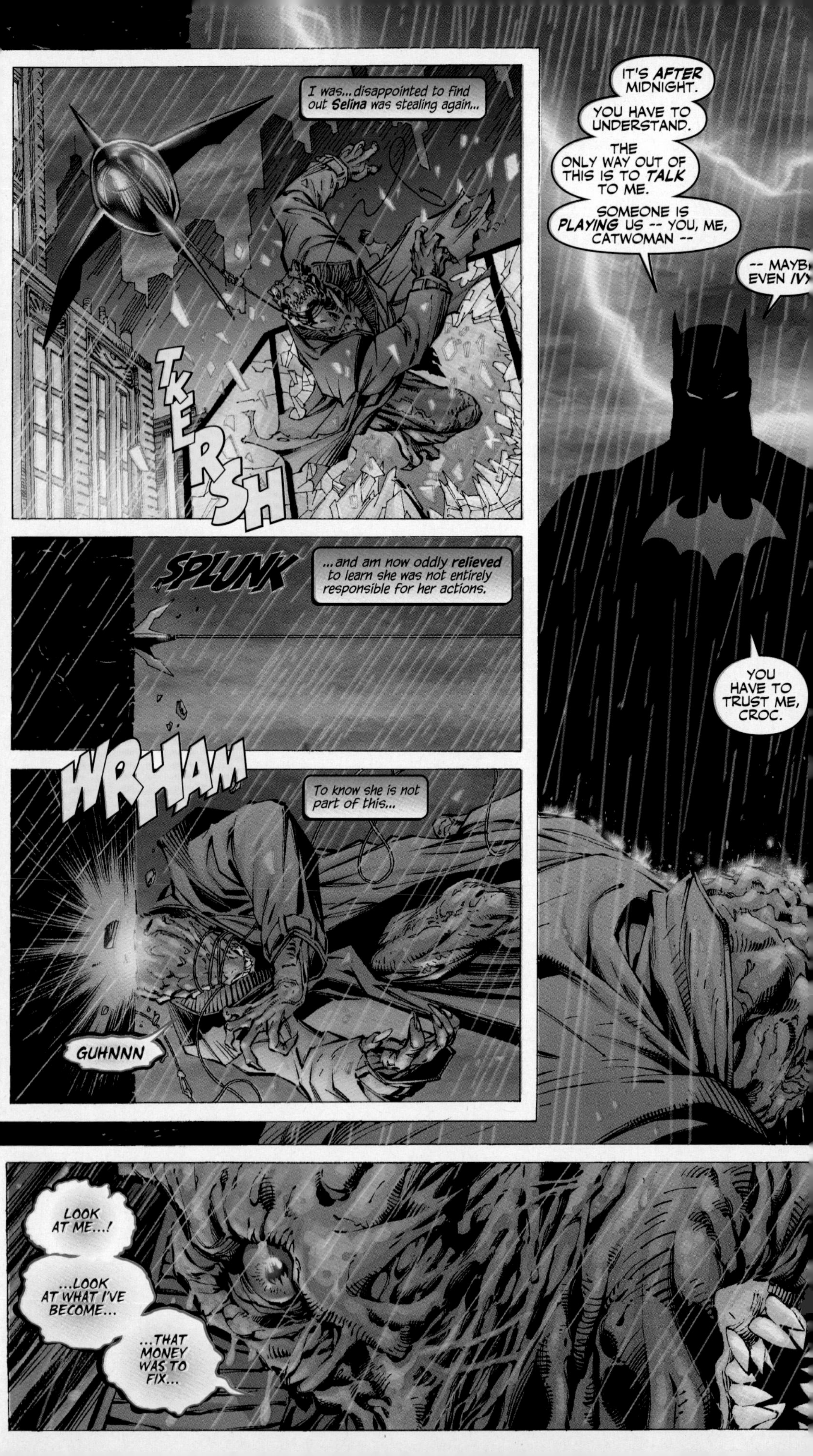
I was... disappointed to find out Selina was stealing again...
TKERSH
IT'S AFTER MIDNIGHT.
YOU HAVE TO UNDERSTAND.
THE ONLY WAY OUT OF THIS IS TO TALK TO ME.
SOMEONE IS PLAYING US -- YOU, ME, CATWOMAN --
-- MAYB EVEN IV
SPLUNK
...and am now oddly relieved to learn she was not entirely responsible for her actions.
YOU HAVE TO TRUST ME, CROC.
WRHAM
To know she is not part of this...
GUHNNN
LOOK AT ME...!
...LOOK AT WHAT I'VE BECOME...
...THAT MONEY WAS TO FIX...

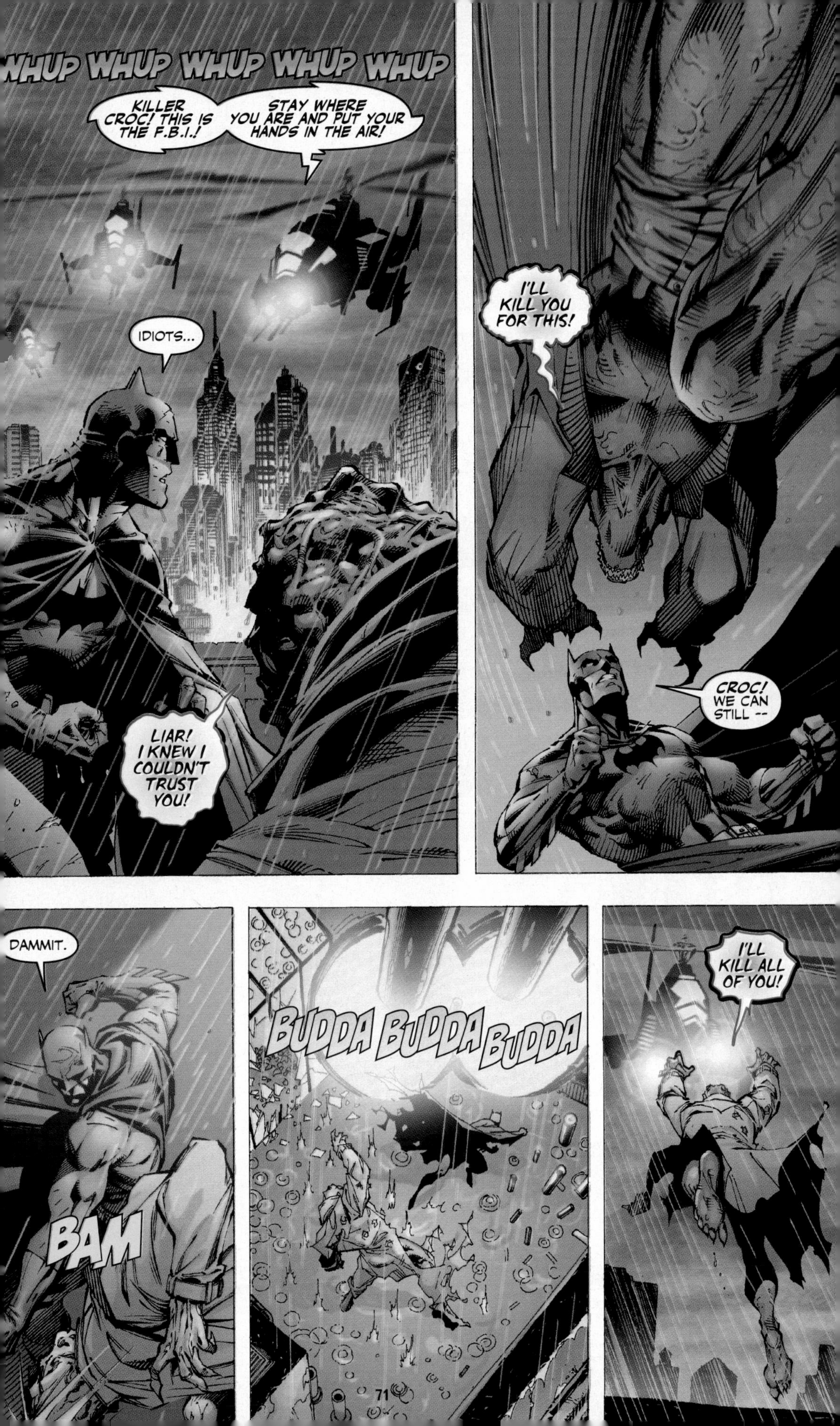
WHUP WHUP WHUP WHUP WHUP
KILLER CROC! THIS IS THE F.B.I.!
STAY WHERE YOU ARE AND PUT YOUR HANDS IN THE AIR!
IDIOTS...
LIAR! I KNEW I COULDN'T TRUST YOU!
I'LL KILL YOU FOR THIS!
CROC! WE CAN STILL --
DAMMIT.
BAM
BUDDA BUDDA BUDDA
I'LL KILL ALL OF YOU!

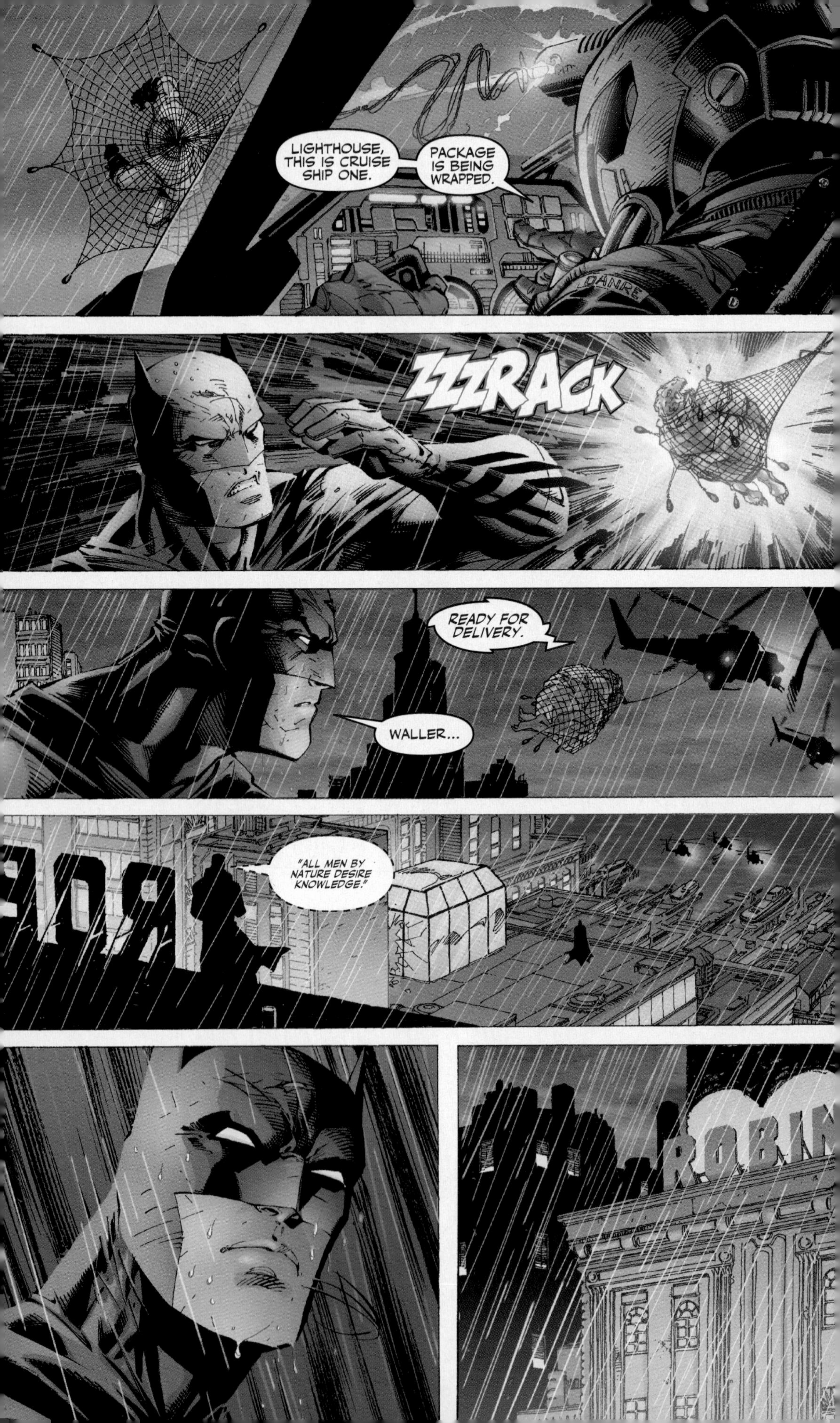
LIGHTHOUSE, THIS IS CRUISE SHIP ONE.
PACKAGE IS BEING WRAPPED.
ZZZRACK
READY FOR DELIVERY.
WALLER...
"ALL MEN BY NATURE DESIRE KNOWLEDGE."
ROBIN

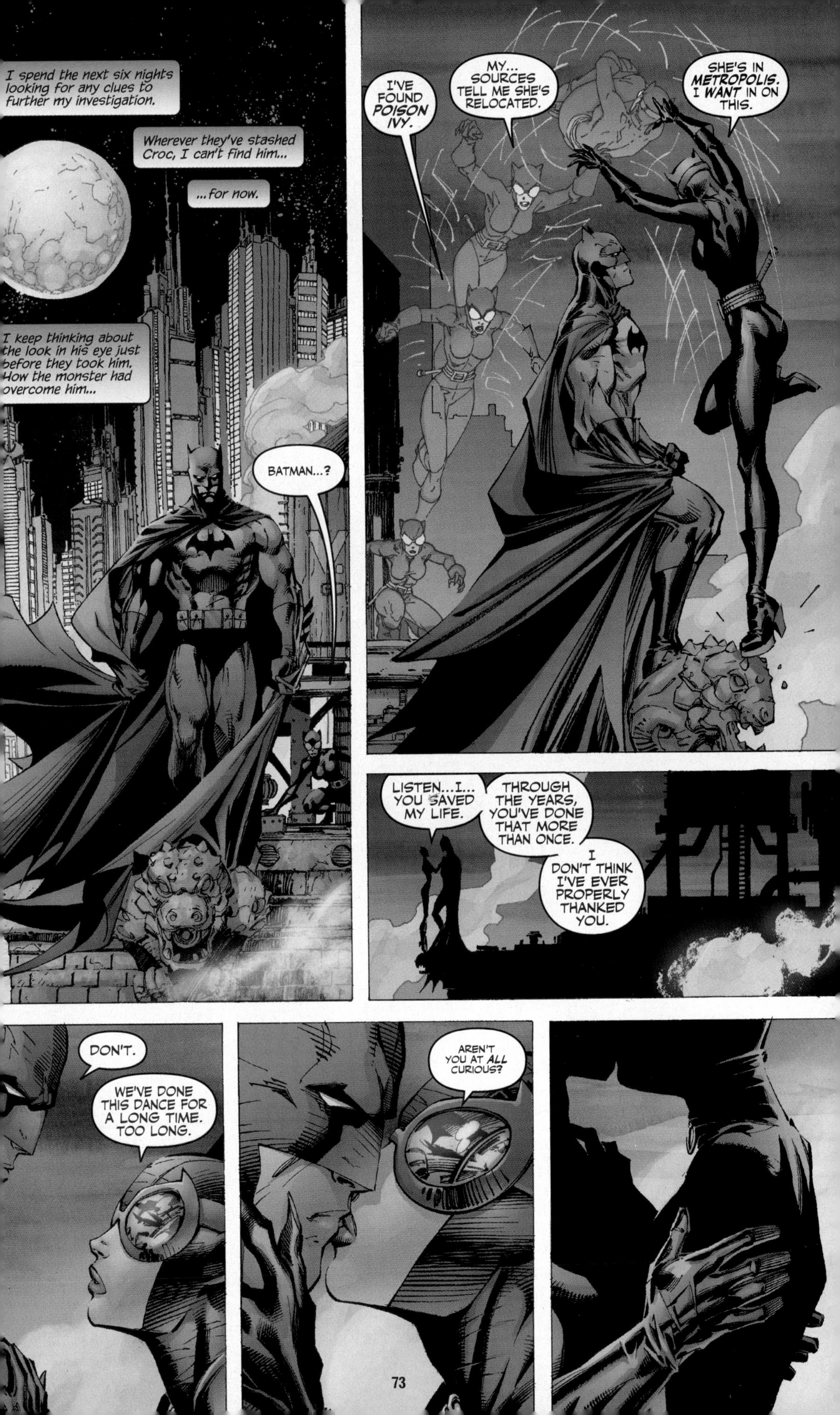

I spend the next six nights looking for any clues to further my investigation.
Wherever they've stashed Croc, I can't find him...
...for now.
I keep thinking about the look in his eye just before they took him. How the monster had overcome him...
BATMAN...?
I'VE FOUND POISON IVY.
MY... SOURCES TELL ME SHE'S RELOCATED.
SHE'S IN METROPOLIS. I WANT IN ON THIS.
LISTEN...I... YOU SAVED MY LIFE.
THROUGH THE YEARS, YOU'VE DONE THAT MORE THAN ONCE.
I DON'T THINK I'VE EVER PROPERLY THANKED YOU.
DON'T.
WE'VE DONE THIS DANCE FOR A LONG TIME. TOO LONG.
AREN'T YOU AT ALL CURIOUS?

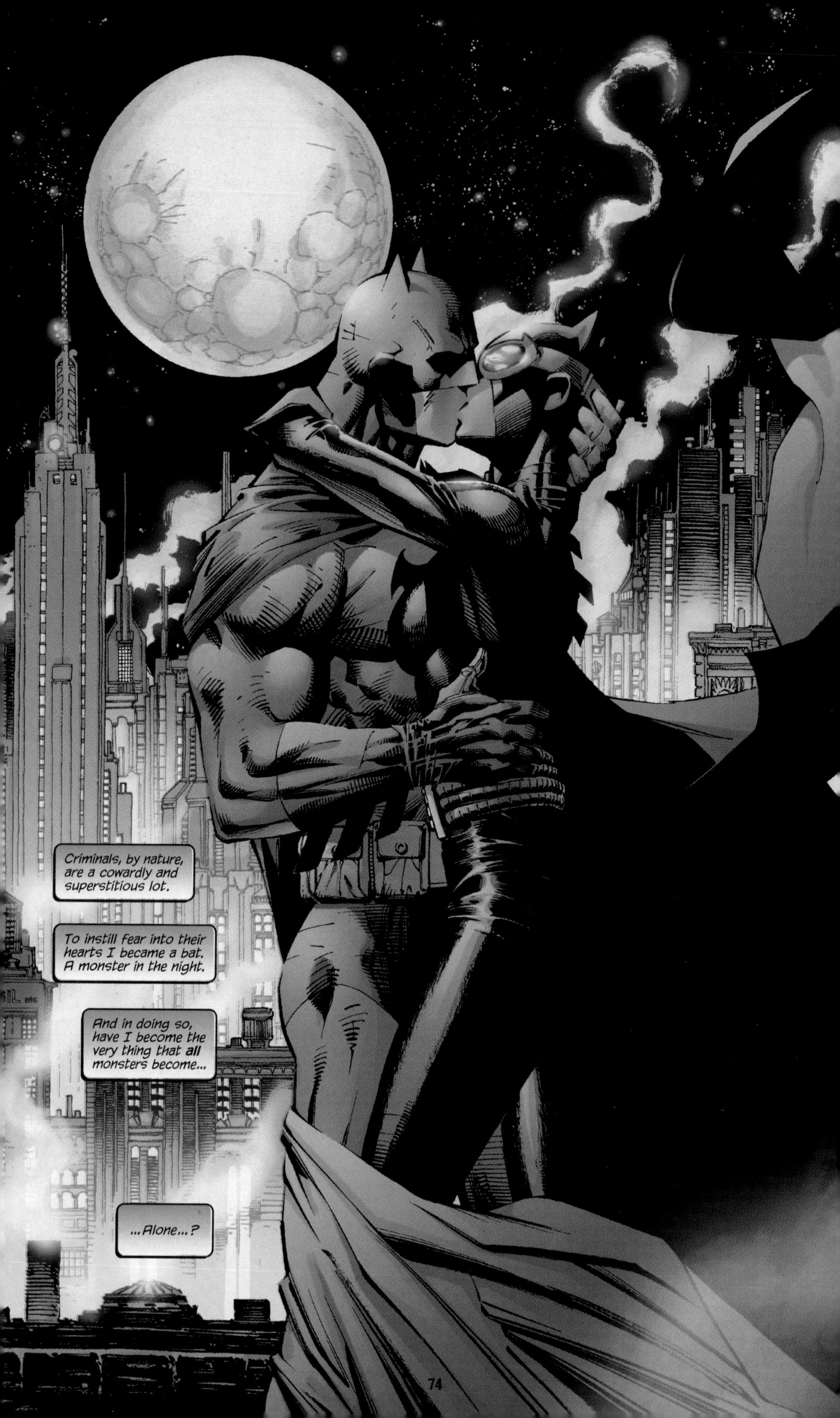
Criminals, by nature, are a cowardly and superstitious lot.
To instill fear into their hearts I became a bat. A monster in the night.
And in doing so, have I become the very thing that **all** monsters become...
...Alone...?

Metropolis.

It is very different from *Gotham City* and for that alone...

...I try to avoid coming here.

There are not many reasons for *Batman* to be in this city.

WAYNETECH

But, no one will raise an eyebrow when *Bruce Wayne* comes to town.

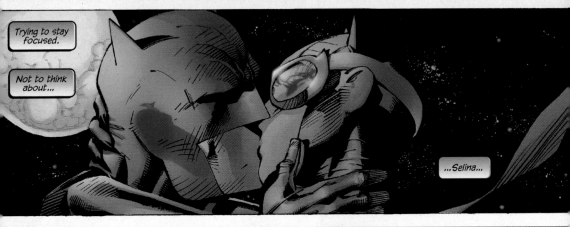

Trying to stay focused.

Not to think about...

...*Selina*...

The last time I remember actually *wanting* to be here was years ago.

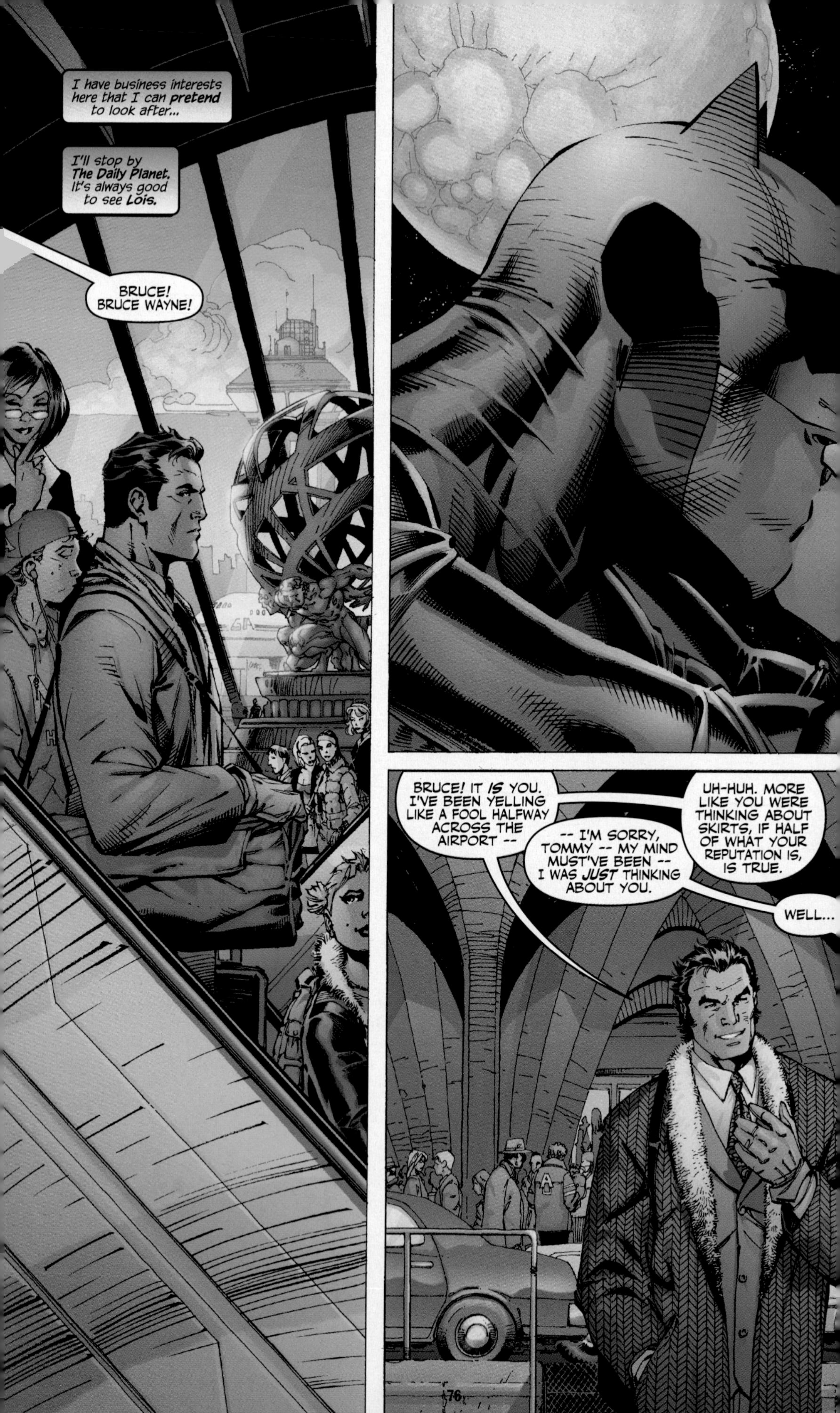

I have business interests here that I can **pretend** to look after...
I'll stop by **The Daily Planet.** It's always good to see **Lois.**
BRUCE! BRUCE WAYNE!
BRUCE! IT ***IS*** YOU. I'VE BEEN YELLING LIKE A FOOL HALFWAY ACROSS THE AIRPORT --
-- I'M SORRY, TOMMY -- MY MIND MUST'VE BEEN -- I WAS ***JUST*** THINKING ABOUT YOU.
UH-HUH. MORE LIKE YOU WERE THINKING ABOUT SKIRTS, IF HALF OF WHAT YOUR REPUTATION IS, IS TRUE.
WELL...

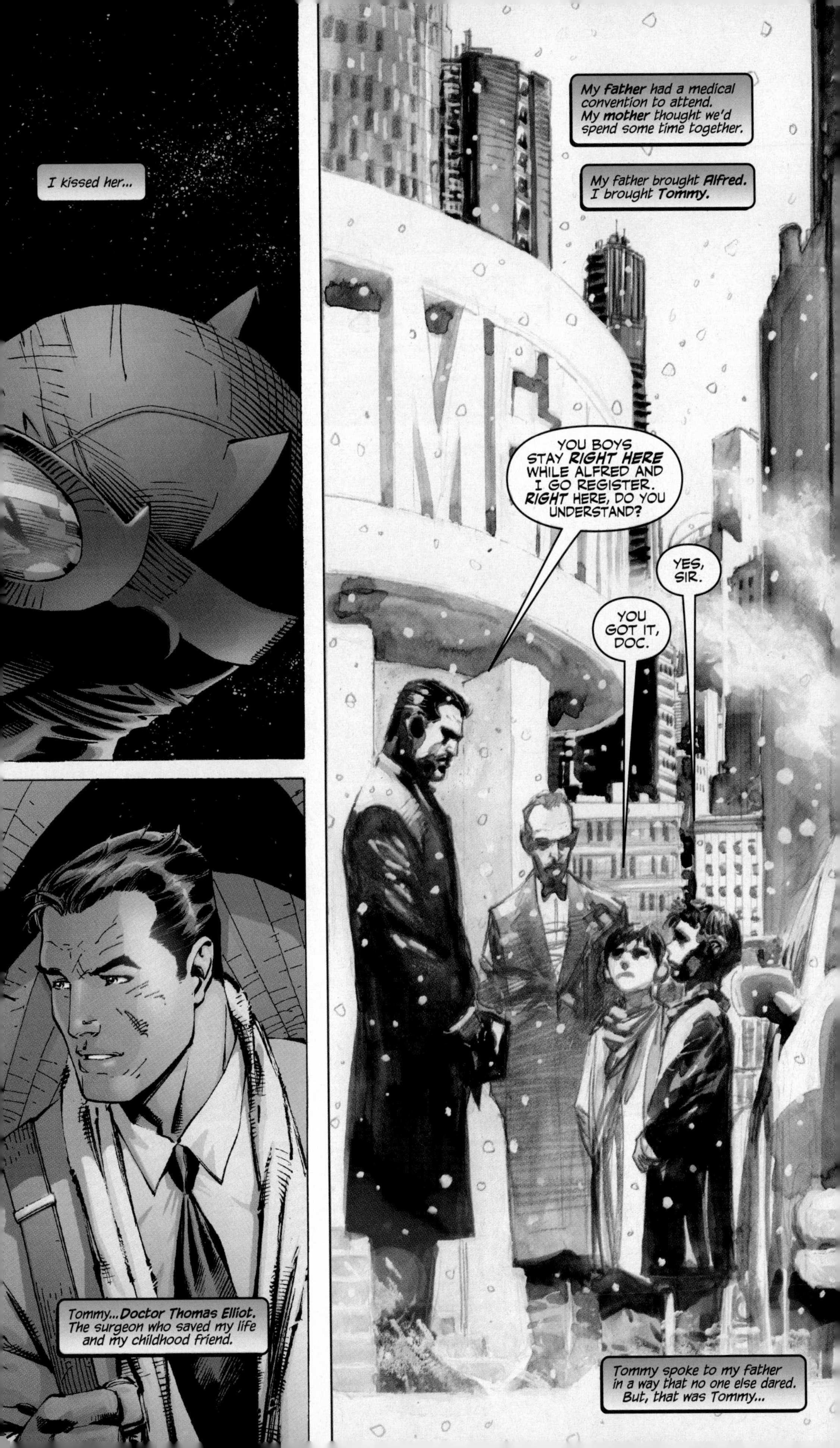
I kissed her...
Tommy...Doctor Thomas Elliot. The surgeon who saved my life and my childhood friend.
My father had a medical convention to attend. My mother thought we'd spend some time together.
My father brought Alfred. I brought Tommy.
YOU BOYS STAY RIGHT HERE WHILE ALFRED AND I GO REGISTER. RIGHT HERE, DO YOU UNDERSTAND?
YES, SIR.
YOU GOT IT, DOC.
Tommy spoke to my father in a way that no one else dared. But, that was Tommy...

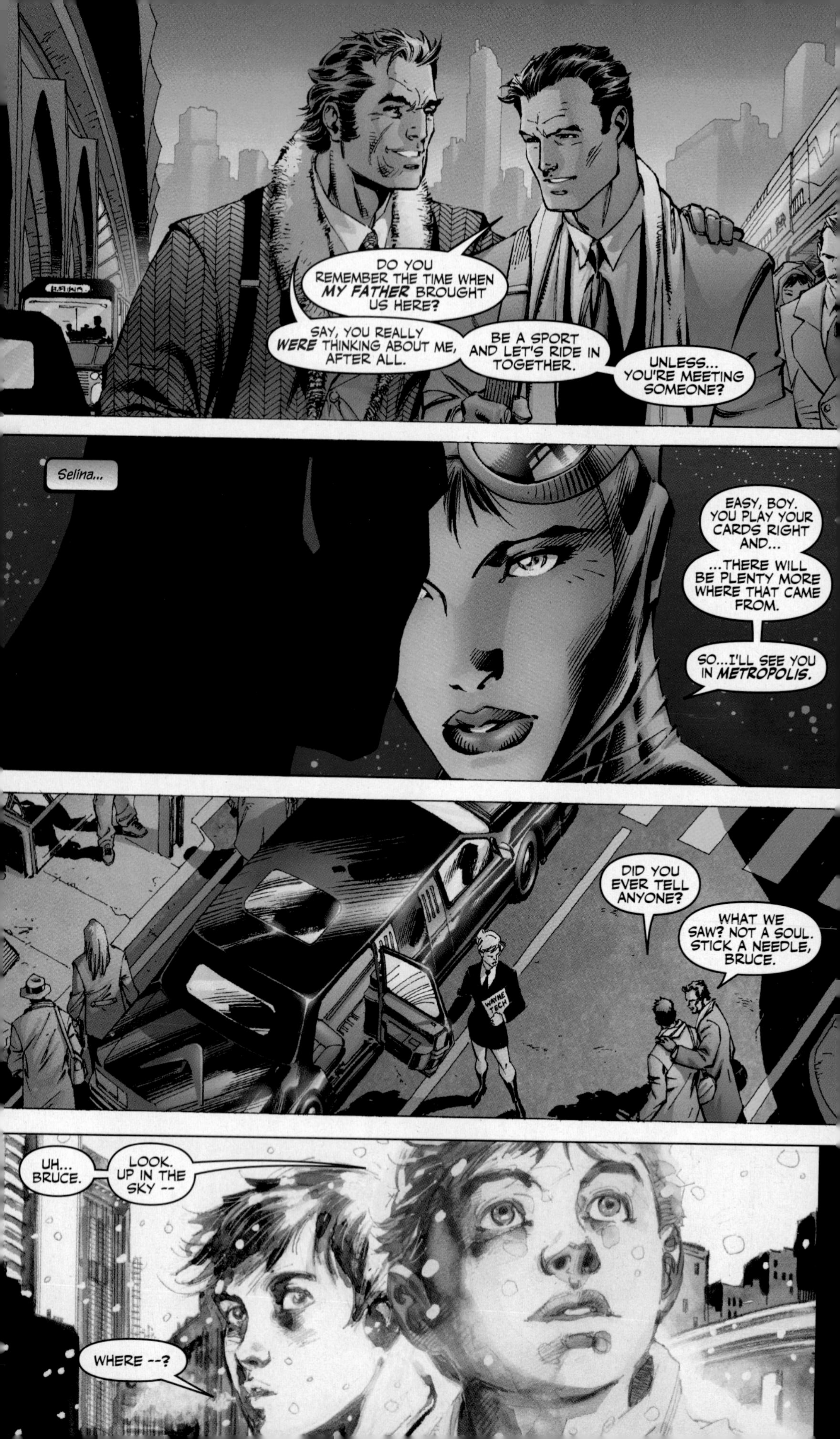
DO YOU REMEMBER THE TIME WHEN MY FATHER BROUGHT US HERE?
SAY, YOU REALLY WERE THINKING ABOUT ME, AFTER ALL.
BE A SPORT AND LET'S RIDE IN TOGETHER.
UNLESS... YOU'RE MEETING SOMEONE?
Selina...
EASY, BOY. YOU PLAY YOUR CARDS RIGHT AND...
...THERE WILL BE PLENTY MORE WHERE THAT CAME FROM.
SO...I'LL SEE YOU IN METROPOLIS.
DID YOU EVER TELL ANYONE?
WHAT WE SAW? NOT A SOUL. STICK A NEEDLE, BRUCE.
WAYNE TECH
UH... BRUCE.
LOOK. UP IN THE SKY --
WHERE --?

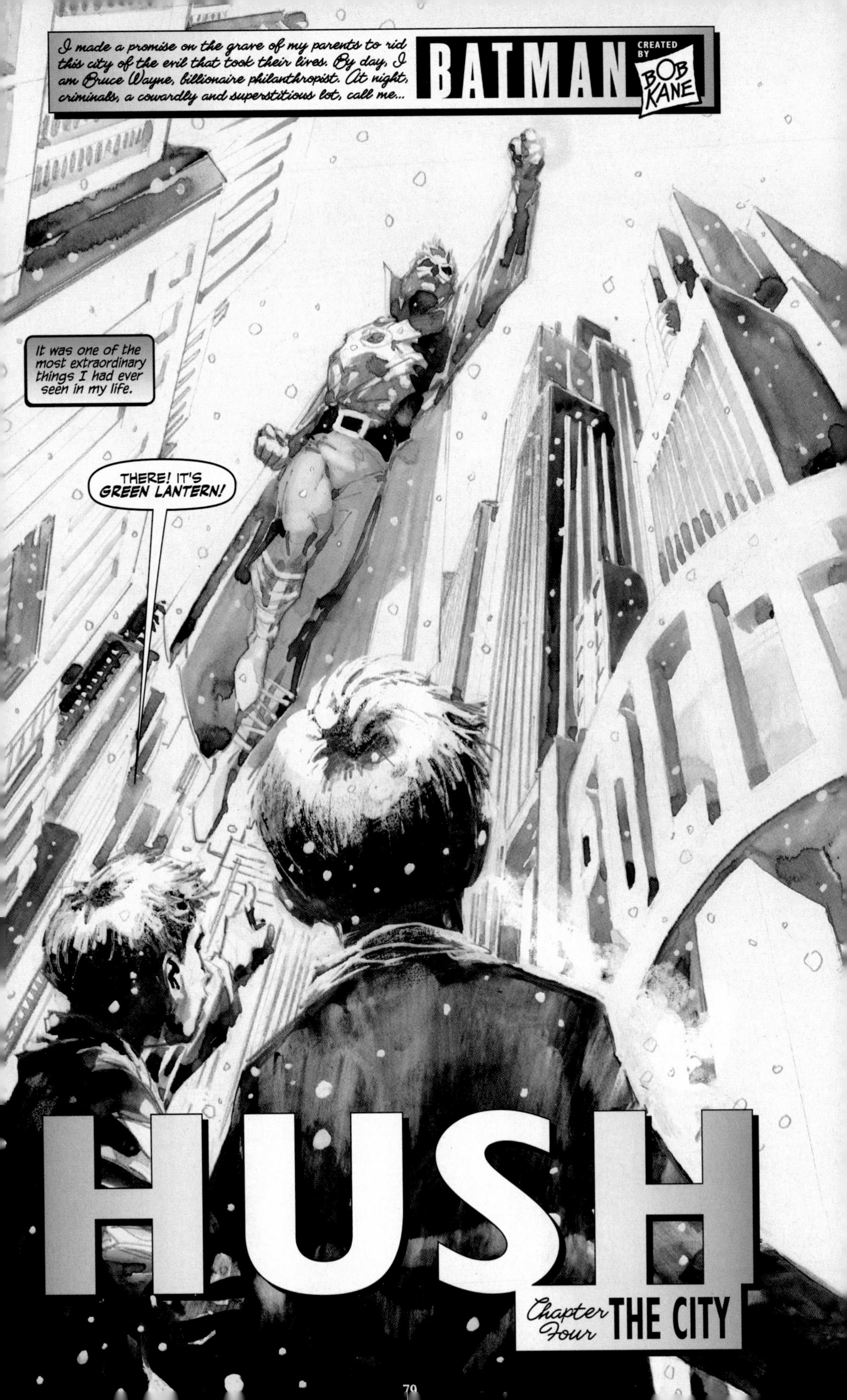

I made a promise on the grave of my parents to rid this city of the evil that took their lives. By day, I am Bruce Wayne, billionaire philanthropist. At night, criminals, a cowardly and superstitious lot, call me...
BATMAN
CREATED BY BOB KANE
It was one of the most extraordinary things I had ever seen in my life.
THERE! IT'S GREEN LANTERN!
HUSH
Chapter Four THE CITY

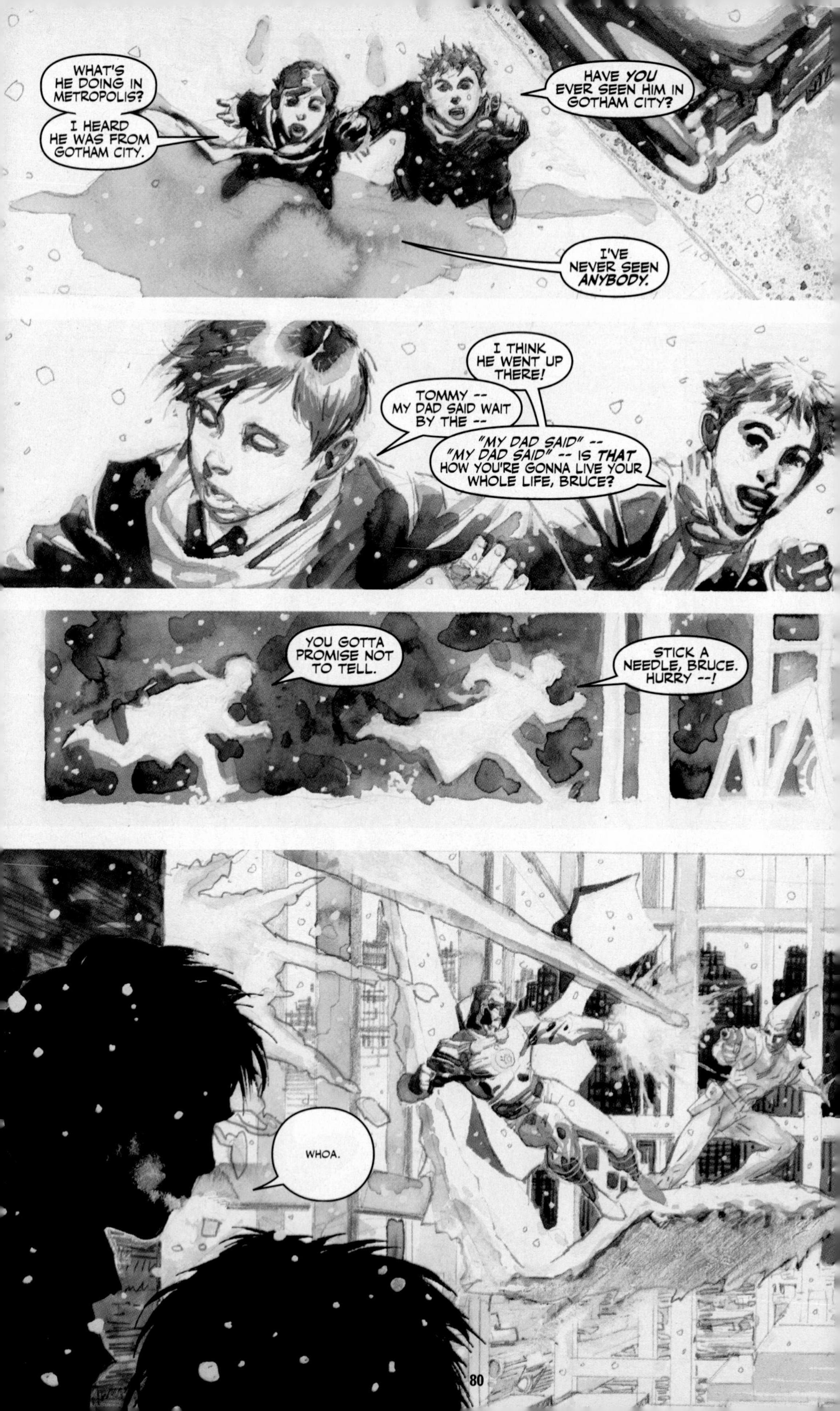
WHAT'S HE DOING IN METROPOLIS?
I HEARD HE WAS FROM GOTHAM CITY.
HAVE YOU EVER SEEN HIM IN GOTHAM CITY?
I'VE NEVER SEEN ANYBODY.
TOMMY -- MY DAD SAID WAIT BY THE --
I THINK HE WENT UP THERE!
"MY DAD SAID" -- "MY DAD SAID" -- IS THAT HOW YOU'RE GONNA LIVE YOUR WHOLE LIFE, BRUCE?
YOU GOTTA PROMISE NOT TO TELL.
STICK A NEEDLE, BRUCE. HURRY --!
WHOA.

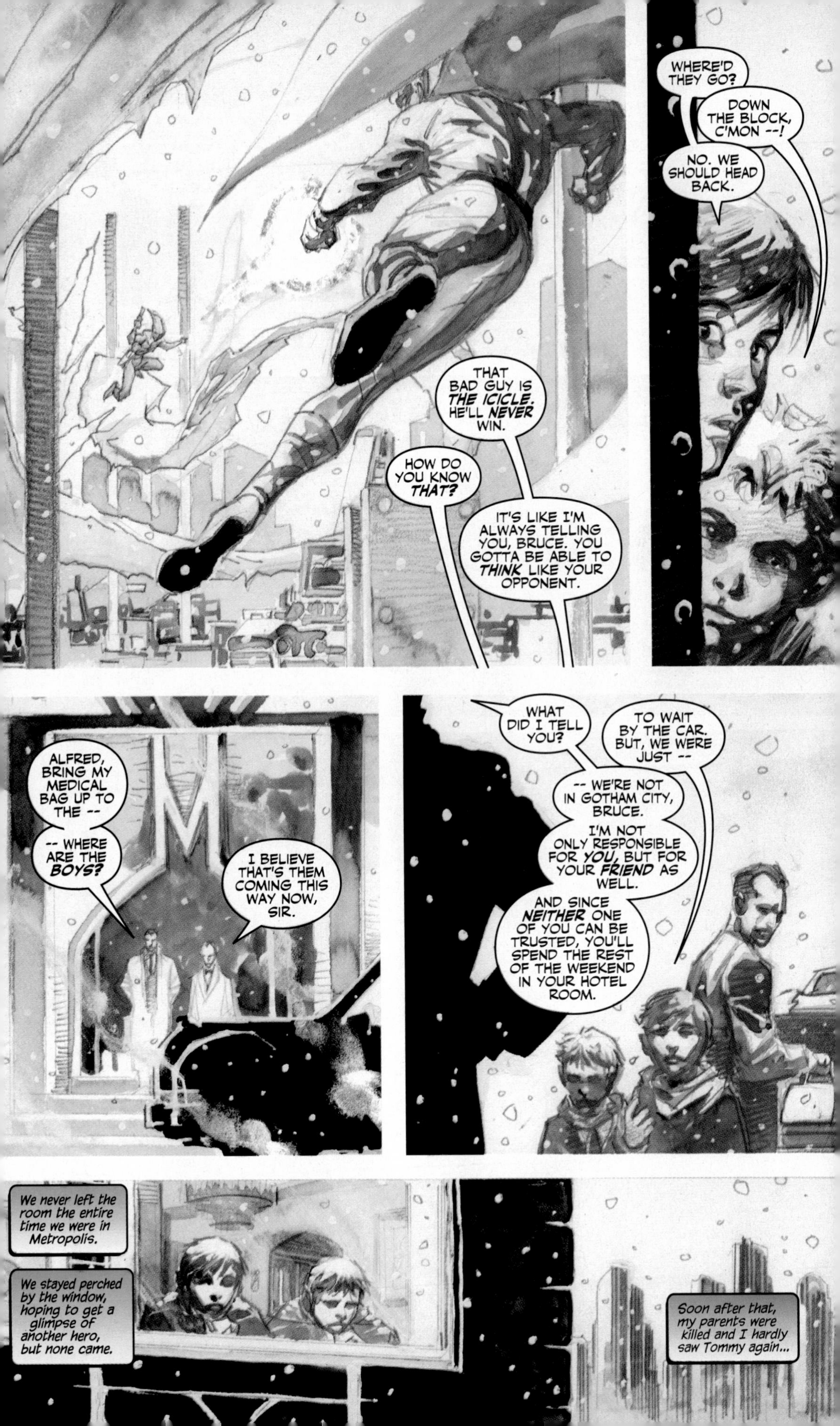
WHERE'D THEY GO?
DOWN THE BLOCK, C'MON --!
NO. WE SHOULD HEAD BACK.
THAT BAD GUY IS THE ICICLE. HE'LL NEVER WIN.
HOW DO YOU KNOW THAT?
IT'S LIKE I'M ALWAYS TELLING YOU, BRUCE. YOU GOTTA BE ABLE TO THINK LIKE YOUR OPPONENT.
ALFRED, BRING MY MEDICAL BAG UP TO THE --
-- WHERE ARE THE BOYS?
I BELIEVE THAT'S THEM COMING THIS WAY NOW, SIR.
WHAT DID I TELL YOU?
TO WAIT BY THE CAR. BUT, WE WERE JUST --
-- WE'RE NOT IN GOTHAM CITY, BRUCE.
I'M NOT ONLY RESPONSIBLE FOR YOU, BUT FOR YOUR FRIEND AS WELL.
AND SINCE NEITHER ONE OF YOU CAN BE TRUSTED, YOU'LL SPEND THE REST OF THE WEEKEND IN YOUR HOTEL ROOM.
We never left the room the entire time we were in Metropolis.
We stayed perched by the window, hoping to get a glimpse of another hero, but none came.
Soon after that, my parents were killed and I hardly saw Tommy again...

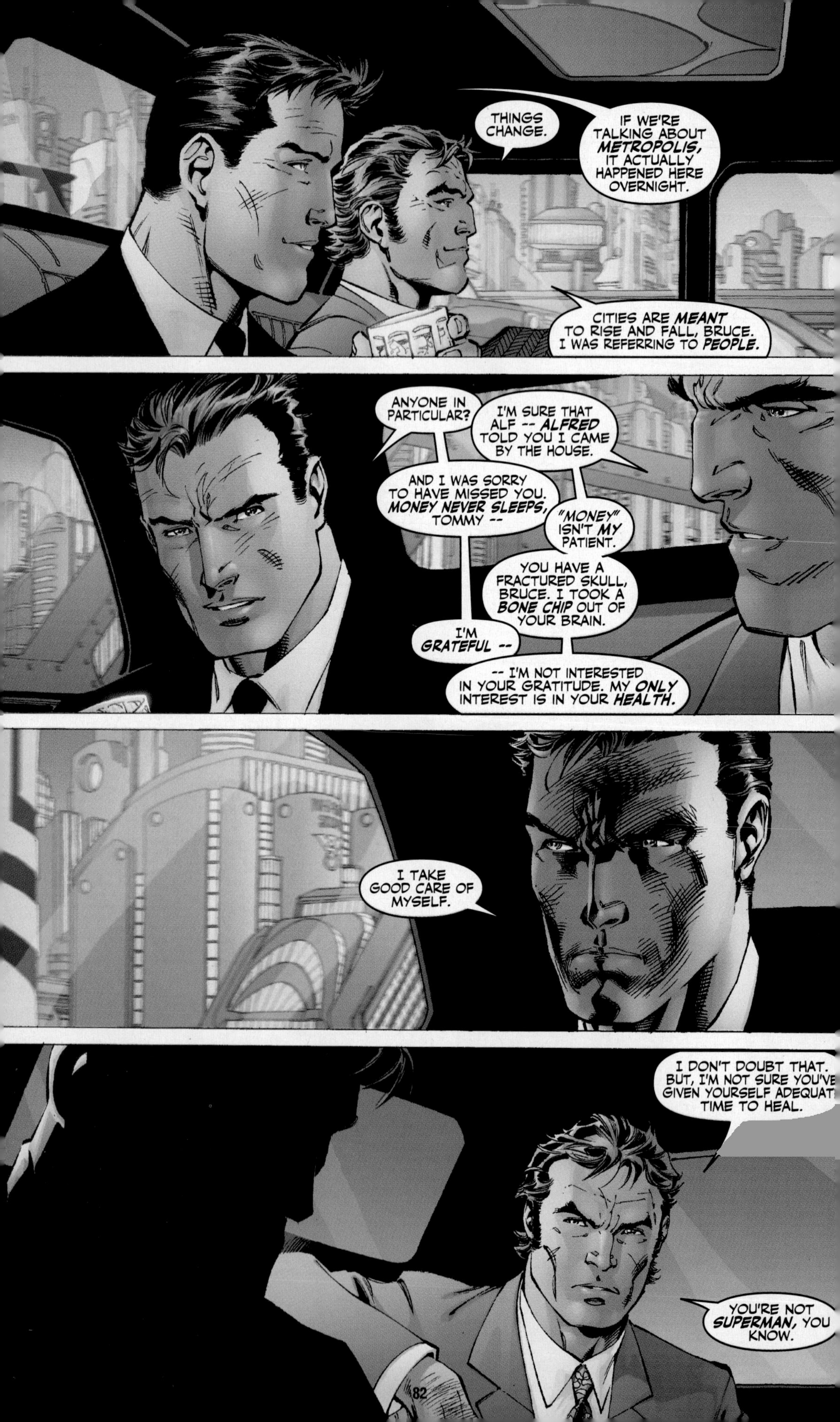

THINGS CHANGE.
IF WE'RE TALKING ABOUT METROPOLIS, IT ACTUALLY HAPPENED HERE OVERNIGHT.
CITIES ARE MEANT TO RISE AND FALL, BRUCE. I WAS REFERRING TO PEOPLE.
ANYONE IN PARTICULAR?
I'M SURE THAT ALF -- ALFRED TOLD YOU I CAME BY THE HOUSE.
AND I WAS SORRY TO HAVE MISSED YOU. MONEY NEVER SLEEPS, TOMMY --
"MONEY" ISN'T MY PATIENT.
YOU HAVE A FRACTURED SKULL, BRUCE. I TOOK A BONE CHIP OUT OF YOUR BRAIN.
I'M GRATEFUL --
-- I'M NOT INTERESTED IN YOUR GRATITUDE. MY ONLY INTEREST IS IN YOUR HEALTH.
I TAKE GOOD CARE OF MYSELF.
I DON'T DOUBT THAT. BUT, I'M NOT SURE YOU'VE GIVEN YOURSELF ADEQUATE TIME TO HEAL.
YOU'RE NOT SUPERMAN, YOU KNOW.

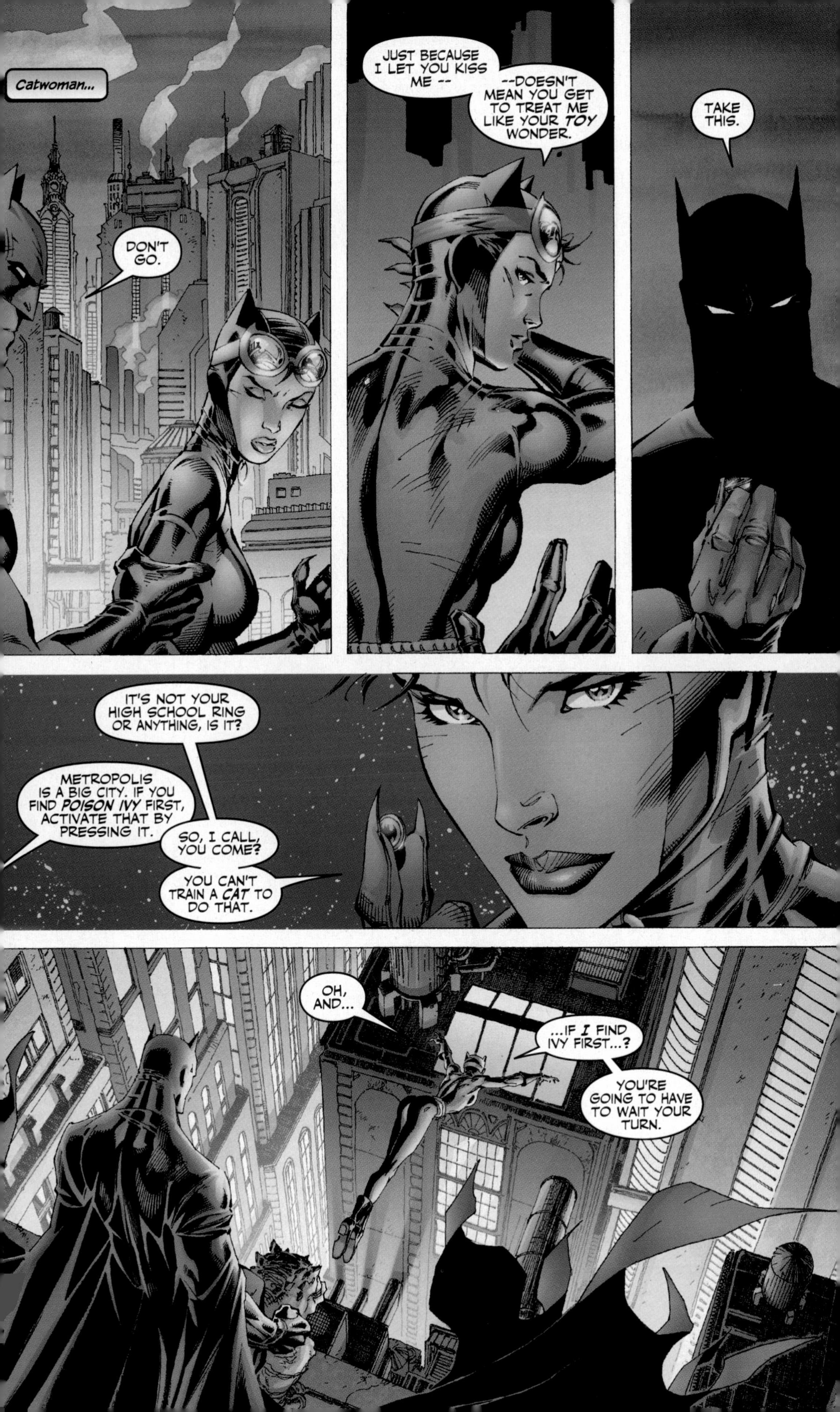

Catwoman...
DON'T GO.
JUST BECAUSE I LET YOU KISS ME --
--DOESN'T MEAN YOU GET TO TREAT ME LIKE YOUR TOY WONDER.
TAKE THIS.
IT'S NOT YOUR HIGH SCHOOL RING OR ANYTHING, IS IT?
METROPOLIS IS A BIG CITY. IF YOU FIND POISON IVY FIRST, ACTIVATE THAT BY PRESSING IT.
SO, I CALL, YOU COME?
YOU CAN'T TRAIN A CAT TO DO THAT.
OH, AND...
...IF I FIND IVY FIRST...?
YOU'RE GOING TO HAVE TO WAIT YOUR TURN.

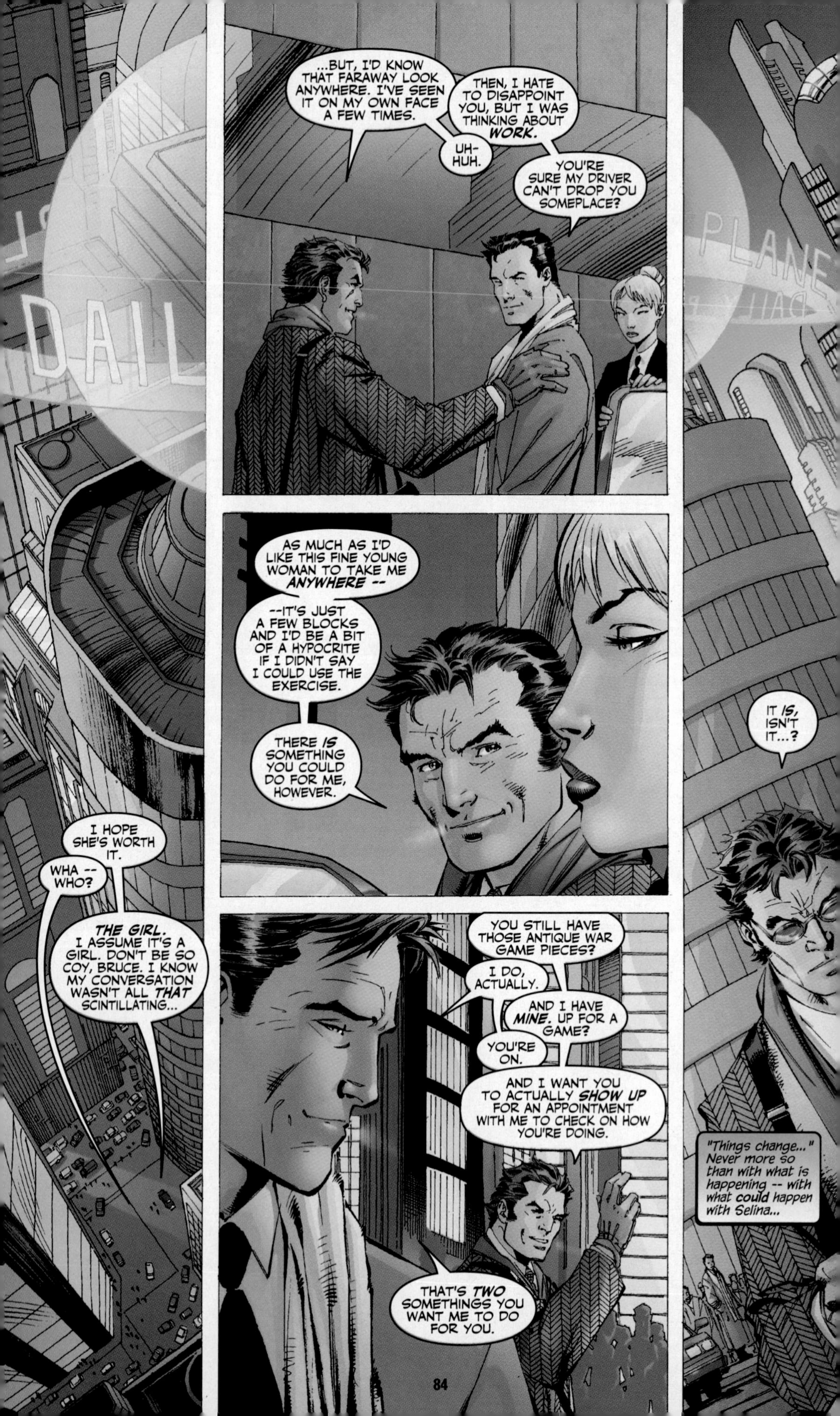
...BUT, I'D KNOW THAT FARAWAY LOOK ANYWHERE. I'VE SEEN IT ON MY OWN FACE A FEW TIMES.
THEN, I HATE TO DISAPPOINT YOU, BUT I WAS THINKING ABOUT *WORK.*
UH-HUH.
YOU'RE SURE MY DRIVER CAN'T DROP YOU SOMEPLACE?
AS MUCH AS I'D LIKE THIS FINE YOUNG WOMAN TO TAKE ME *ANYWHERE* --
--IT'S JUST A FEW BLOCKS AND I'D BE A BIT OF A HYPOCRITE IF I DIDN'T SAY I COULD USE THE EXERCISE.
THERE *IS* SOMETHING YOU COULD DO FOR ME, HOWEVER.
YOU STILL HAVE THOSE ANTIQUE WAR GAME PIECES?
I DO, ACTUALLY.
AND I HAVE *MINE.* UP FOR A GAME?
YOU'RE ON.
AND I WANT YOU TO ACTUALLY *SHOW UP* FOR AN APPOINTMENT WITH ME TO CHECK ON HOW YOU'RE DOING.
THAT'S *TWO* SOMETHINGS YOU WANT ME TO DO FOR YOU.
I HOPE SHE'S WORTH IT.
WHA -- WHO?
THE GIRL. I ASSUME IT'S A GIRL. DON'T BE SO COY, BRUCE. I KNOW MY CONVERSATION WASN'T ALL *THAT* SCINTILLATING...
IT *IS,* ISN'T IT...?
*"Things change..." Never more so than with what is happening -- with what **could** happen with Selina...*

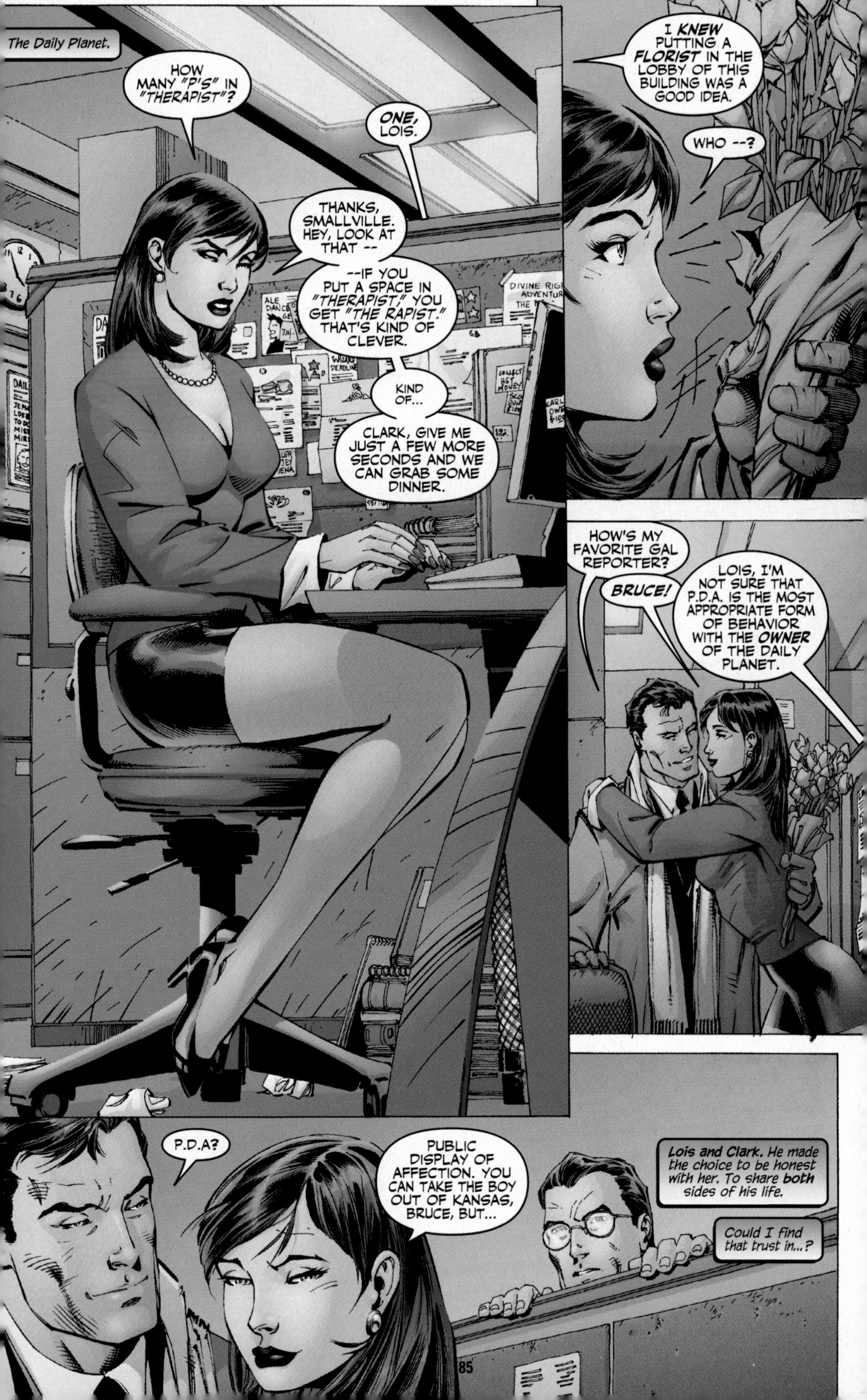
The Daily Planet.
HOW MANY "P'S" IN "THERAPIST"?
ONE, LOIS.
THANKS, SMALLVILLE. HEY, LOOK AT THAT --
--IF YOU PUT A SPACE IN "THERAPIST," YOU GET "THE RAPIST." THAT'S KIND OF CLEVER.
KIND OF...
CLARK, GIVE ME JUST A FEW MORE SECONDS AND WE CAN GRAB SOME DINNER.
I KNEW PUTTING A FLORIST IN THE LOBBY OF THIS BUILDING WAS A GOOD IDEA.
WHO --?
HOW'S MY FAVORITE GAL REPORTER?
BRUCE!
LOIS, I'M NOT SURE THAT P.D.A. IS THE MOST APPROPRIATE FORM OF BEHAVIOR WITH THE OWNER OF THE DAILY PLANET.
P.D.A?
PUBLIC DISPLAY OF AFFECTION. YOU CAN TAKE THE BOY OUT OF KANSAS, BRUCE, BUT...
Lois and Clark. He made the choice to be honest with her. To share both sides of his life.
Could I find that trust in...?

MIND IF I LOG ONTO YOUR COMPUTER, LOIS?
STOCK TIP.
ANYTHING YOU NEED, BRUCE.
CLARK, DINNER IS...
...GOING TO HAVE TO WAIT. I UNDERSTAND.
>Instant Message From:
B: O?
O: Metropolis?
B: Secure this line.
O: Done.
B: News on Aztec gilia?
>Instant Message From:
O: Requires ethylene.
B: Fairly common.
O: Not the way they make it at LEXCORP.
O: They've reengineered it to withstand changes in temperature.
O: Perfect if you're on the move.
>Instant Mess
O: Before you ask, it'll take time.
O: L.C. not the easiest to hack in
B: Don't. I have another door.
B: gtg.
IF I HAD READ ALL THAT, WOULD I HAVE BEEN JEALOUS OR RICH?
NEITHER. YOU'D HAVE BEEN BORED TO TEARS.
NO, SERIOUSLY, BRUCE, OTHER THAN MY SPARKLING PERSONALITY, WHAT BRINGS YOU TO --?
BRUCE!

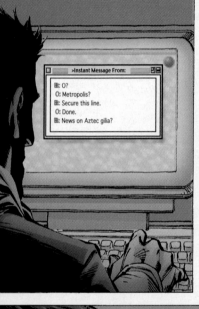

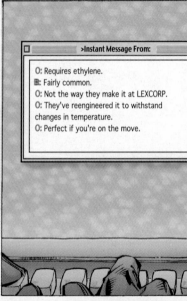

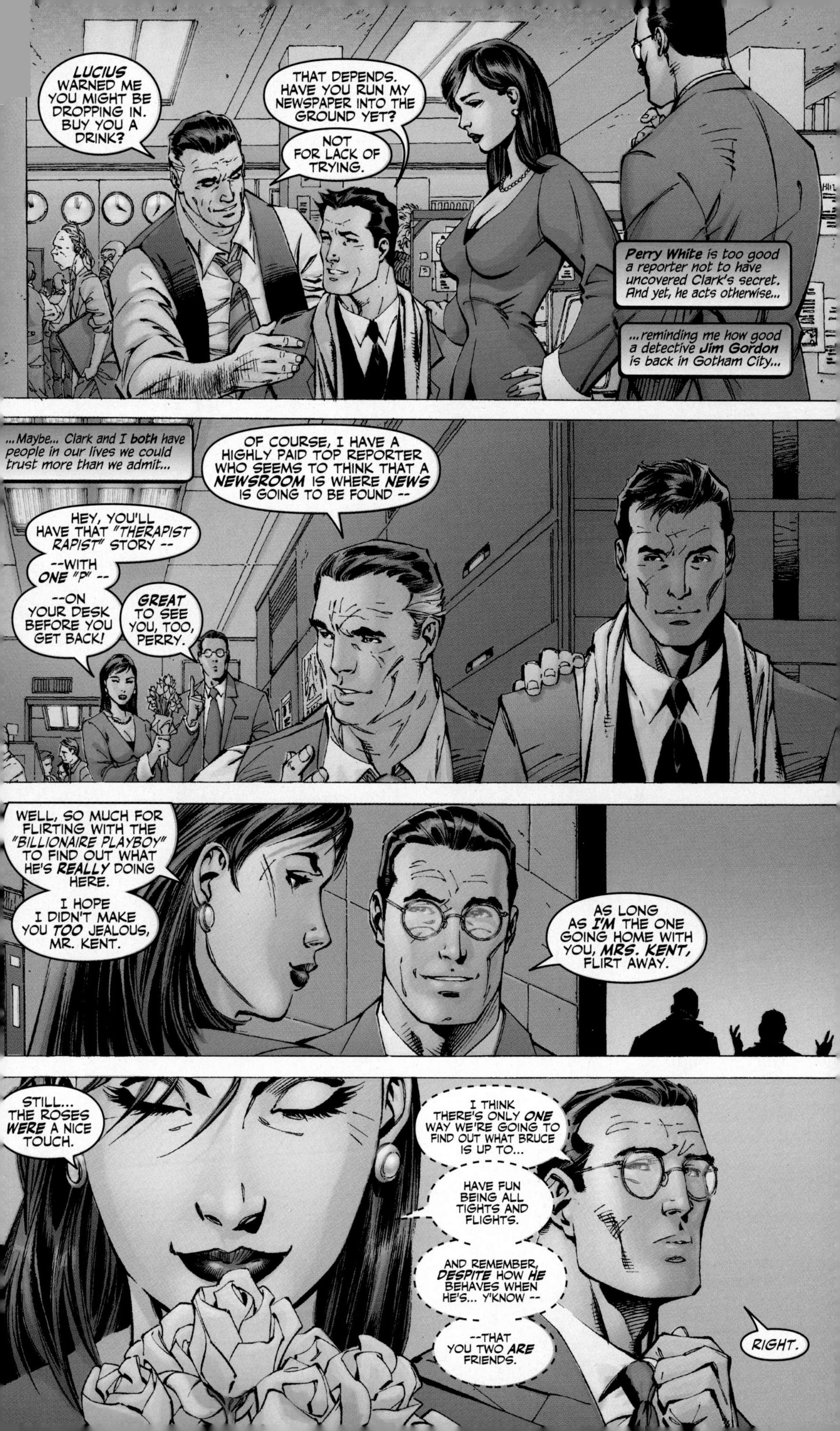
LUCIUS WARNED ME YOU MIGHT BE DROPPING IN. BUY YOU A DRINK?
THAT DEPENDS. HAVE YOU RUN MY NEWSPAPER INTO THE GROUND YET?
NOT FOR LACK OF TRYING.
Perry White is too good a reporter not to have uncovered Clark's secret. And yet, he acts otherwise...
...reminding me how good a detective Jim Gordon is back in Gotham City...
...Maybe... Clark and I both have people in our lives we could trust more than we admit...
OF COURSE, I HAVE A HIGHLY PAID TOP REPORTER WHO SEEMS TO THINK THAT A NEWSROOM IS WHERE NEWS IS GOING TO BE FOUND --
HEY, YOU'LL HAVE THAT "THERAPIST RAPIST" STORY --
--WITH ONE "P" --
--ON YOUR DESK BEFORE YOU GET BACK!
GREAT TO SEE YOU, TOO, PERRY.
WELL, SO MUCH FOR FLIRTING WITH THE "BILLIONAIRE PLAYBOY" TO FIND OUT WHAT HE'S REALLY DOING HERE.
I HOPE I DIDN'T MAKE YOU TOO JEALOUS, MR. KENT.
AS LONG AS I'M THE ONE GOING HOME WITH YOU, MRS. KENT, FLIRT AWAY.
STILL... THE ROSES WERE A NICE TOUCH.
I THINK THERE'S ONLY ONE WAY WE'RE GOING TO FIND OUT WHAT BRUCE IS UP TO...
HAVE FUN BEING ALL TIGHTS AND FLIGHTS.
AND REMEMBER, DESPITE HOW HE BEHAVES WHEN HE'S... Y'KNOW --
--THAT YOU TWO ARE FRIENDS.
RIGHT.

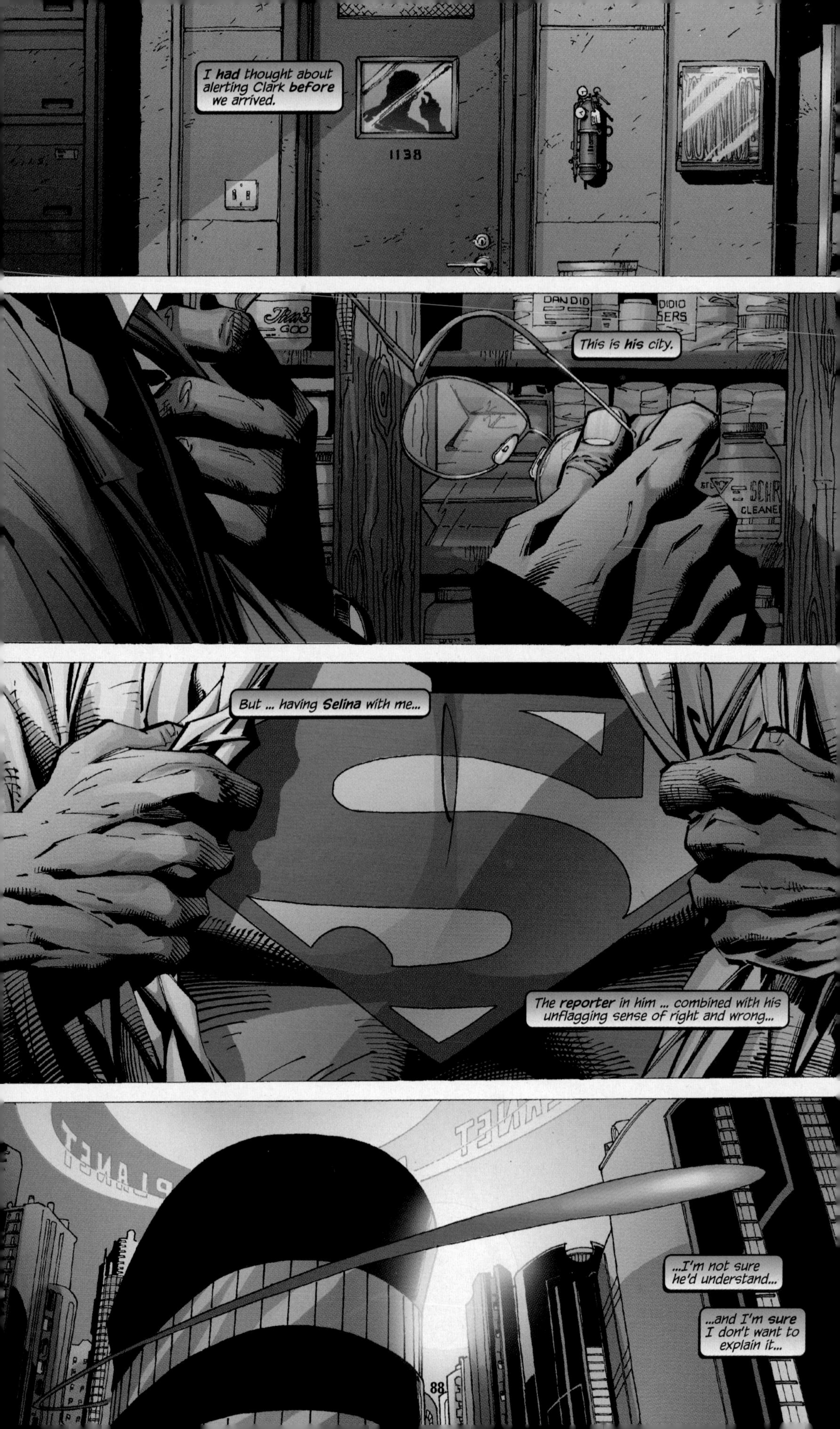
I had thought about alerting Clark before we arrived.
This is his city.
But ... having Selina with me...
The reporter in him ... combined with his unflagging sense of right and wrong...
...I'm not sure he'd understand...
...and I'm sure I don't want to explain it...

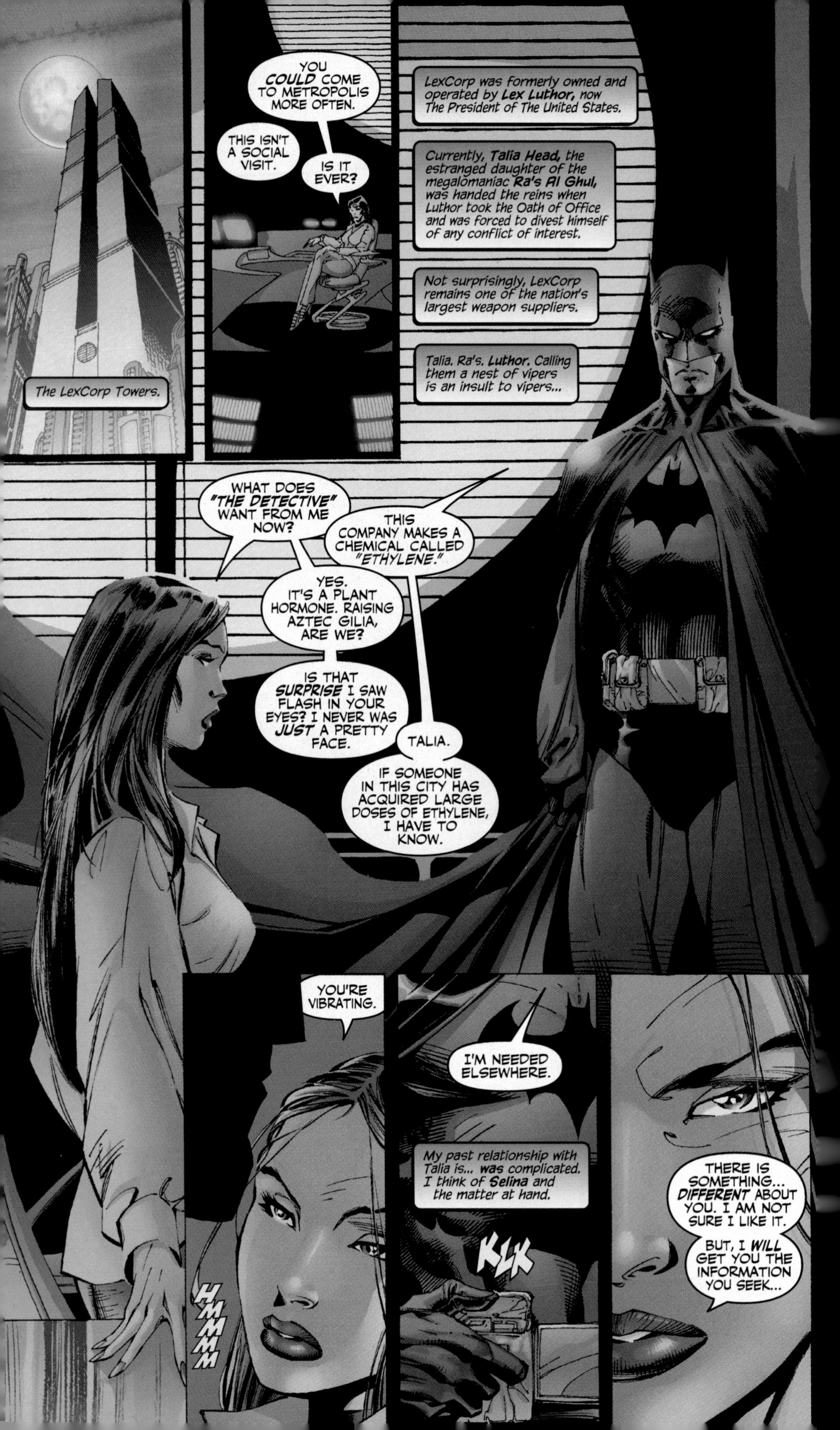

The LexCorp Towers.
YOU COULD COME TO METROPOLIS MORE OFTEN.
THIS ISN'T A SOCIAL VISIT.
IS IT EVER?
LexCorp was formerly owned and operated by Lex Luthor, now The President of The United States.
Currently, Talia Head, the estranged daughter of the megalomaniac Ra's Al Ghul, was handed the reins when Luthor took the Oath of Office and was forced to divest himself of any conflict of interest.
Not surprisingly, LexCorp remains one of the nation's largest weapon suppliers.
Talia. Ra's. Luthor. Calling them a nest of vipers is an insult to vipers...
WHAT DOES "THE DETECTIVE" WANT FROM ME NOW?
THIS COMPANY MAKES A CHEMICAL CALLED "ETHYLENE."
YES. IT'S A PLANT HORMONE. RAISING AZTEC GILIA, ARE WE?
IS THAT SURPRISE I SAW FLASH IN YOUR EYES? I NEVER WAS JUST A PRETTY FACE.
TALIA.
IF SOMEONE IN THIS CITY HAS ACQUIRED LARGE DOSES OF ETHYLENE, I HAVE TO KNOW.
YOU'RE VIBRATING.
HMMMM
I'M NEEDED ELSEWHERE.
My past relationship with Talia is... was complicated. I think of Selina and the matter at hand.
KLK
THERE IS SOMETHING... DIFFERENT ABOUT YOU. I AM NOT SURE I LIKE IT.
BUT, I WILL GET YOU THE INFORMATION YOU SEEK...

DOES IT *EVER* GET DARK IN THIS CITY?

EVEN AT NIGHT, IT'S LIT UP LIKE IT'S IMPORTANT OR SOMETHING.

YOUR "PAGER/HOMING-DEVICE THING" WORKS.

OBVIOUSLY.

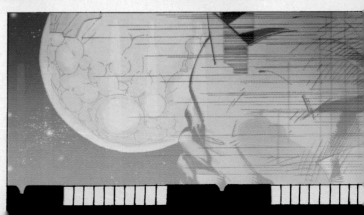

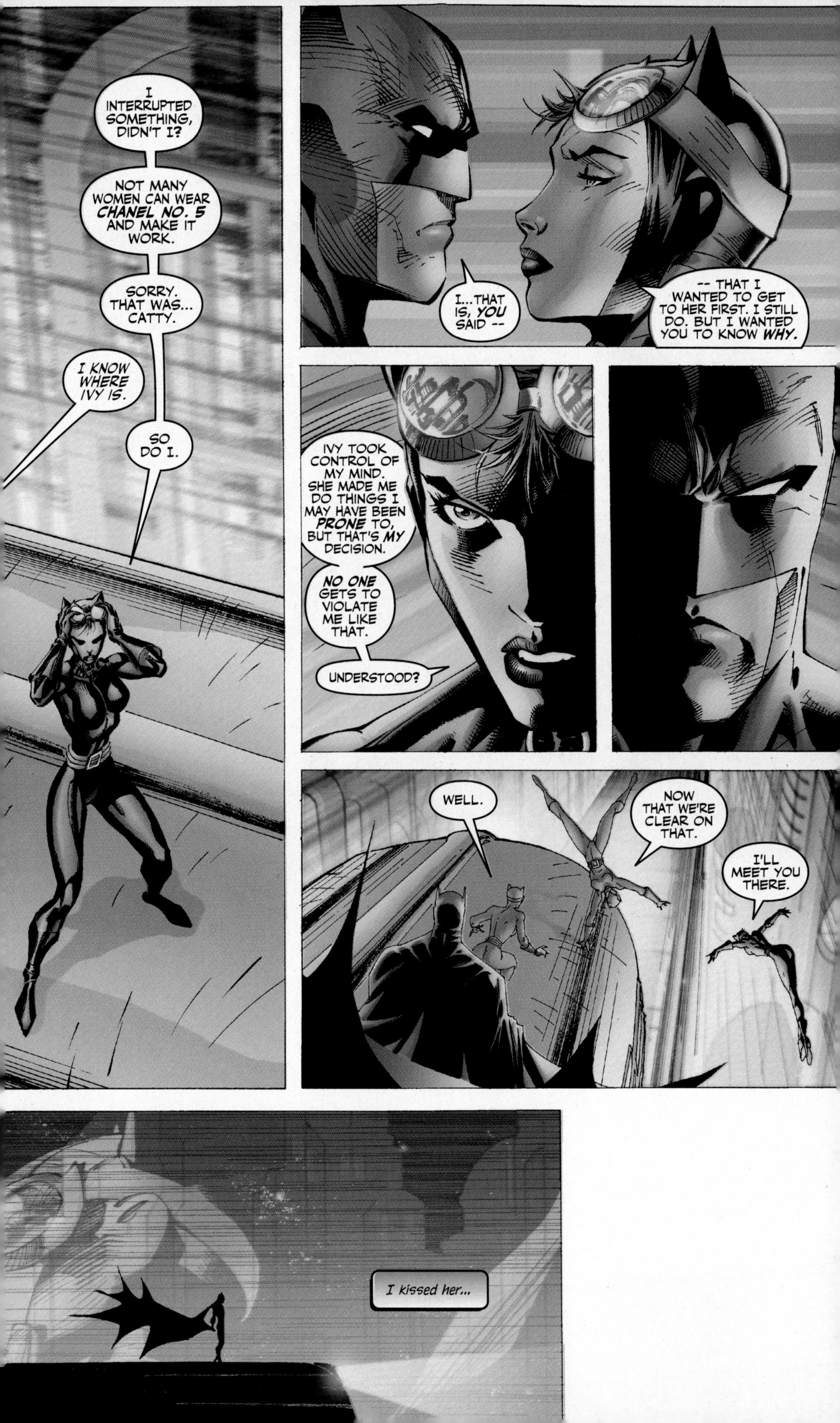
I INTERRUPTED SOMETHING, DIDN'T I?
NOT MANY WOMEN CAN WEAR **CHANEL NO. 5** AND MAKE IT WORK.
SORRY. THAT WAS... CATTY.
I KNOW **WHERE** IVY IS.
SO DO I.
I...THAT IS, **YOU** SAID --
-- THAT I WANTED TO GET TO HER FIRST. I STILL DO. BUT I WANTED YOU TO KNOW **WHY.**
IVY TOOK CONTROL OF MY MIND. SHE MADE ME DO THINGS I MAY HAVE BEEN **PRONE** TO, BUT THAT'S **MY** DECISION.
NO ONE GETS TO VIOLATE ME LIKE THAT.
UNDERSTOOD?
WELL.
NOW THAT WE'RE CLEAR ON THAT.
I'LL MEET YOU THERE.
I kissed her...

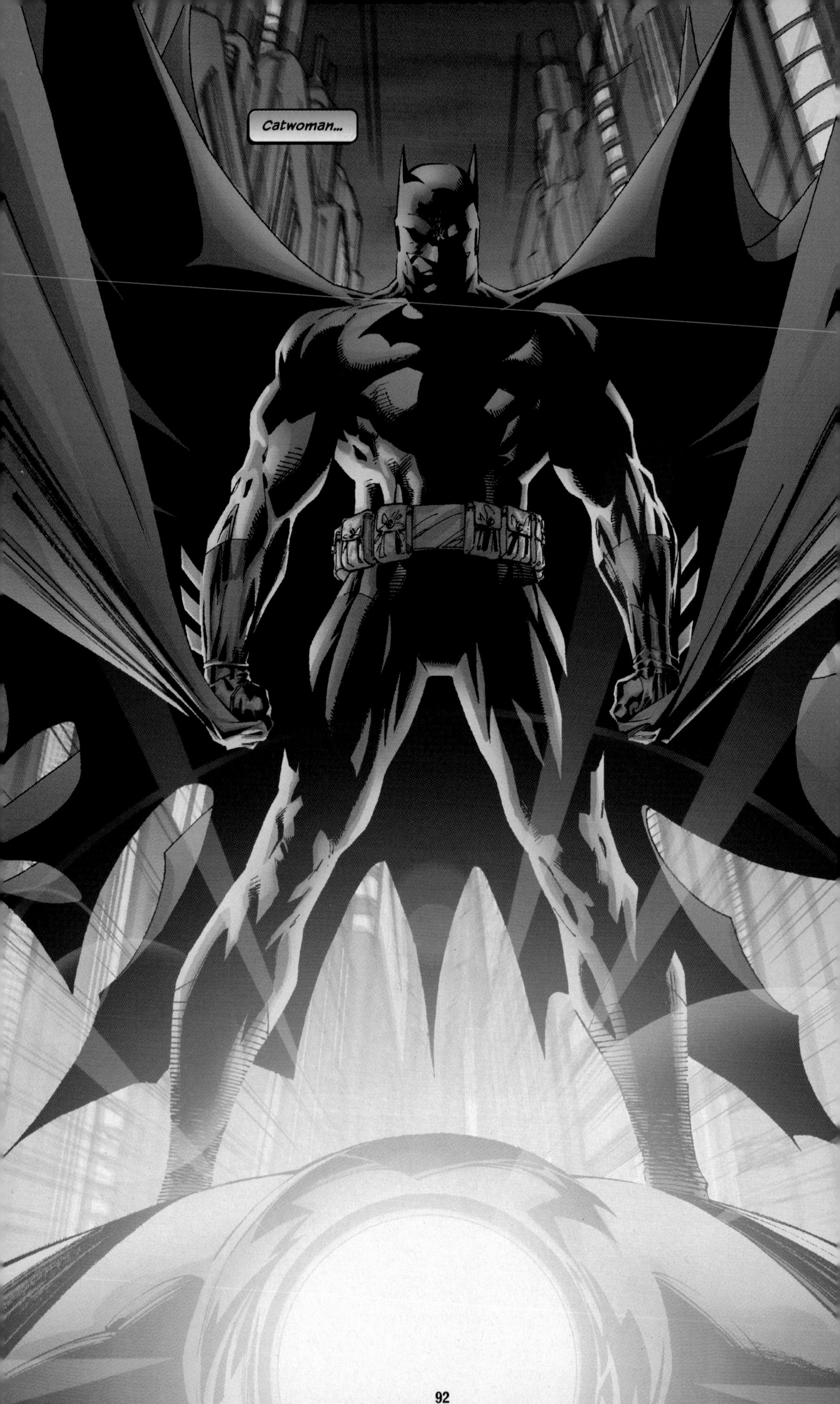
Catwoman...

Gotham City, [kil]ler Croc led me [to] a penthouse [whe]re he believed [Po]ison Ivy would be.

[Th]e plants I [fou]nd there were [Az]tec gilia. [Th]ey are, at best, [dif]ficult to grow [in] an indoor [en]vironment.

[I] could no more [ab]andon them [th]an a mother [wo]uld her child, [ta]king them [with] her to [M]etropolis.

I'VE COME BACK TO YOU.

HAVE YOU?

IT'S LIKE YOU SAID --

-- NO ONE CAN RESIST YOU.

YESSS...

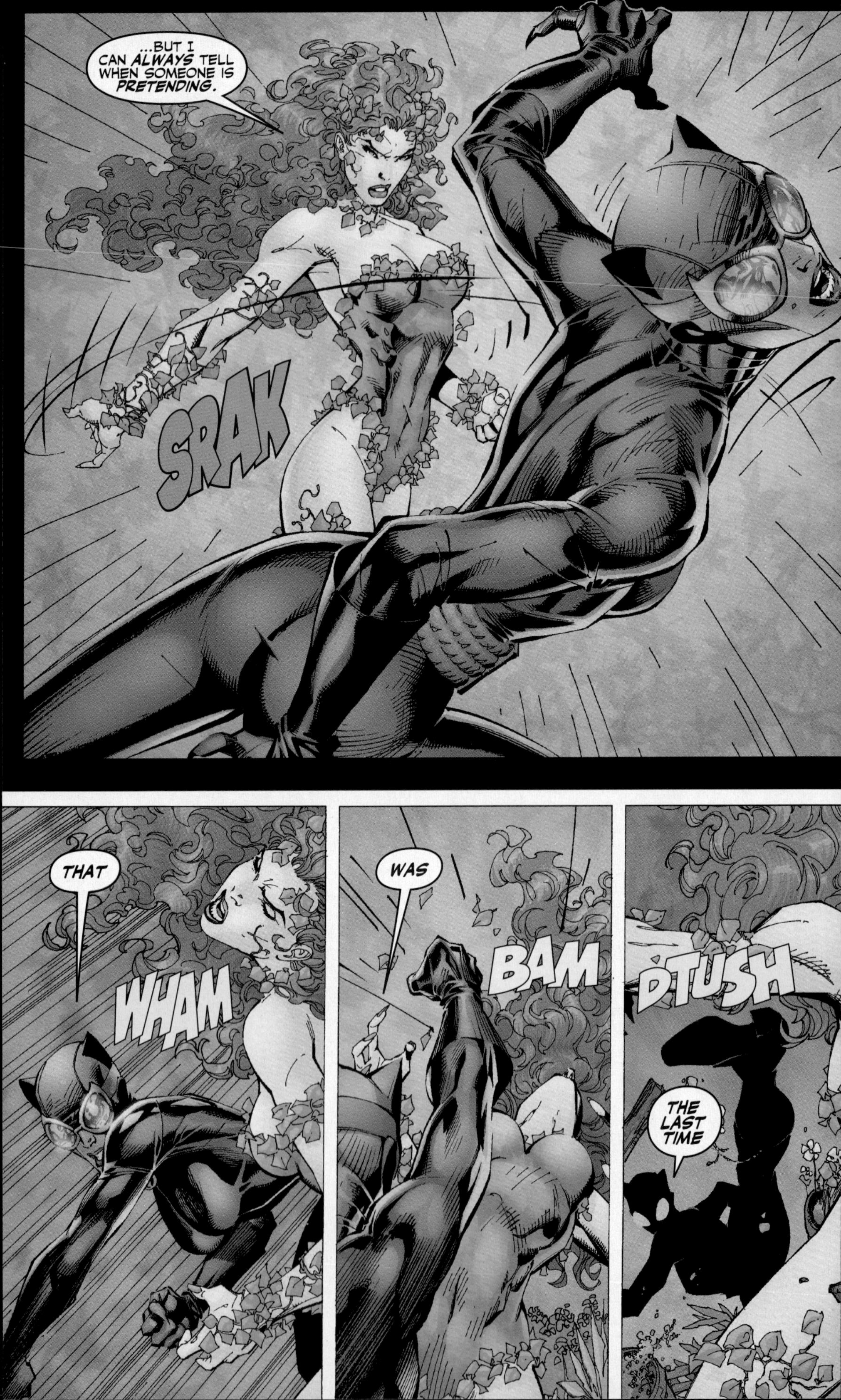

...BUT I CAN ALWAYS TELL WHEN SOMEONE IS PRETENDING.
SRAK
THAT
WHAM
WAS
BAM
DTUSH
THE LAST TIME

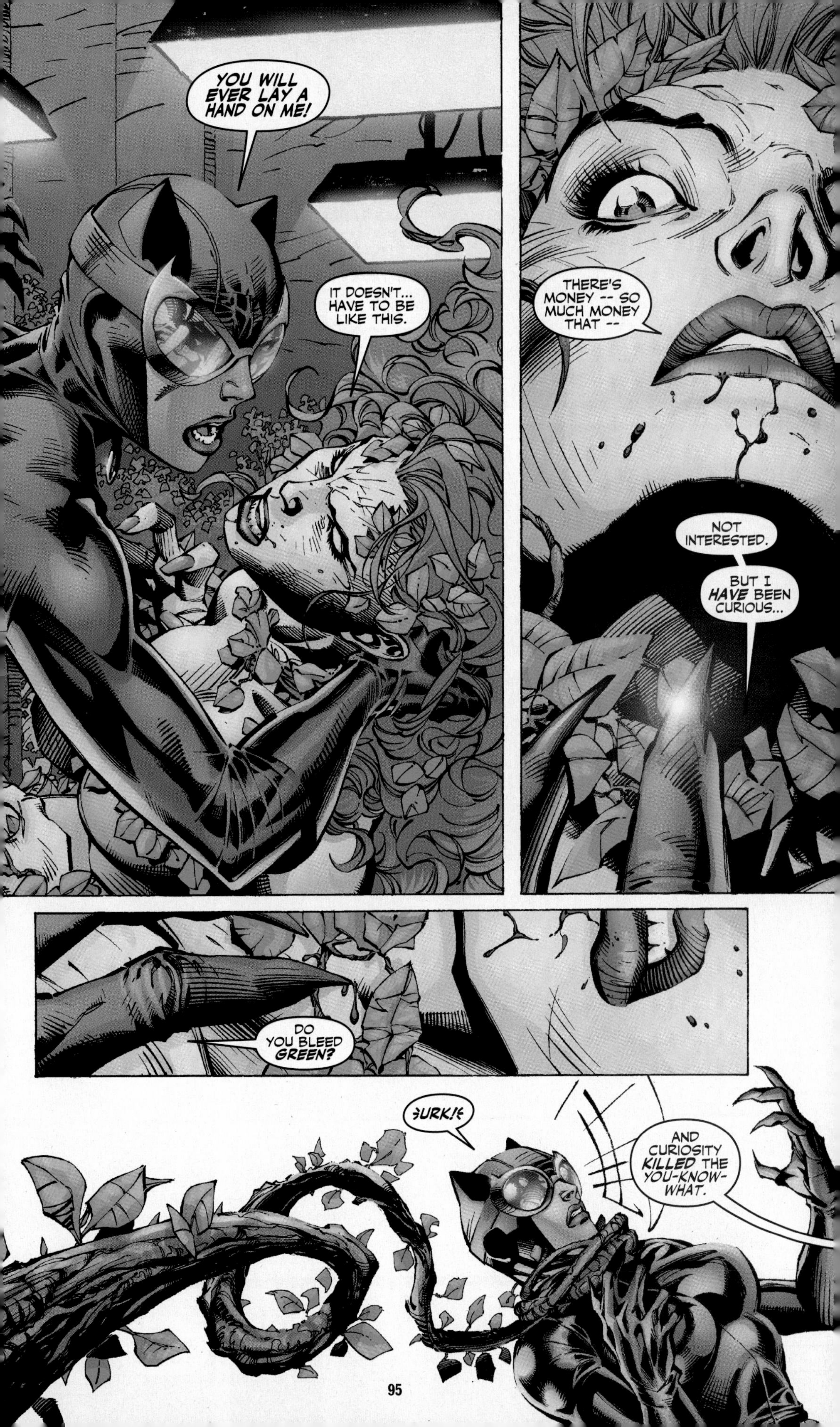
YOU WILL EVER LAY A HAND ON ME!
IT DOESN'T... HAVE TO BE LIKE THIS.
THERE'S MONEY -- SO MUCH MONEY THAT --
NOT INTERESTED.
BUT I *HAVE* BEEN CURIOUS...
DO YOU BLEED *GREEN?*
ƷURK!Ƹ
AND CURIOSITY *KILLED* THE YOU-KNOW-WHAT.

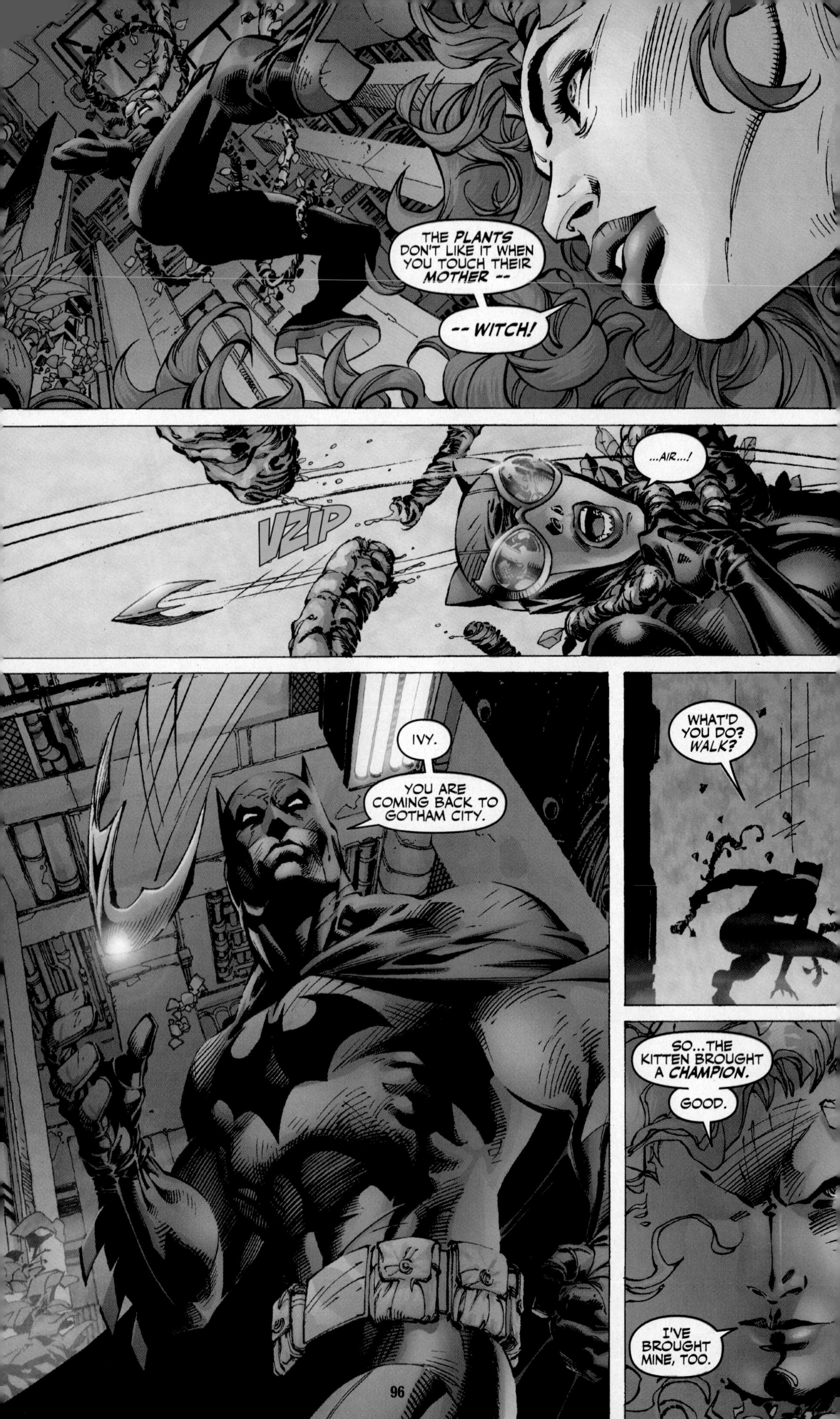
THE PLANTS DON'T LIKE IT WHEN YOU TOUCH THEIR MOTHER --
-- WITCH!
...AIR...!
VZIP
IVY.
YOU ARE COMING BACK TO GOTHAM CITY.
WHAT'D YOU DO? WALK?
SO...THE KITTEN BROUGHT A CHAMPION.
GOOD.
I'VE BROUGHT MINE, TOO.

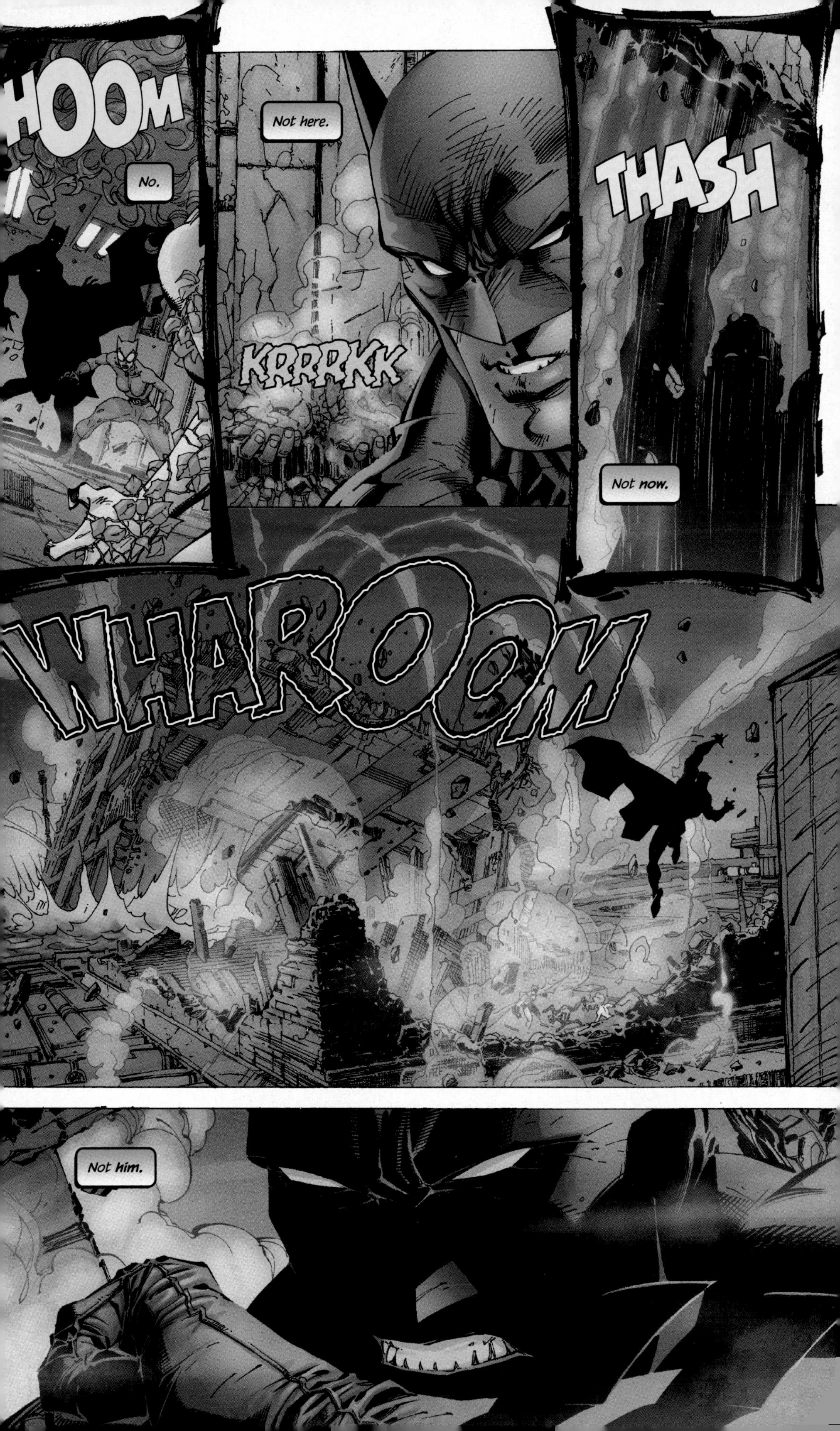
HOOM
No.
Not here.
KRRRKK
THASH
Not now.
WHAROOM
Not him.

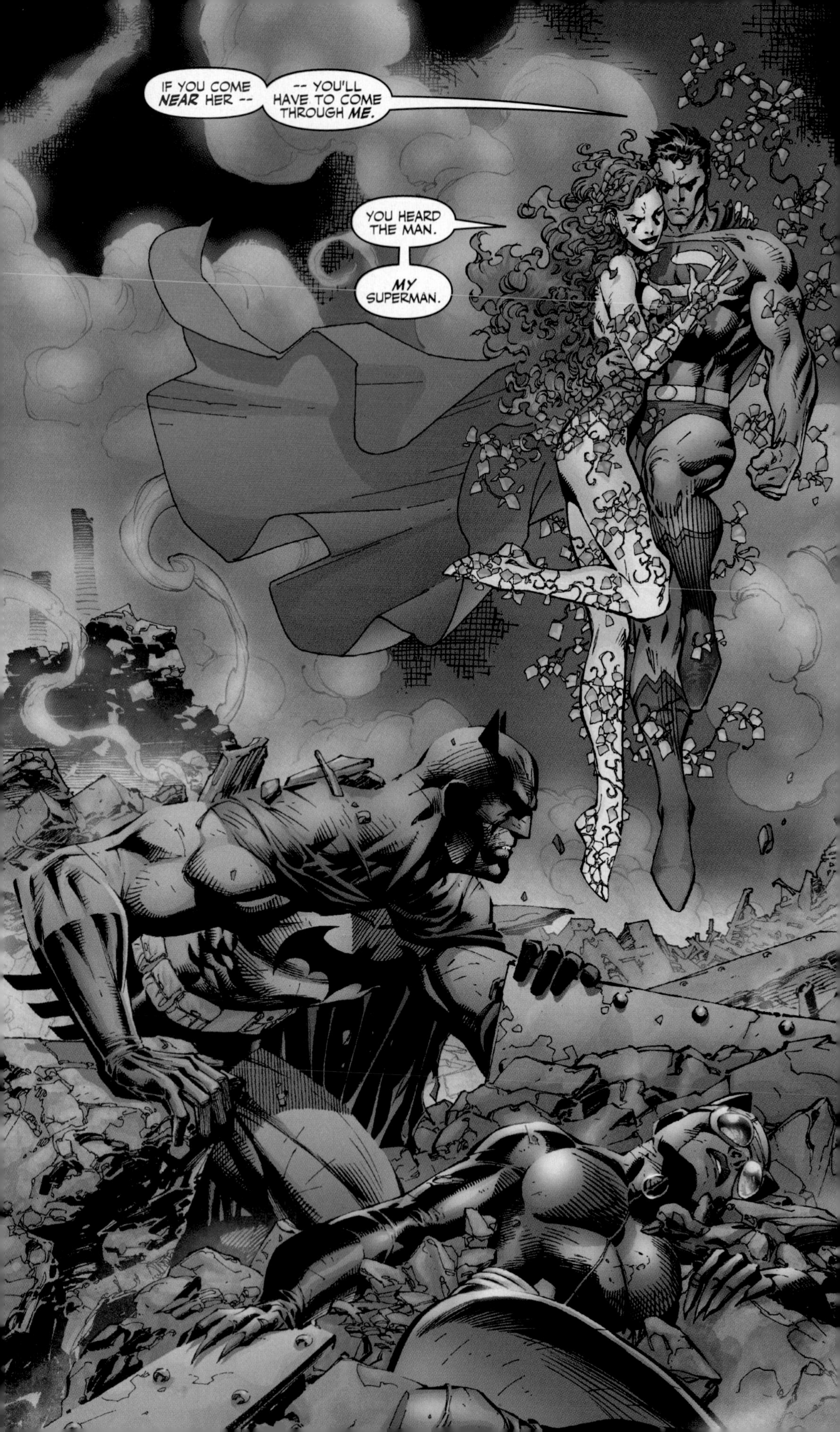
IF YOU COME NEAR HER --
-- YOU'LL HAVE TO COME THROUGH ME.
YOU HEARD THE MAN.
MY SUPERMAN.

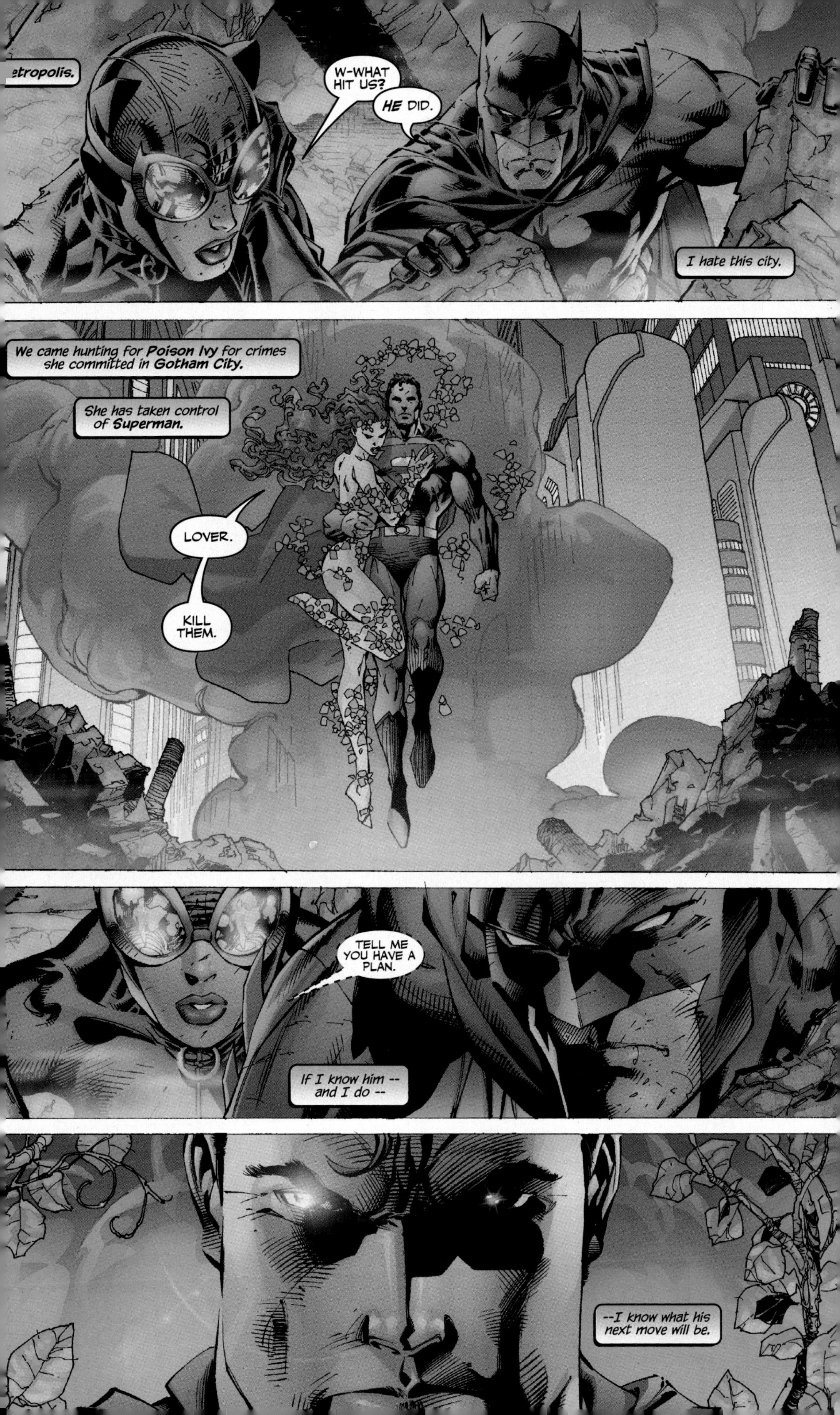
etropolis.
W-WHAT HIT US?
HE DID.
I hate this city.
We came hunting for Poison Ivy for crimes she committed in Gotham City.
She has taken control of Superman.
LOVER.
KILL THEM.
TELL ME YOU HAVE A PLAN.
If I know him -- and I do --
--I know what his next move will be.

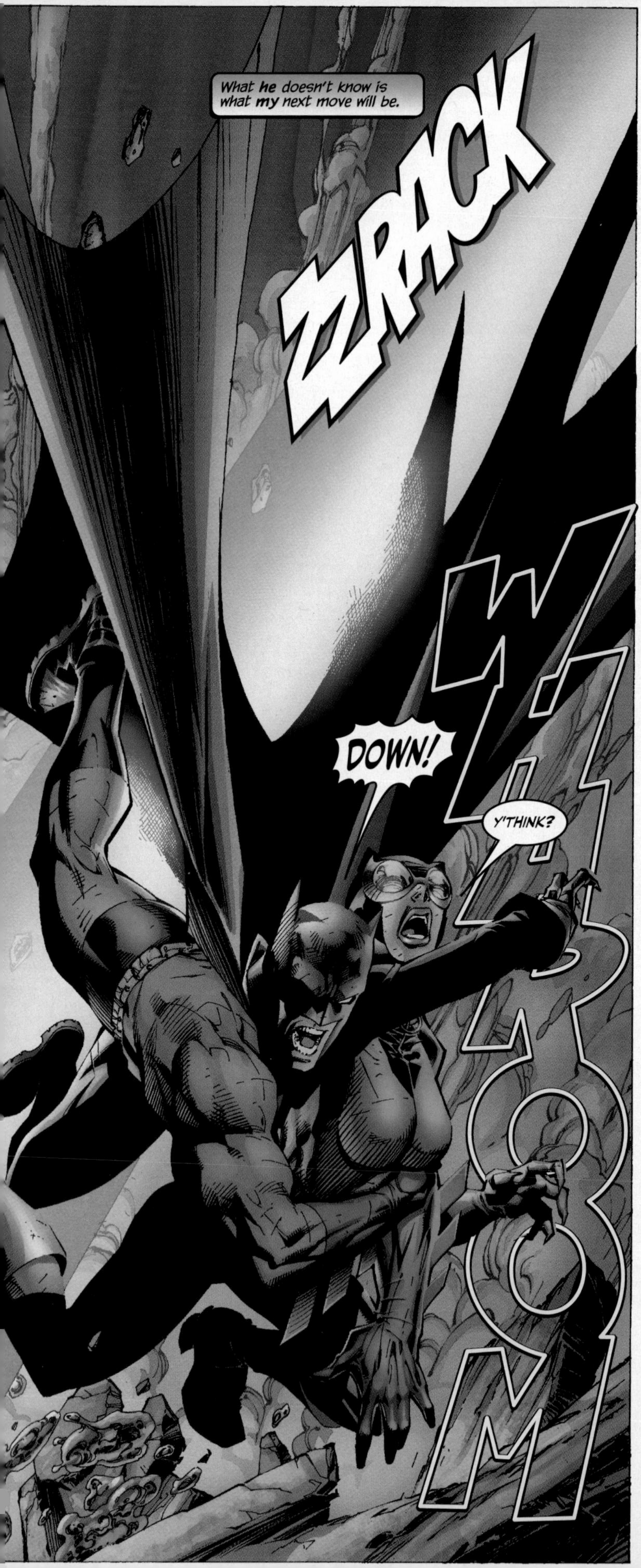
What he doesn't know is what my next move will be.
ZZRACK
DOWN!
Y'THINK?
WHOOM

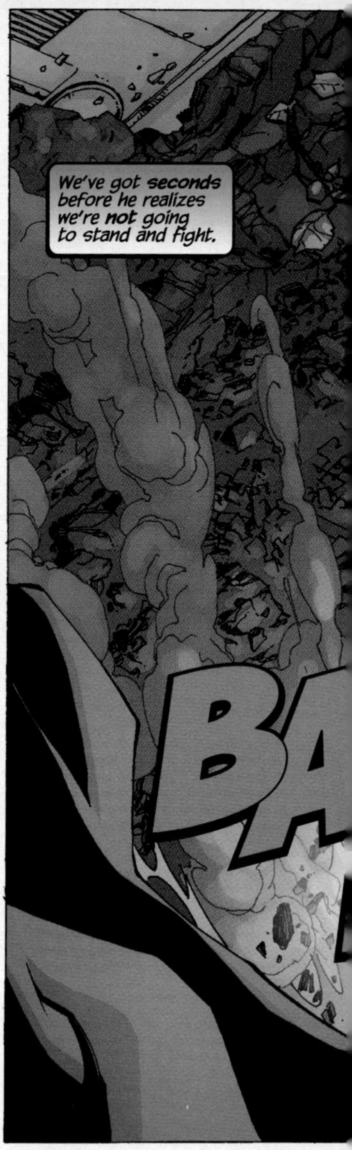
We've got seconds before he realizes we're not going to stand and fight.

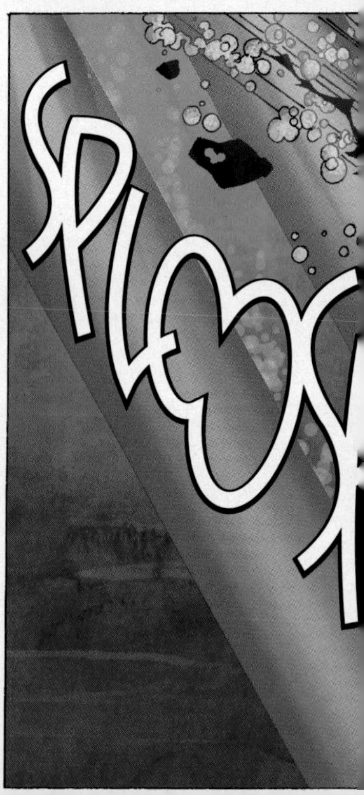

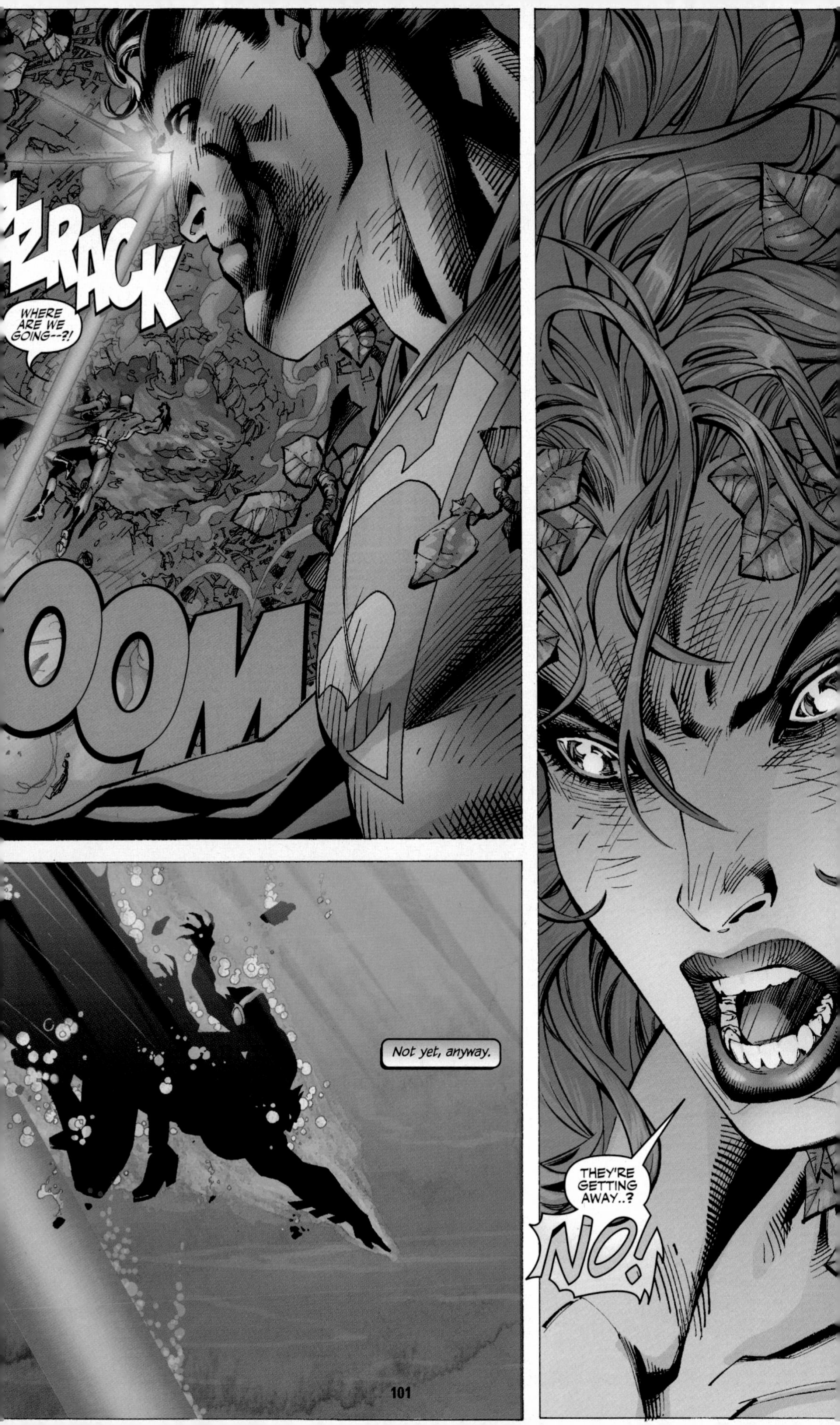

ZRACK
WHERE ARE WE GOING--?!
OOM
Not yet, anyway.
THEY'RE GETTING AWAY..?
NO!

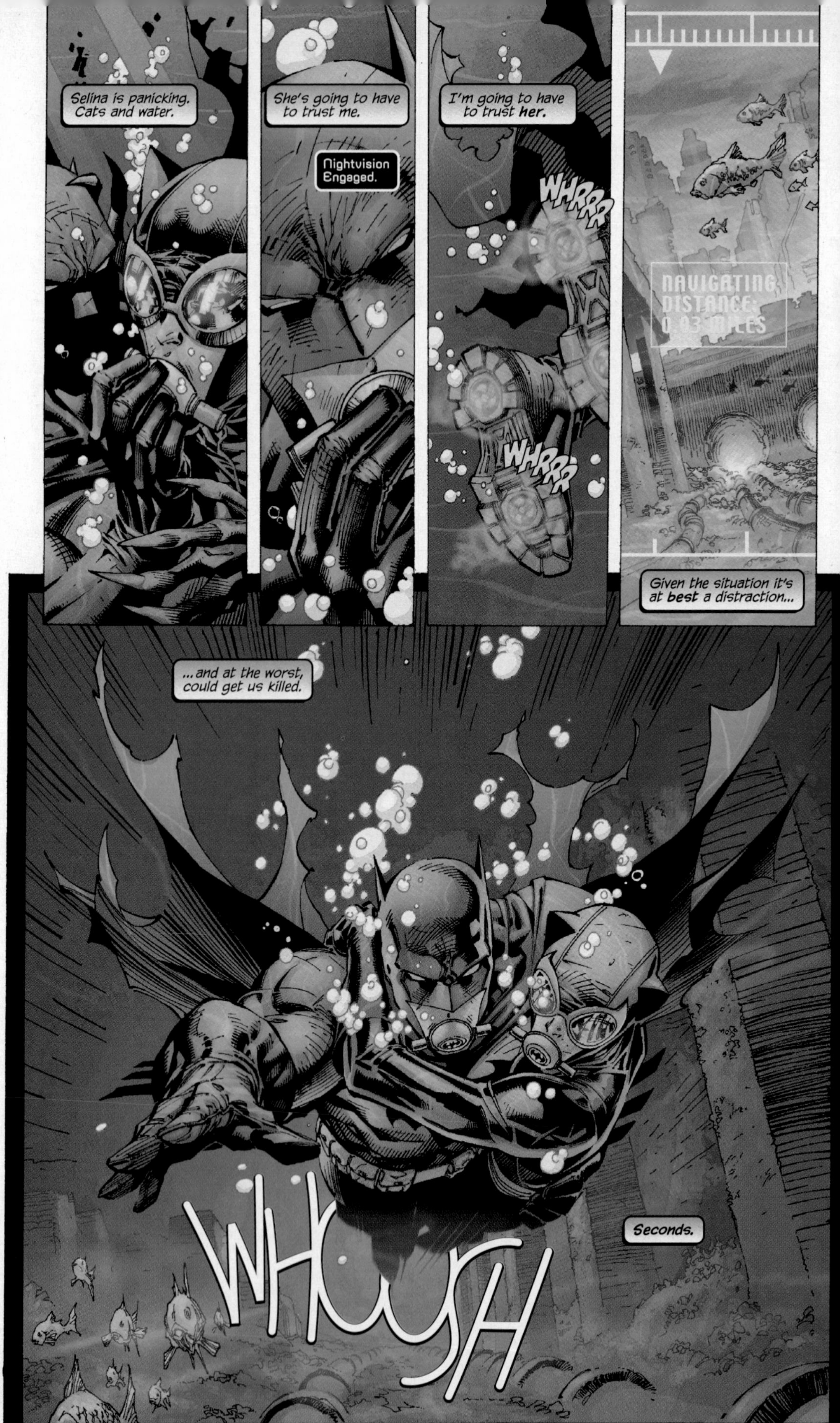

Selina is panicking. Cats and water.
She's going to have to trust me.
Nightvision Engaged.
I'm going to have to trust her.
WHRRR
WHRRR
NAVIGATING DISTANCE: 0.03 MILES
Given the situation it's at best a distraction...
...and at the worst, could get us killed.
WHOOSH
Seconds.

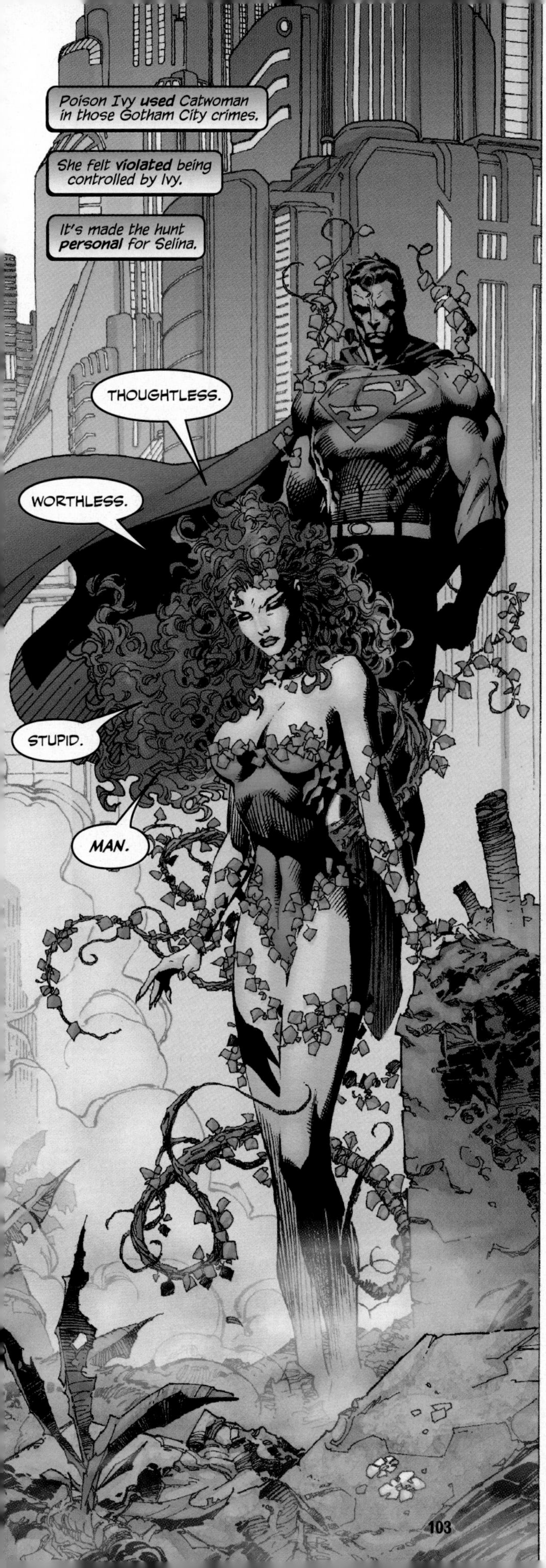
Poison Ivy **used** Catwoman in those Gotham City crimes.
She felt **violated** being controlled by Ivy.
It's made the hunt **personal** for Selina.
THOUGHTLESS.
WORTHLESS.
STUPID.
MAN.

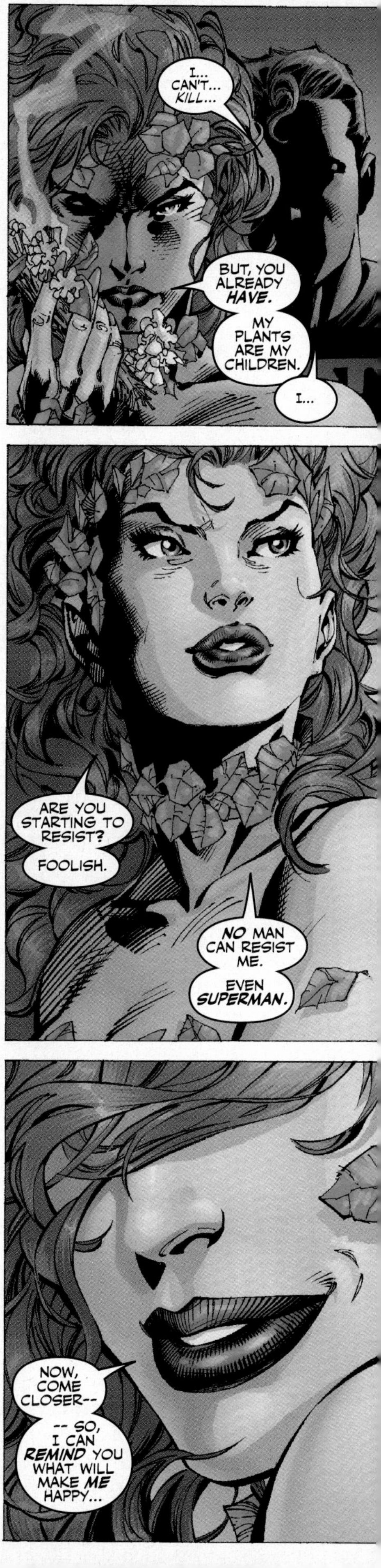
I... CAN'T... KILL...
BUT, YOU ALREADY **HAVE.**
MY PLANTS ARE MY CHILDREN.
I...
ARE YOU STARTING TO RESIST?
FOOLISH.
NO MAN CAN RESIST ME.
EVEN **SUPERMAN.**
NOW, COME CLOSER--
-- SO, I CAN **REMIND** YOU WHAT WILL MAKE **ME** HAPPY...

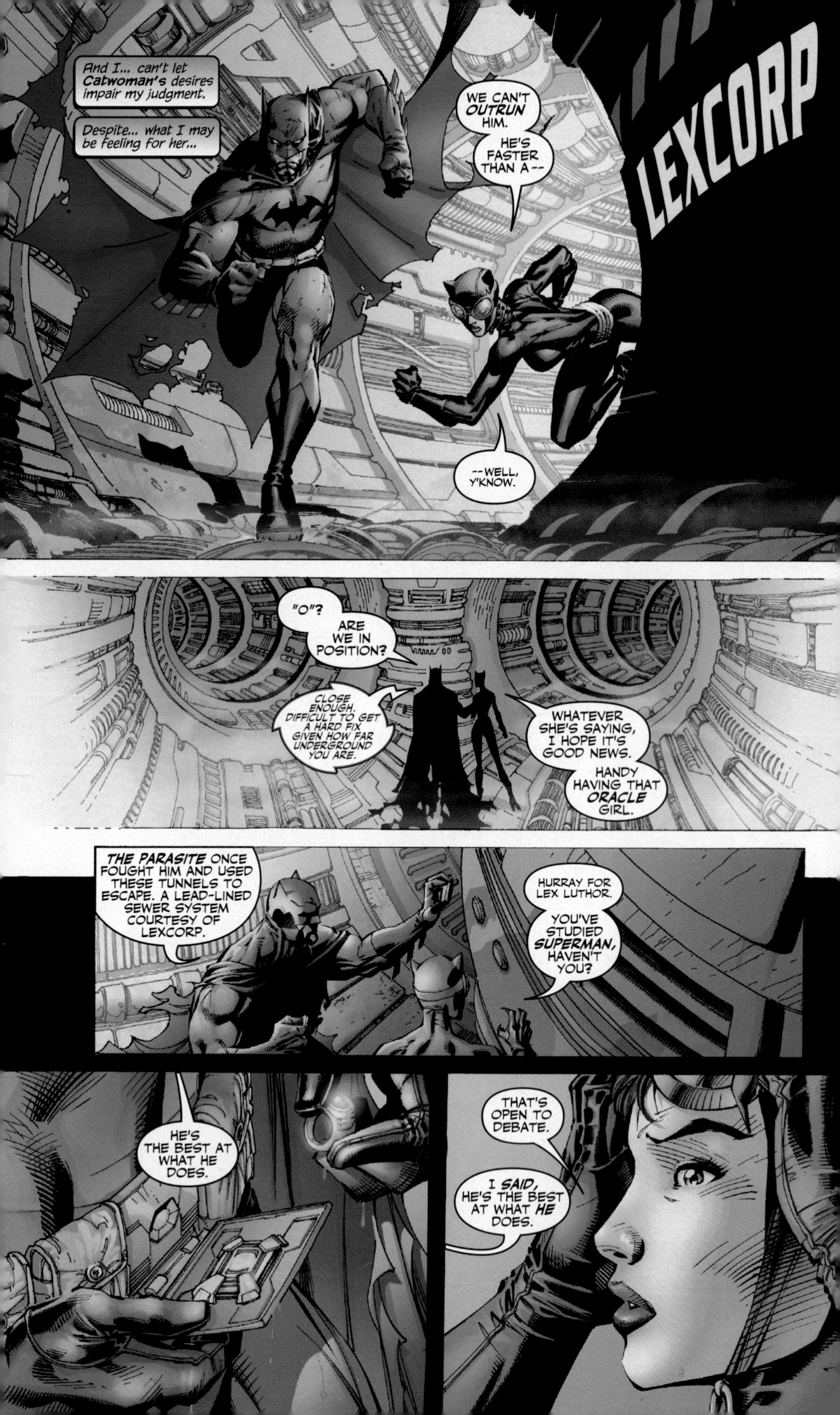

And I... can't let Catwoman's desires impair my judgment.
Despite... what I may be feeling for her...
LEXCORP
WE CAN'T OUTRUN HIM.
HE'S FASTER THAN A--
--WELL, Y'KNOW.
"O"? ARE WE IN POSITION?
CLOSE ENOUGH. DIFFICULT TO GET A HARD FIX GIVEN HOW FAR UNDERGROUND YOU ARE.
WHATEVER SHE'S SAYING, I HOPE IT'S GOOD NEWS.
HANDY HAVING THAT ORACLE GIRL.
THE PARASITE ONCE FOUGHT HIM AND USED THESE TUNNELS TO ESCAPE. A LEAD-LINED SEWER SYSTEM COURTESY OF LEXCORP.
HURRAY FOR LEX LUTHOR.
YOU'VE STUDIED SUPERMAN, HAVEN'T YOU?
HE'S THE BEST AT WHAT HE DOES.
THAT'S OPEN TO DEBATE.
I SAID, HE'S THE BEST AT WHAT HE DOES.

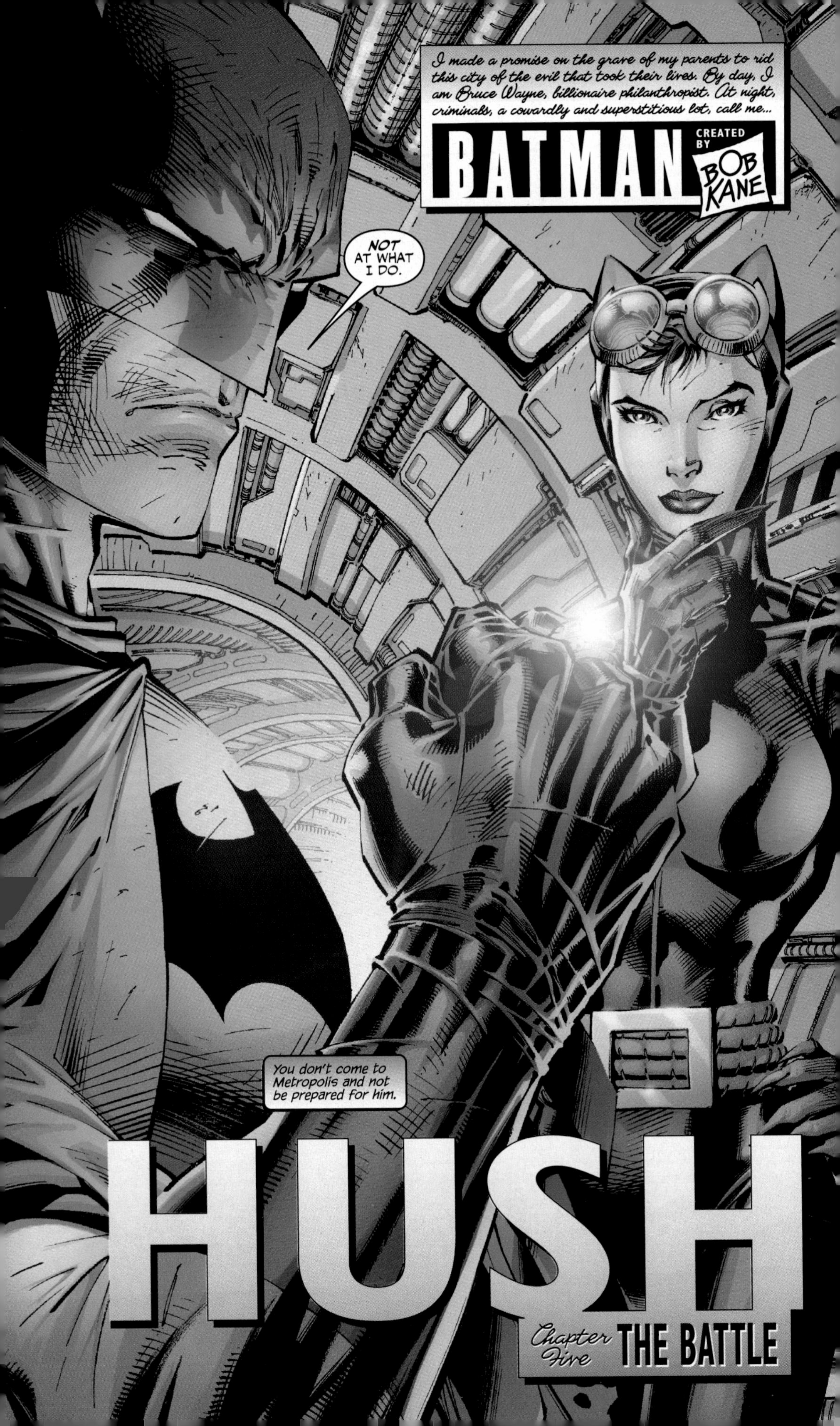

I made a promise on the grave of my parents to rid this city of the evil that took their lives. By day, I am Bruce Wayne, billionaire philanthropist. At night, criminals, a cowardly and superstitious lot, call me...
BATMAN
CREATED BY BOB KANE
NOT AT WHAT I DO.
You don't come to Metropolis and not be prepared for him.
HUSH
Chapter Five THE BATTLE

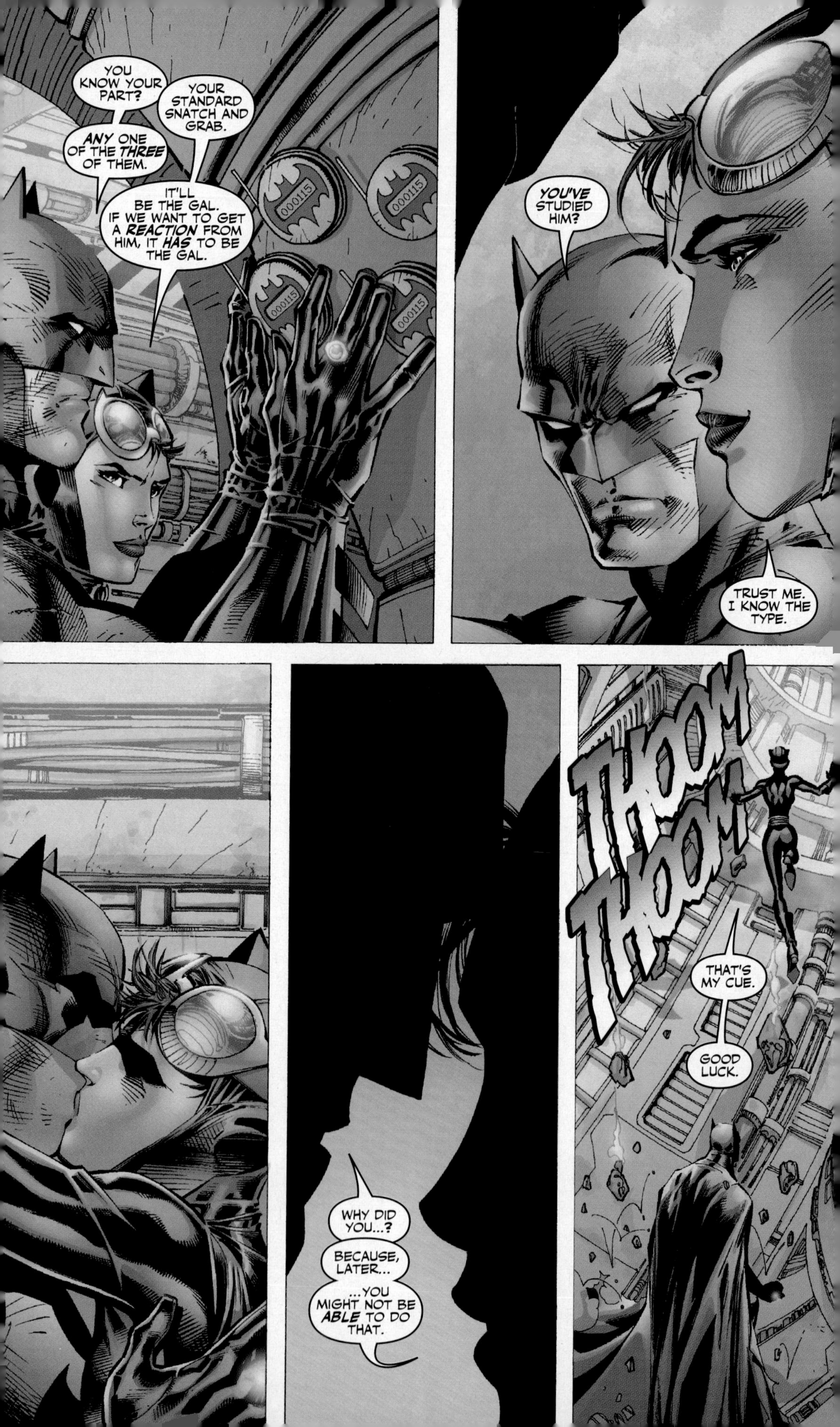
YOU KNOW YOUR PART?
YOUR STANDARD SNATCH AND GRAB.
ANY ONE OF THE THREE OF THEM.
IT'LL BE THE GAL. IF WE WANT TO GET A REACTION FROM HIM, IT HAS TO BE THE GAL.
000115
YOU'VE STUDIED HIM?
TRUST ME. I KNOW THE TYPE.
WHY DID YOU...?
BECAUSE, LATER...
...YOU MIGHT NOT BE ABLE TO DO THAT.
THOOM THOOM
THAT'S MY CUE.
GOOD LUCK.

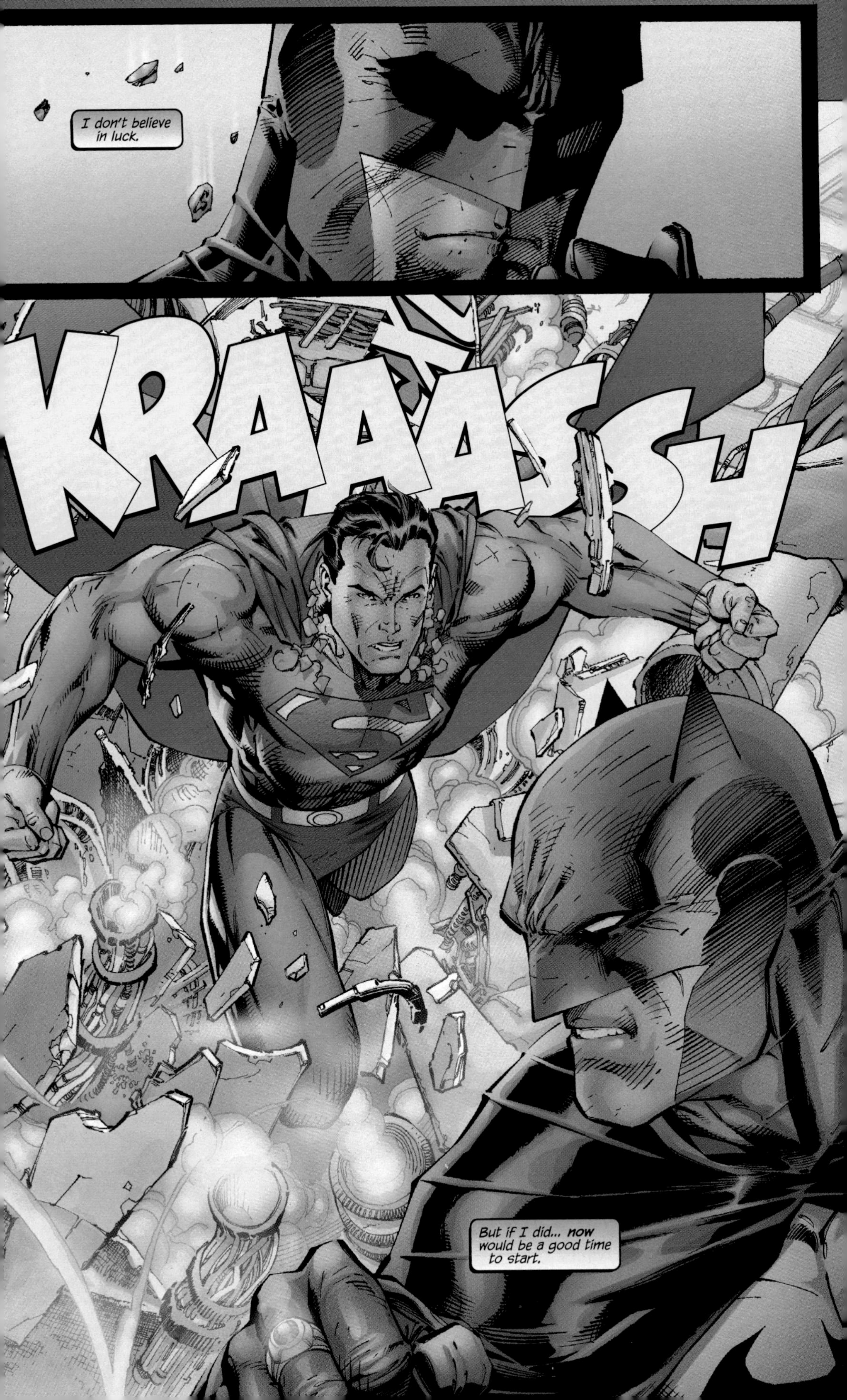

I don't believe in luck.
KRAAASH
But if I did... now would be a good time to start.

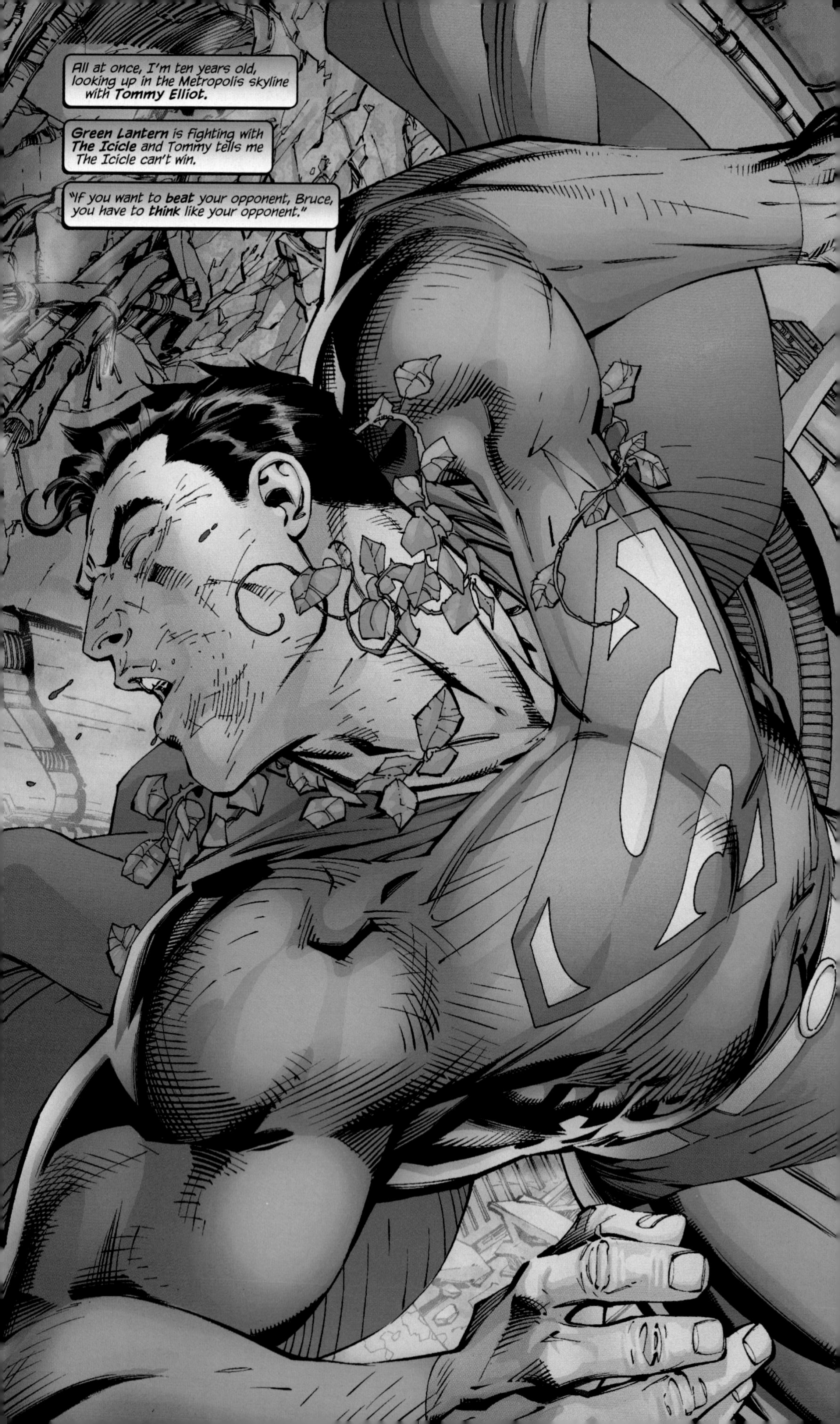
All at once, I'm ten years old, looking up in the Metropolis skyline with Tommy Elliot.
Green Lantern is fighting with The Icicle and Tommy tells me The Icicle can't win.
"If you want to beat your opponent, Bruce, you have to think like your opponent."

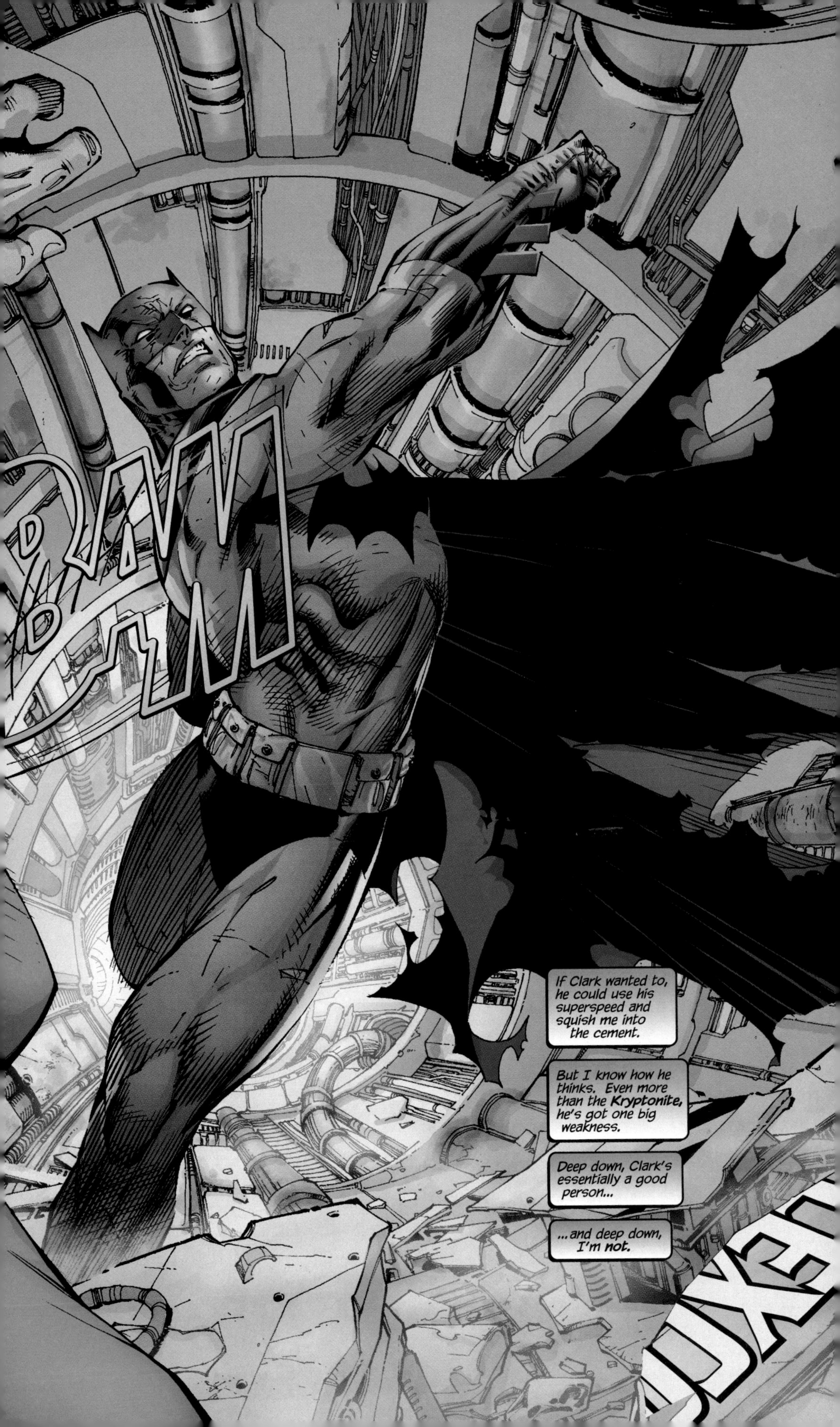
If Clark wanted to, he could use his superspeed and squish me into the cement.
But I know how he thinks. Even more than the **Kryptonite,** he's got one big weakness.
Deep down, Clark's essentially a good person...
...and deep down, I'm **not.**

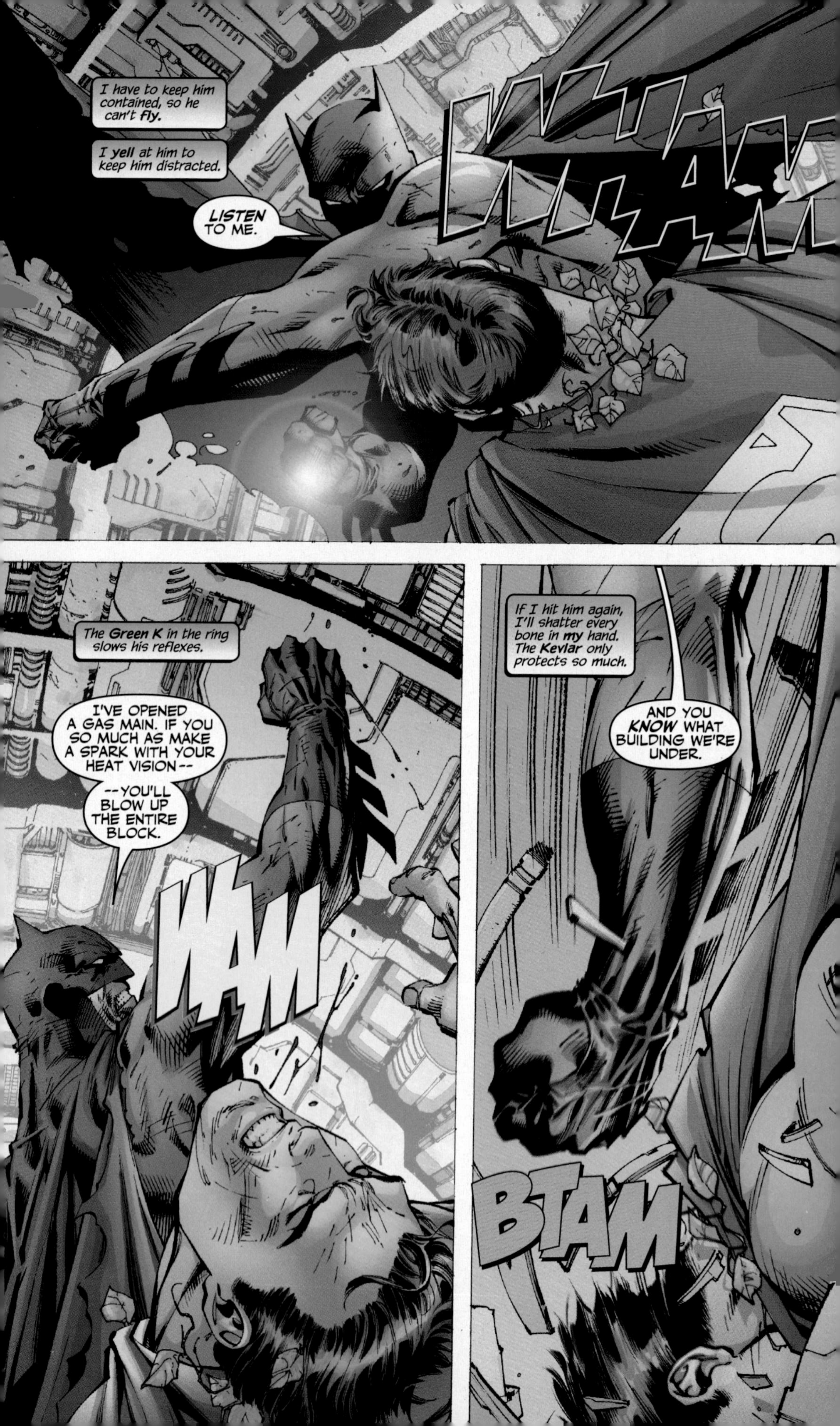
I have to keep him contained, so he can't **fly.**
I **yell** at him to keep him distracted.
LISTEN TO ME.
WHAM
The **Green K** in the ring slows his reflexes.
I'VE OPENED A GAS MAIN. IF YOU SO MUCH AS MAKE A SPARK WITH YOUR HEAT VISION--
--YOU'LL BLOW UP THE ENTIRE BLOCK.
WAM
If I hit him again, I'll shatter every bone in **my** hand. The **Kevlar** only protects so much.
AND YOU ***KNOW*** WHAT BUILDING WE'RE UNDER.
BTAM

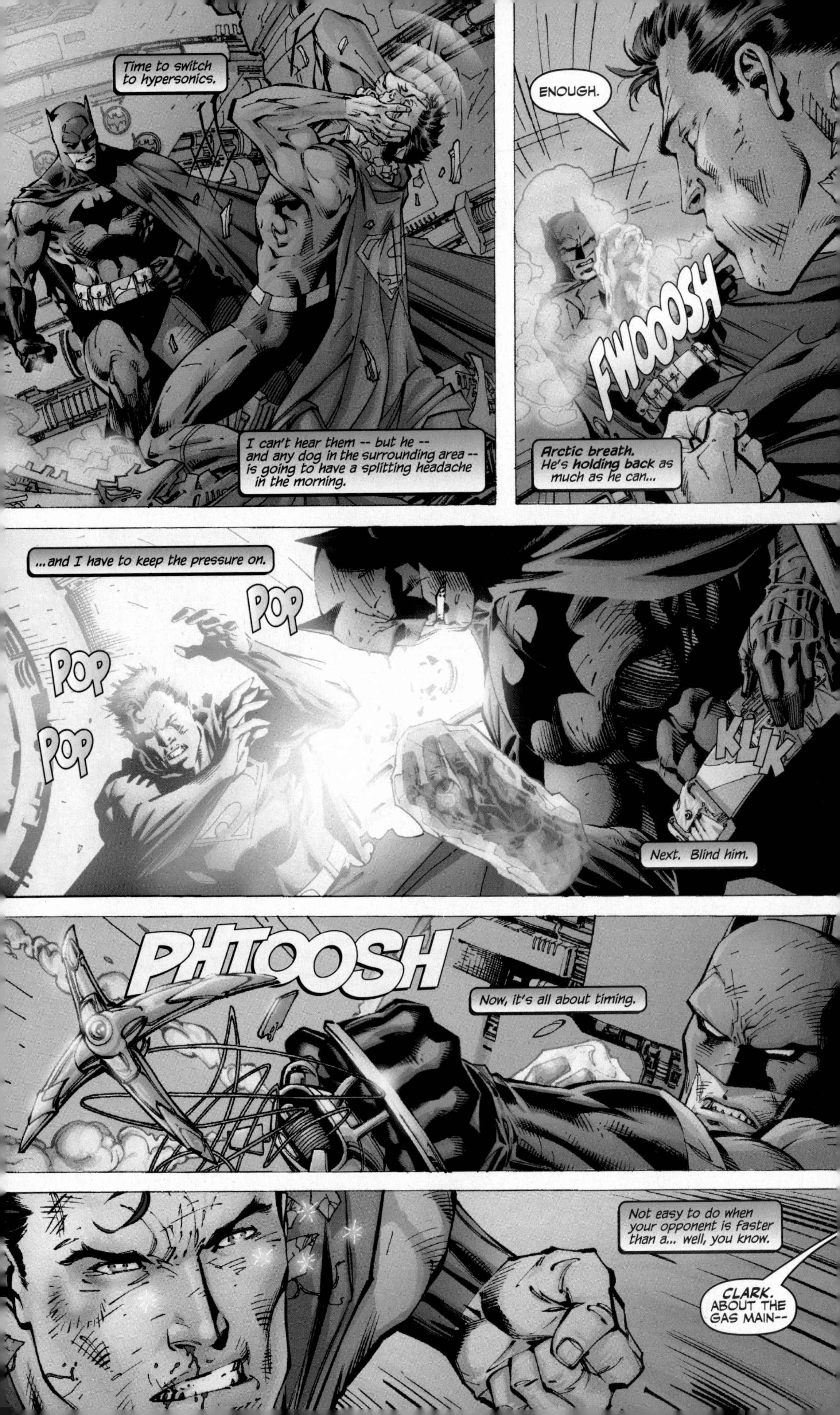
Time to switch to hypersonics.
I can't hear them -- but he -- and any dog in the surrounding area -- is going to have a splitting headache in the morning.
ENOUGH.
FWOOOSH
Arctic breath. He's holding back as much as he can...
...and I have to keep the pressure on.
POP
POP
POP
KLIK
Next. Blind him.
PHTOOSH
Now, it's all about timing.
Not easy to do when your opponent is faster than a... well, you know.
CLARK. ABOUT THE GAS MAIN--

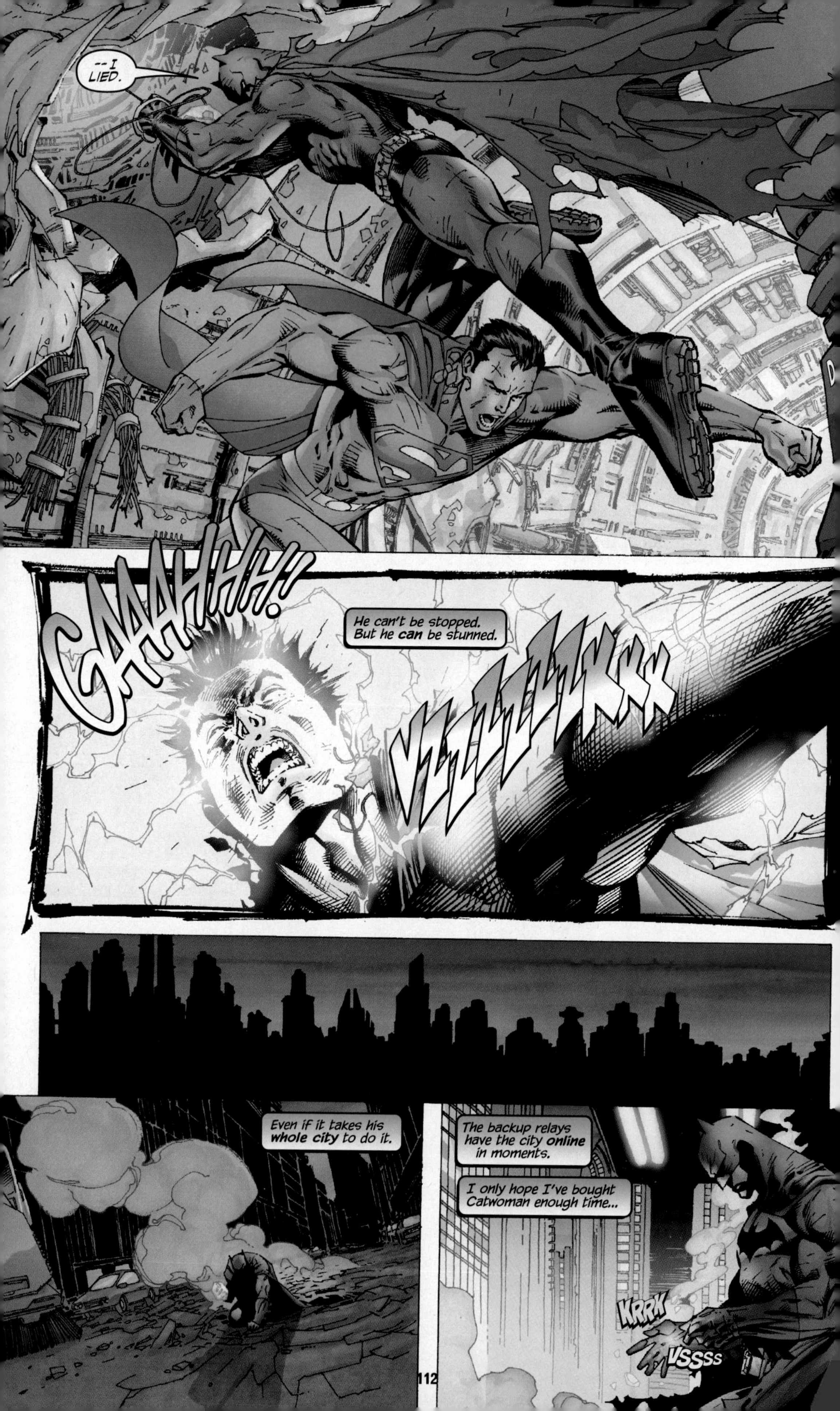
--I LIED.
GAAHHH!
He can't be stopped. But he can be stunned.
VZZZZZKXX
Even if it takes his whole city to do it.
The backup relays have the city online in moments.
I only hope I've bought Catwoman enough time...
KRRK
VSSSS

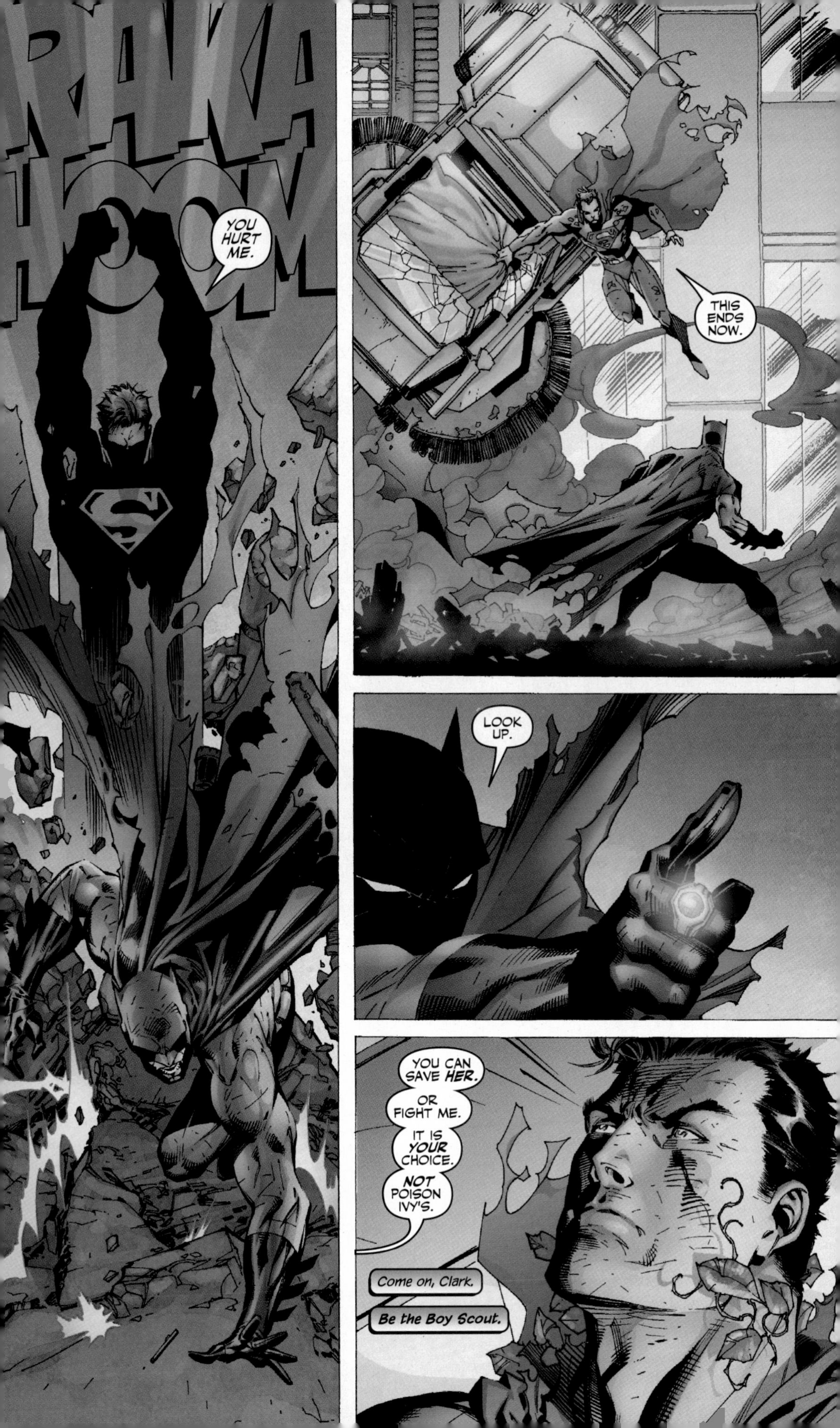
KRAKA-THOOM
YOU HURT ME.
THIS ENDS NOW.
LOOK UP.
YOU CAN SAVE **HER**.
OR FIGHT ME.
IT IS ***YOUR*** CHOICE.
NOT POISON IVY'S.
Come on, Clark.
Be the Boy Scout.

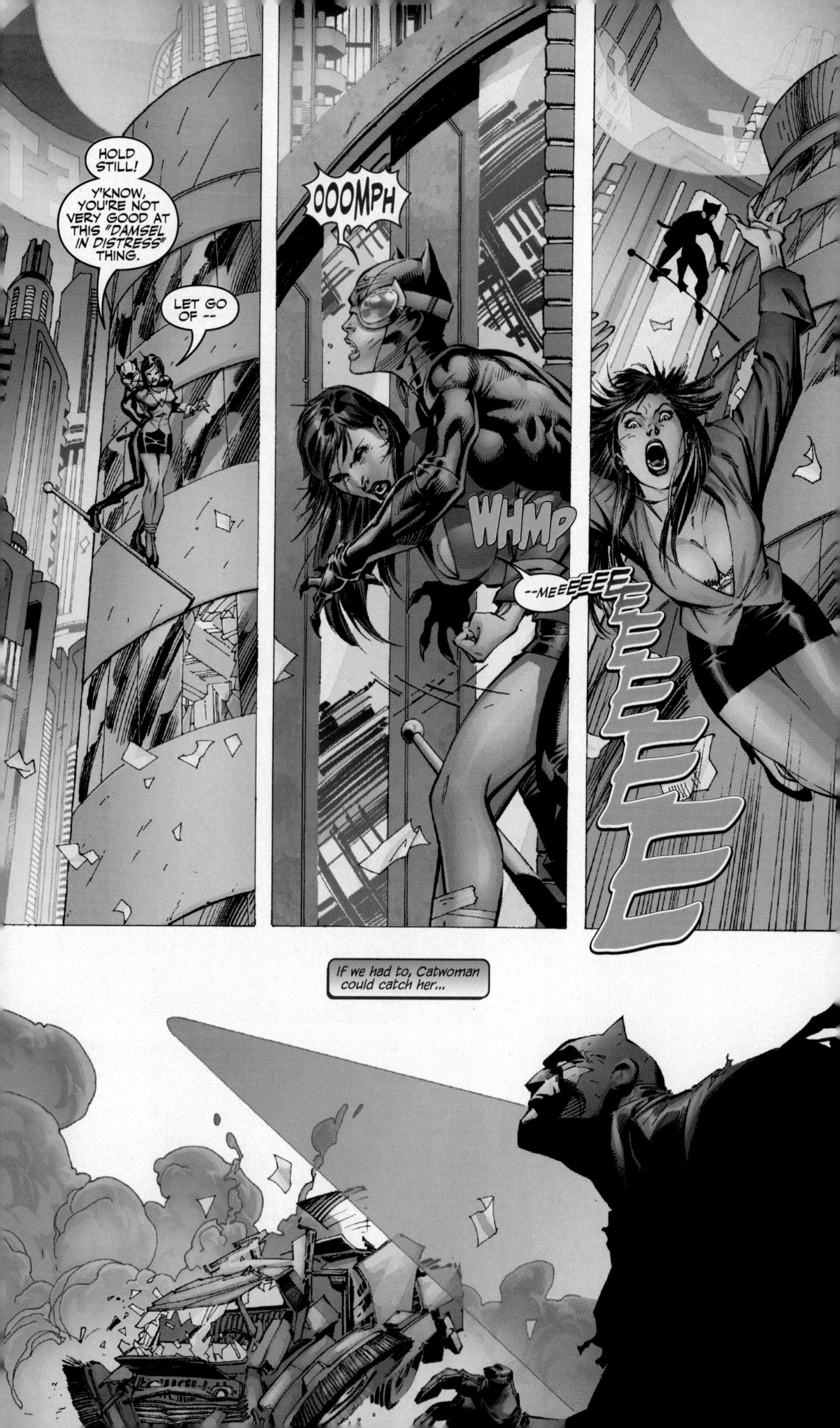
HOLD STILL!
Y'KNOW, YOU'RE NOT VERY GOOD AT THIS "DAMSEL IN DISTRESS" THING.
LET GO OF --
OOOMPH
WHMP
--MEEEEEEEEEEEEEEE
If we had to, Catwoman could catch her...

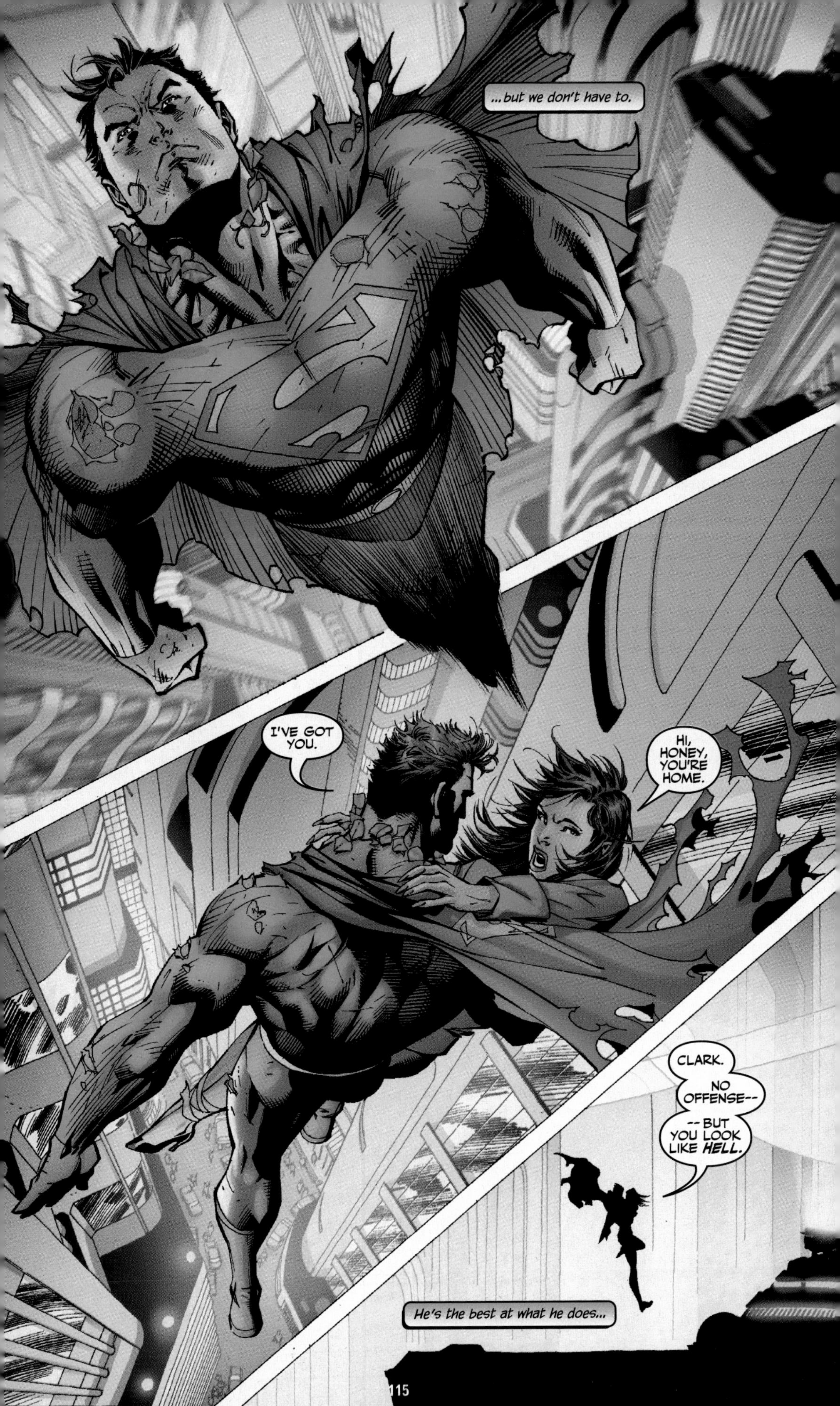
...but we don't have to.
I'VE GOT YOU.
HI, HONEY, YOU'RE HOME.
CLARK.
NO OFFENSE--
--BUT YOU LOOK LIKE HELL.
He's the best at what he does...

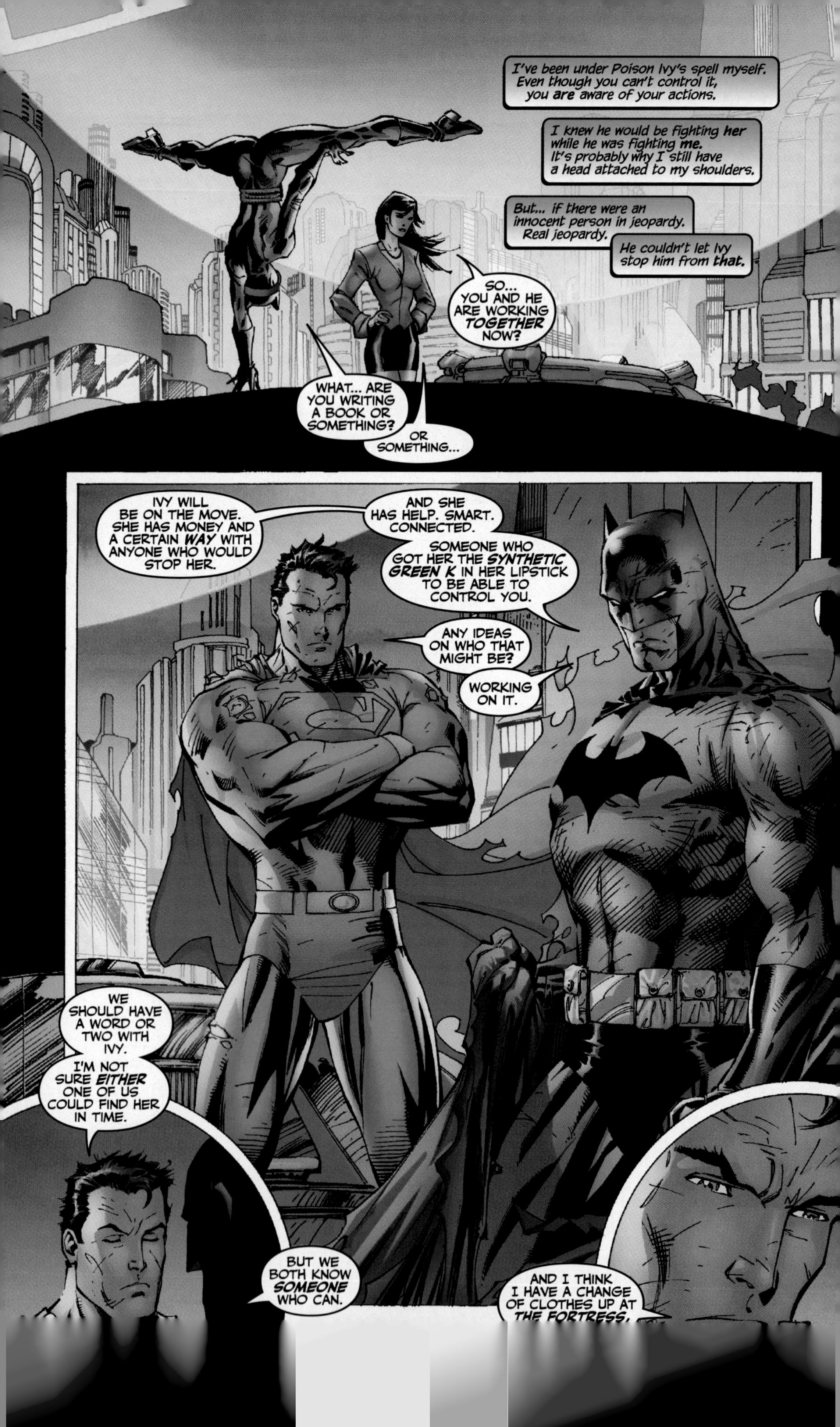

I've been under Poison Ivy's spell myself. Even though you can't control it, you are aware of your actions.
I knew he would be fighting her while he was fighting me. It's probably why I still have a head attached to my shoulders.
But... if there were an innocent person in jeopardy. Real jeopardy.
He couldn't let Ivy stop him from that.
SO... YOU AND HE ARE WORKING TOGETHER NOW?
WHAT... ARE YOU WRITING A BOOK OR SOMETHING?
OR SOMETHING...
IVY WILL BE ON THE MOVE. SHE HAS MONEY AND A CERTAIN WAY WITH ANYONE WHO WOULD STOP HER.
AND SHE HAS HELP. SMART. CONNECTED.
SOMEONE WHO GOT HER THE SYNTHETIC GREEN K IN HER LIPSTICK TO BE ABLE TO CONTROL YOU.
ANY IDEAS ON WHO THAT MIGHT BE?
WORKING ON IT.
WE SHOULD HAVE A WORD OR TWO WITH IVY.
I'M NOT SURE EITHER ONE OF US COULD FIND HER IN TIME.
BUT WE BOTH KNOW SOMEONE WHO CAN.
AND I THINK I HAVE A CHANGE OF CLOTHES UP AT THE FORTRESS.

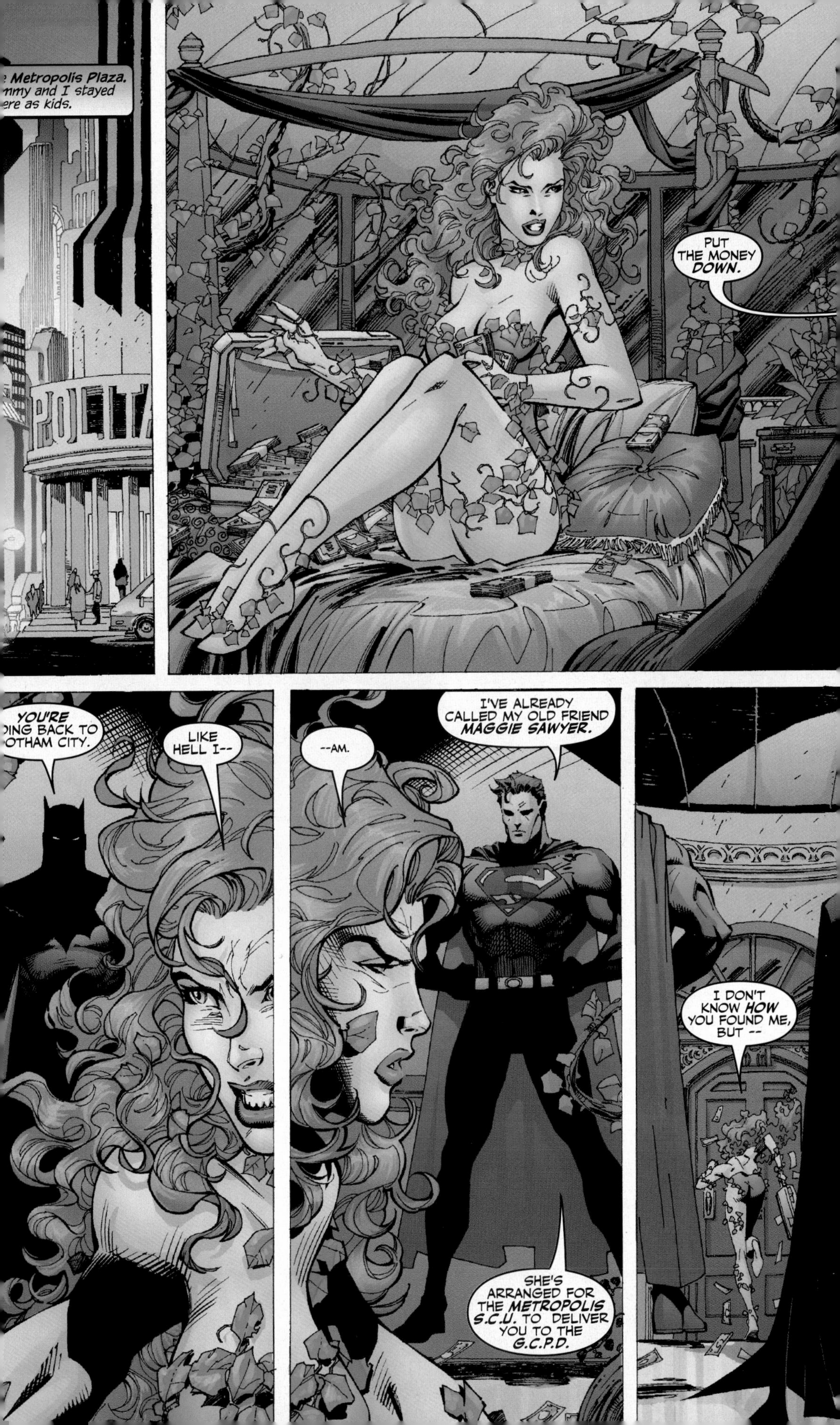

e Metropolis Plaza. mmy and I stayed ere as kids.
PUT THE MONEY DOWN.
YOU'RE ...ING BACK TO ...OTHAM CITY.
LIKE HELL I--
--AM.
I'VE ALREADY CALLED MY OLD FRIEND MAGGIE SAWYER.
SHE'S ARRANGED FOR THE METROPOLIS S.C.U. TO DELIVER YOU TO THE G.C.P.D.
I DON'T KNOW HOW YOU FOUND ME, BUT --

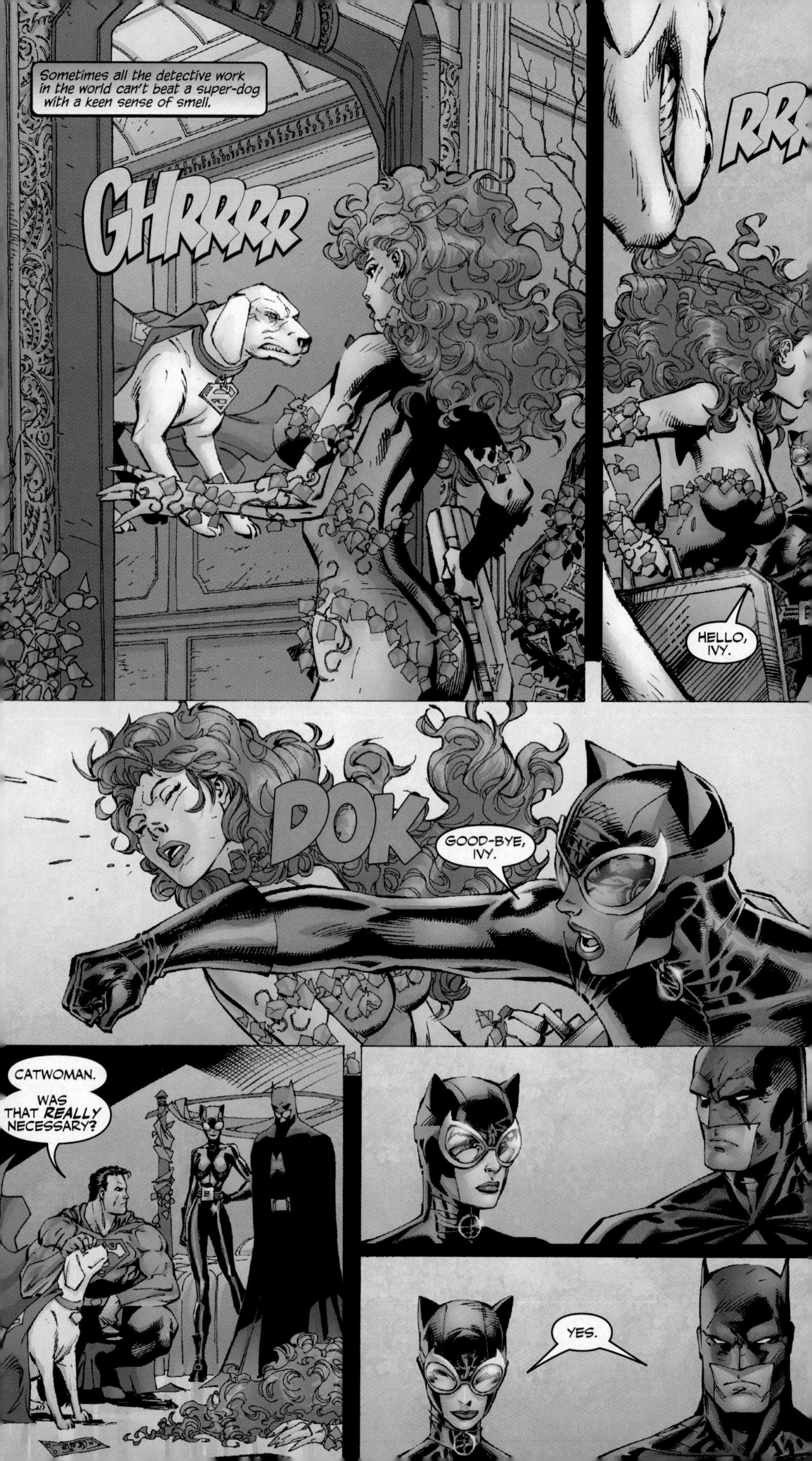
Sometimes all the detective work in the world can't beat a super-dog with a keen sense of smell.
GHRRRR
RR
HELLO, IVY.
DOK
GOOD-BYE, IVY.
CATWOMAN.
WAS THAT *REALLY* NECESSARY?
YES.

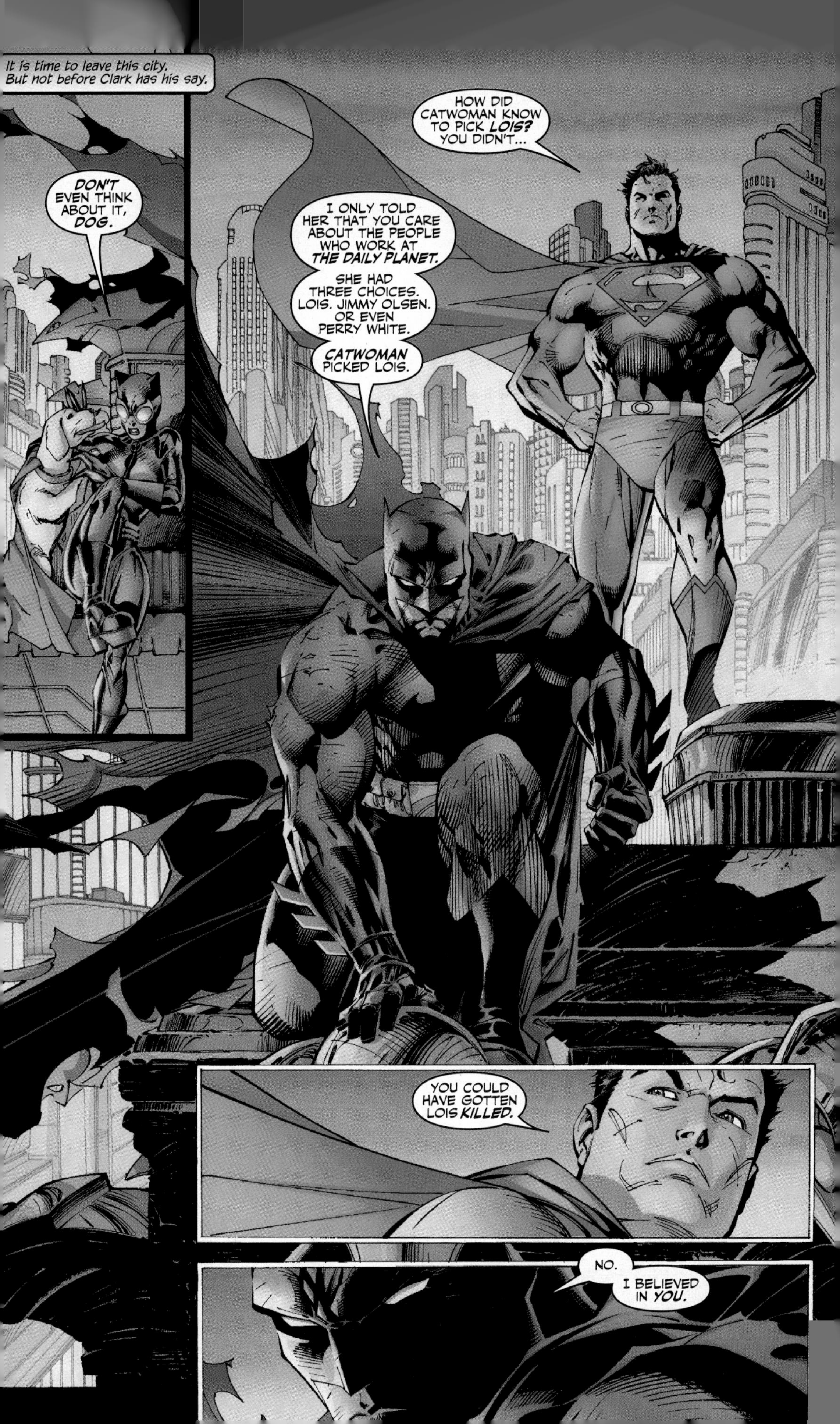
It is time to leave this city. But not before Clark has his say.
DON'T EVEN THINK ABOUT IT, DOG.
HOW DID CATWOMAN KNOW TO PICK LOIS? YOU DIDN'T...
I ONLY TOLD HER THAT YOU CARE ABOUT THE PEOPLE WHO WORK AT THE DAILY PLANET.
SHE HAD THREE CHOICES. LOIS. JIMMY OLSEN. OR EVEN PERRY WHITE.
CATWOMAN PICKED LOIS.
YOU COULD HAVE GOTTEN LOIS KILLED.
NO.
I BELIEVED IN YOU.

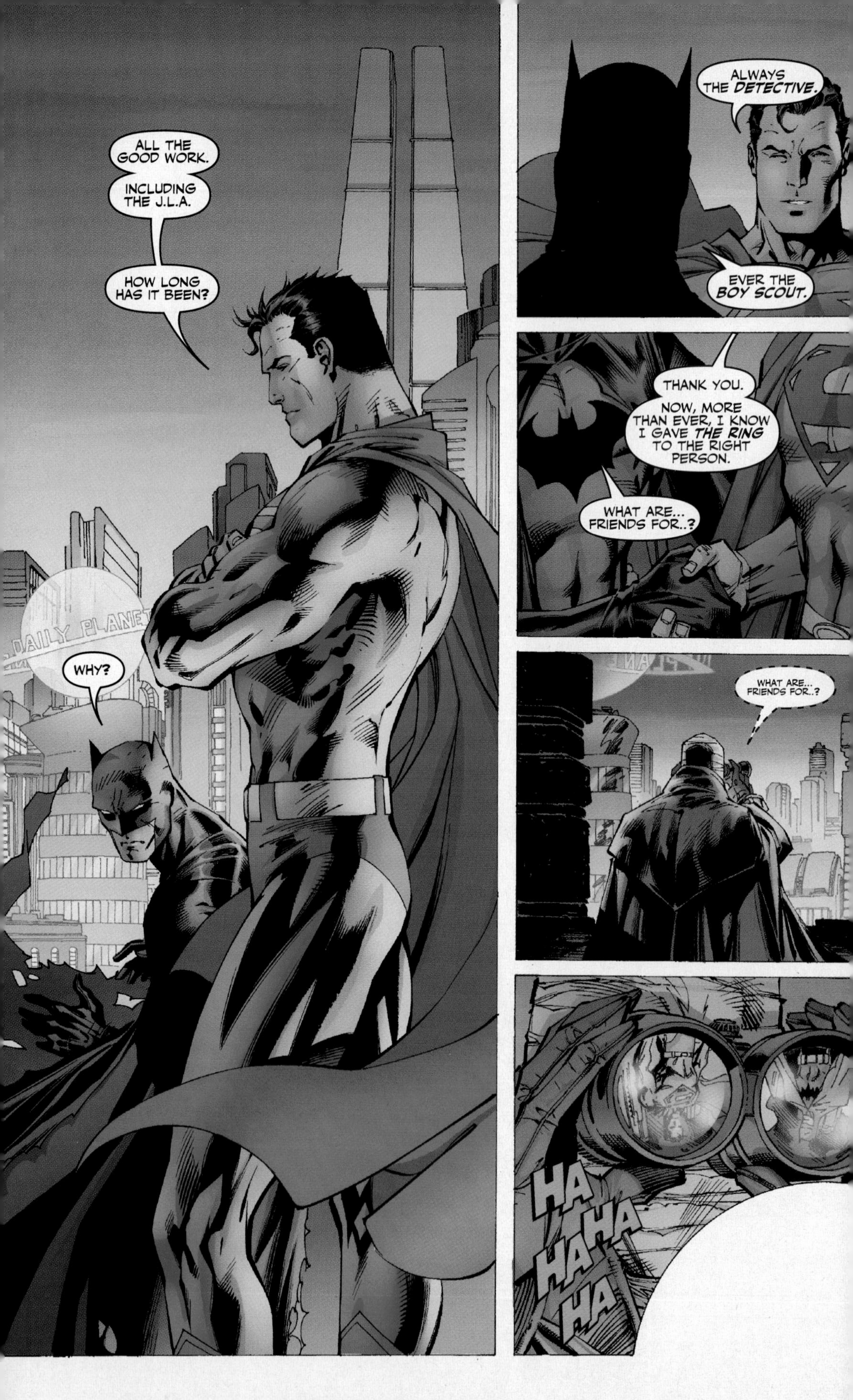
ALL THE GOOD WORK.
INCLUDING THE J.L.A.
HOW LONG HAS IT BEEN?
DAILY PLANET
WHY?
ALWAYS THE DETECTIVE.
EVER THE BOY SCOUT.
THANK YOU.
NOW, MORE THAN EVER, I KNOW I GAVE THE RING TO THE RIGHT PERSON.
WHAT ARE... FRIENDS FOR..?
WHAT ARE... FRIENDS FOR..?
HA HA HA HA HA

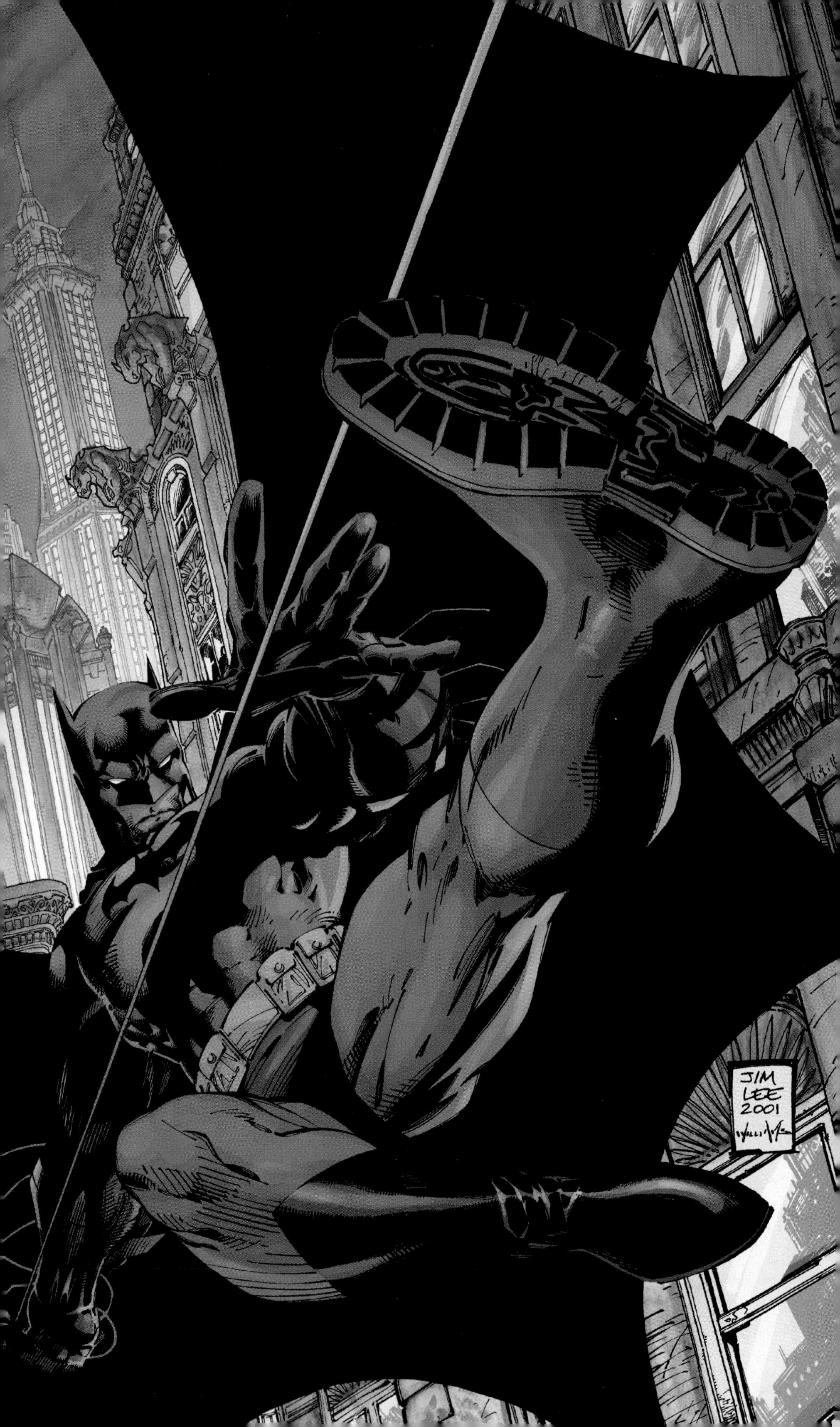
JIM LEE 2001

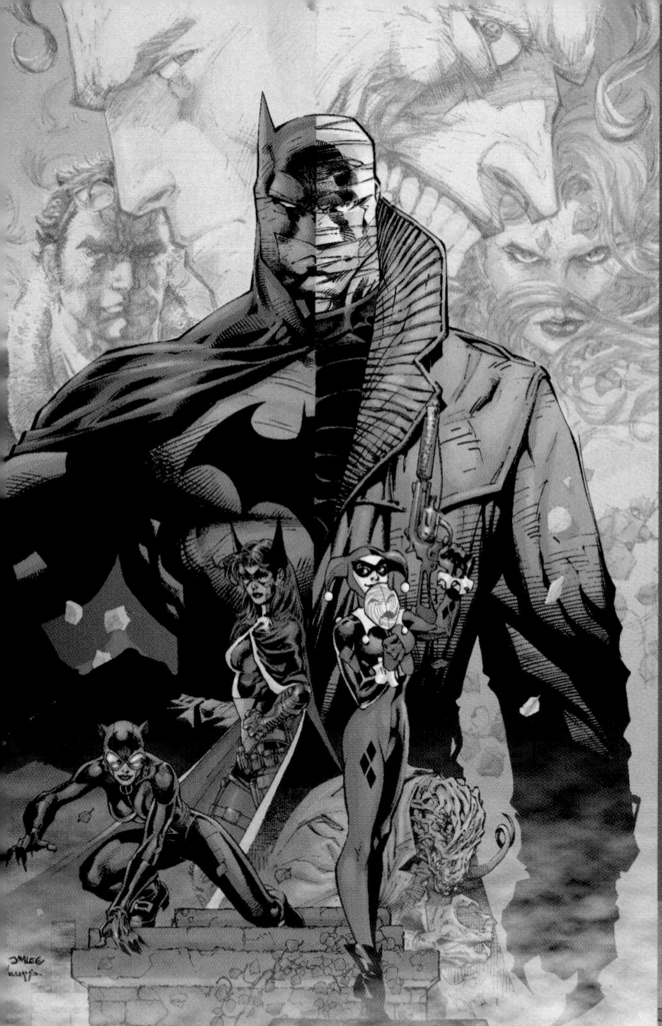

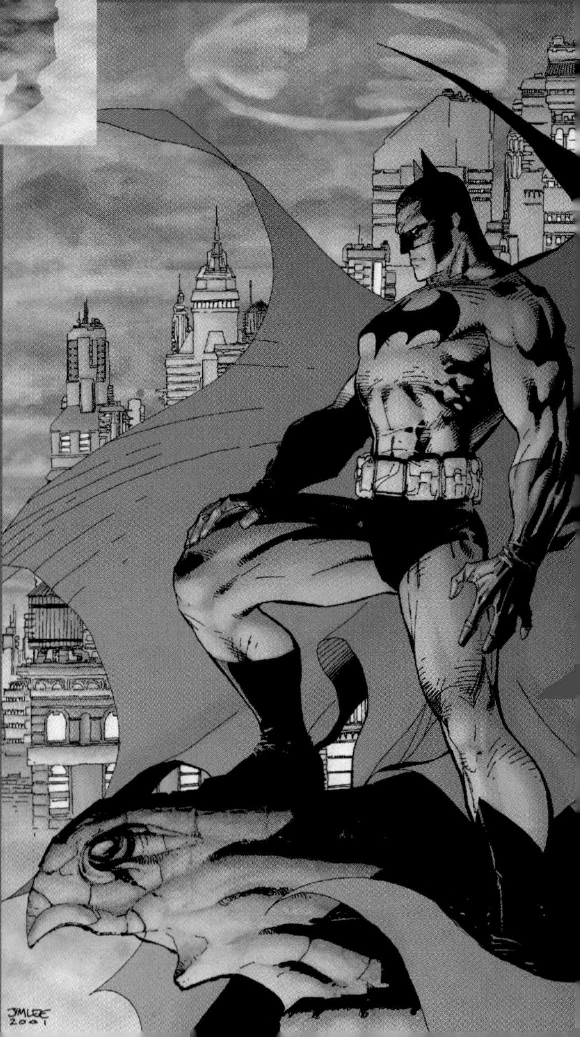

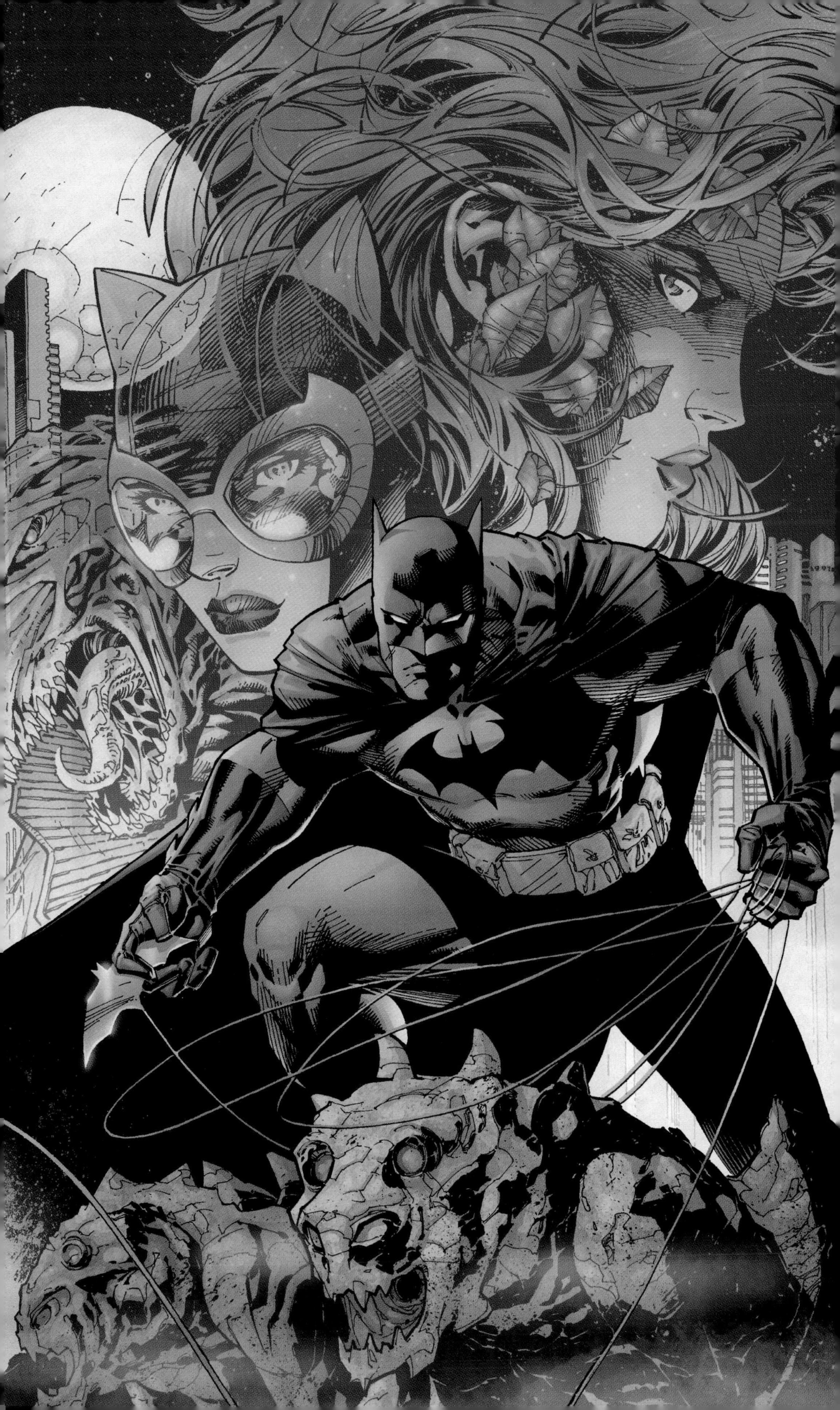

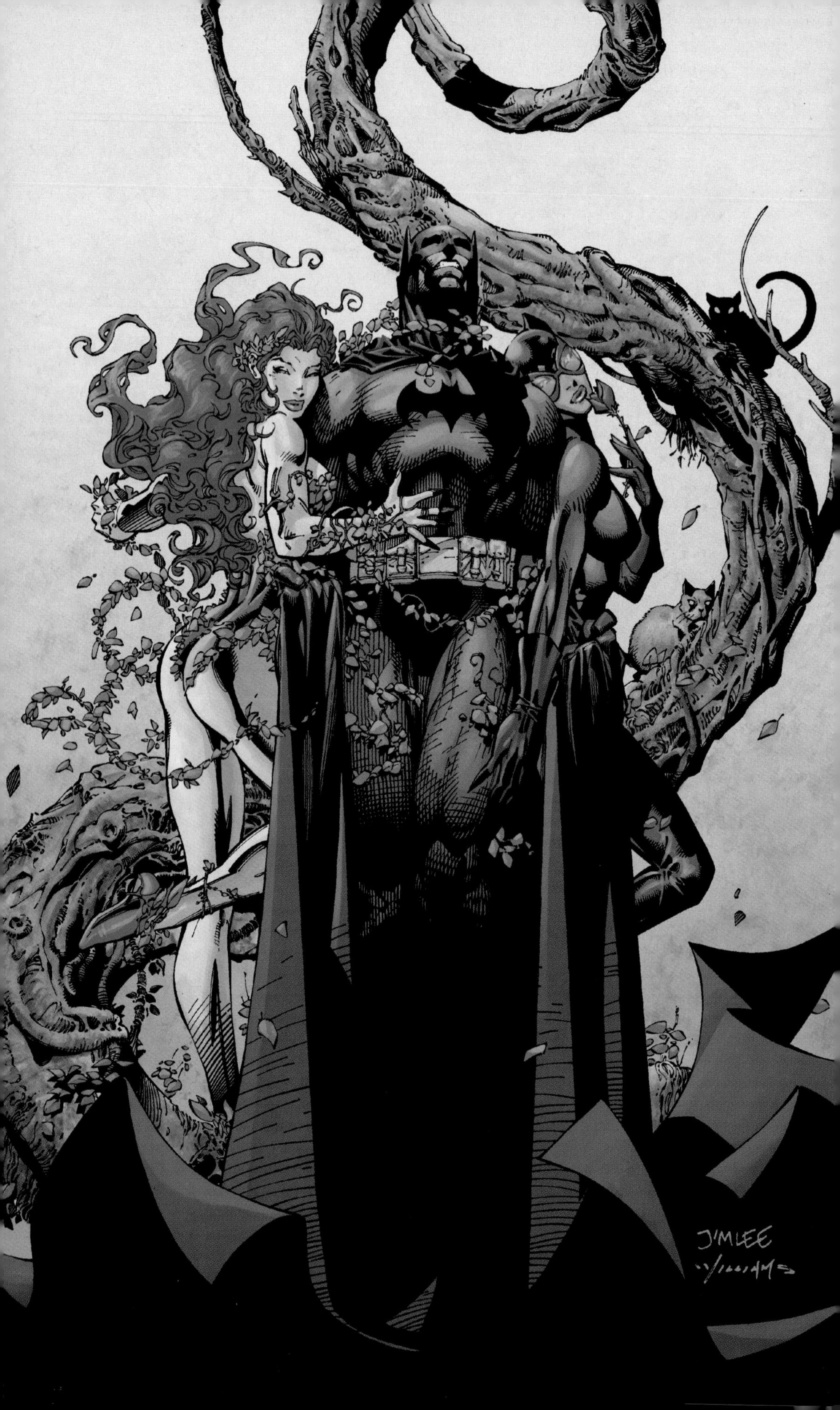

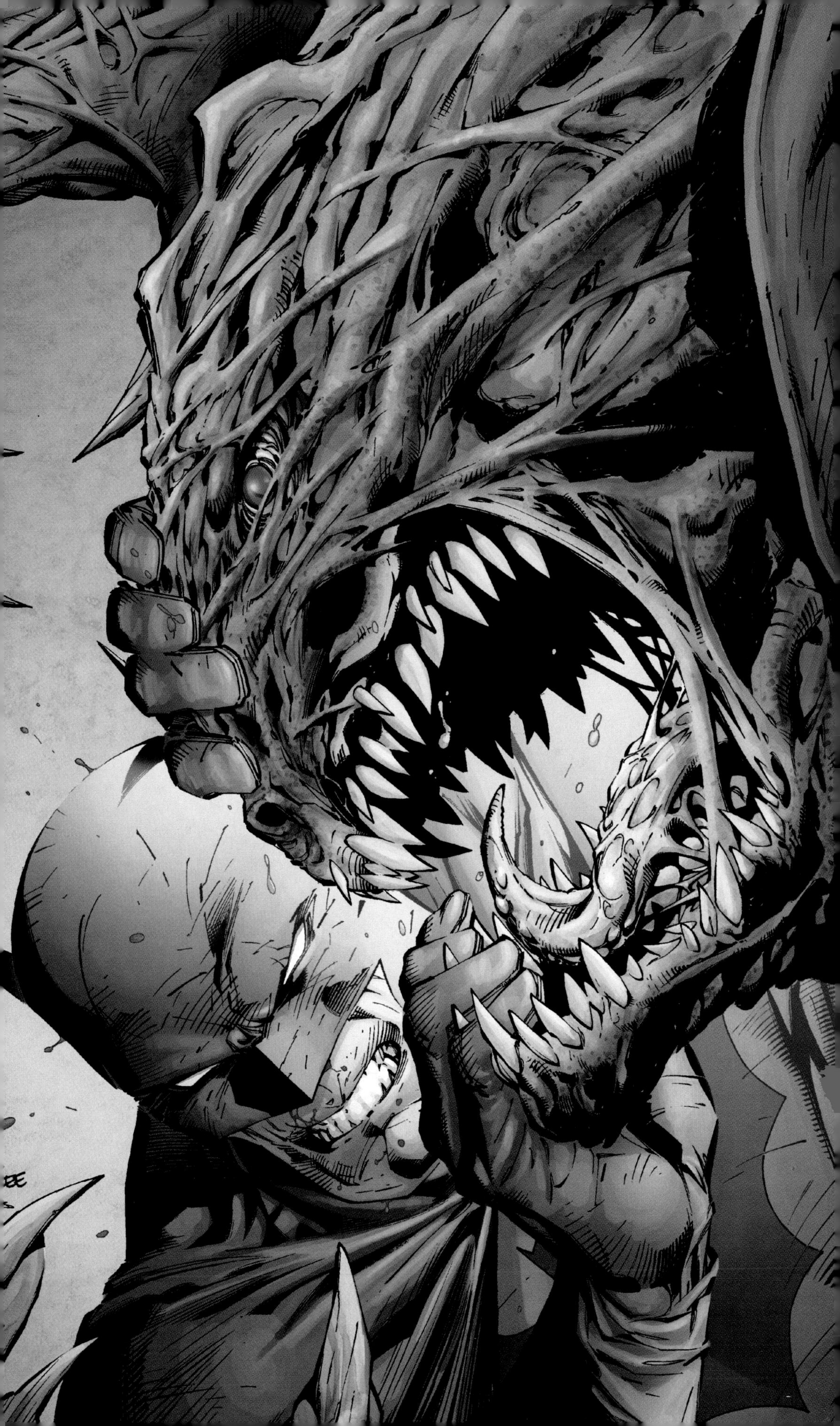

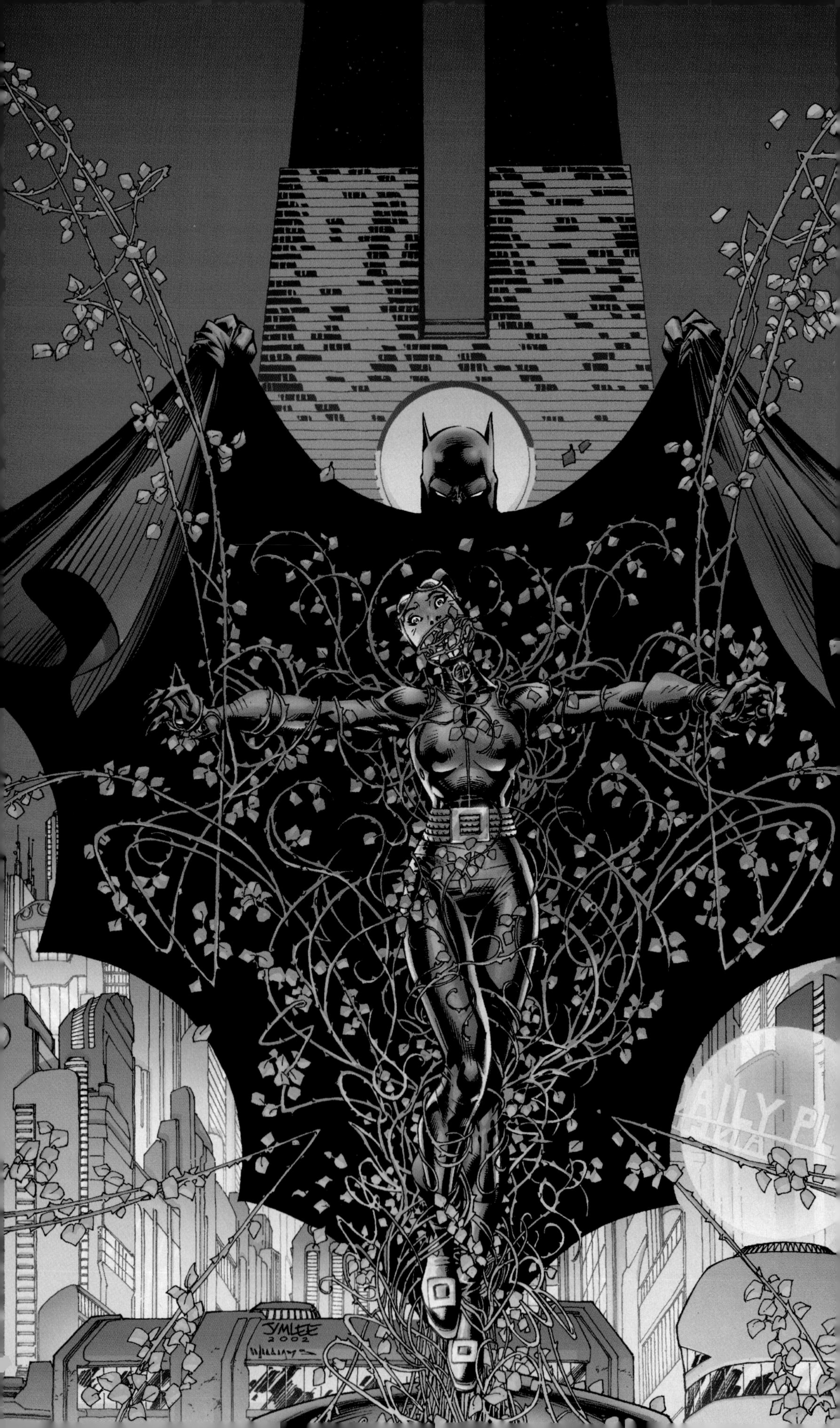
AILY PL

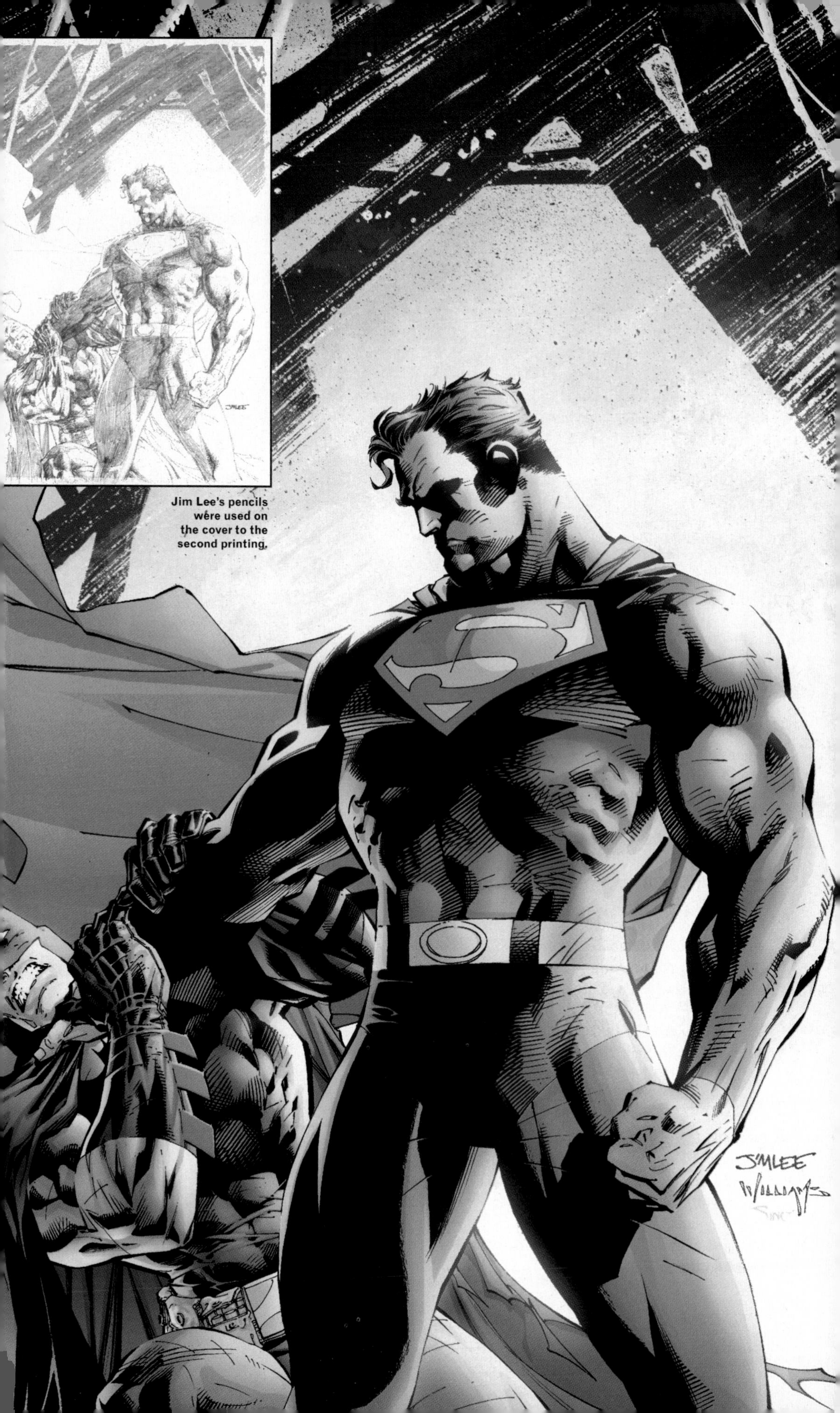

Jim Lee's pencils were used on the cover to the second printing.

JEPH LOEB is the author of BATMAN: THE LONG HALLOWEEN, BATMAN: DARK VICTORY, SUPERMAN FOR ALL SEASONS, *Spider-Man: Blue* and *Daredevil: Yellow*. A writer/producer living in Los Angeles, his credits include *Teen Wolf, Commando, Buffy: The Animated Series* and *Smallville*.

JIM LEE was born in Seoul, South Korea in 1964. He graduated from Princeton University with a degree in psychology but decided to try his hand at comic-book art — his childhood fantasy. He found work at Marvel Comics, where his work quickly proved so popular that the company created a new X-Men title just to showcase it. In 1992, Lee formed his own comics company, WildStorm Productions, which became one of the founding components of Image Comics. There, he launched the best-selling WILDC.A.T.S and introduced scores of new characters such as GEN13. He also helped to discover and train a phalanx of writers, artists, and colorists. With its steady success, WildStorm as a business grew so demanding that Lee found he no longer had any time to draw, leading to his decision to sell the company to DC Comics. He remains WildStorm's editorial director but now concentrates on his first love, art. He lives in La Jolla, California with his wife Angie and his daughters Tyler, Kelsey and Siena.

BIOGRAPHIES

SCOTT WILLIAMS has worked with Jim Lee for more than ten years, and he was voted Favorite Inker for five years in a row (1990-94) in the *Comics Buyer's Guide* Fan Awards. His inking work can be found in WILDCATS, GEN13, JUST IMAGINE STAN LEE... WONDER WOMAN, WILDCATS/X-MEN, *X-Men: Mutant Genesis*, and *X-Men: X-Tinction Agenda*.

ALEX SINCLAIR bought his first comic book — DETECTIVE COMICS #500 — with his brother, Celes, at the local convenience store. He immediately fell in love with comics and with Batman, who continues to be his favorite character. (Alex and Celes still argue over who would win in a fight between Batman and Superman.) He has previously worked on KURT BUSIEK'S ASTRO CITY, TOP 10, HARLEY QUINN, and, with Jim Lee and Scott Williams, on WILDC.A.T.S, GEN13, and DIVINE RIGHT. Sinclair lives in San Diego with his sidekick Rebecca and their four hench-girls: Grace, Blythe, Meredith, and Harley. He would love to fight crime, but the weather's too nice...

RICHARD STARKINGS is best known as the creator of the Comicraft studio, purveyors of unique design and fine lettering — and a copious catalogue of comic-book fonts — since 1992. He is less well known as the creator and publisher of *Hip Flask* and his semi-autobiographical cartoon strip, *Hedge Backwards*. He never seems to get tired of reminding people that he lettered BATMAN: THE KILLING JOKE with a pen.

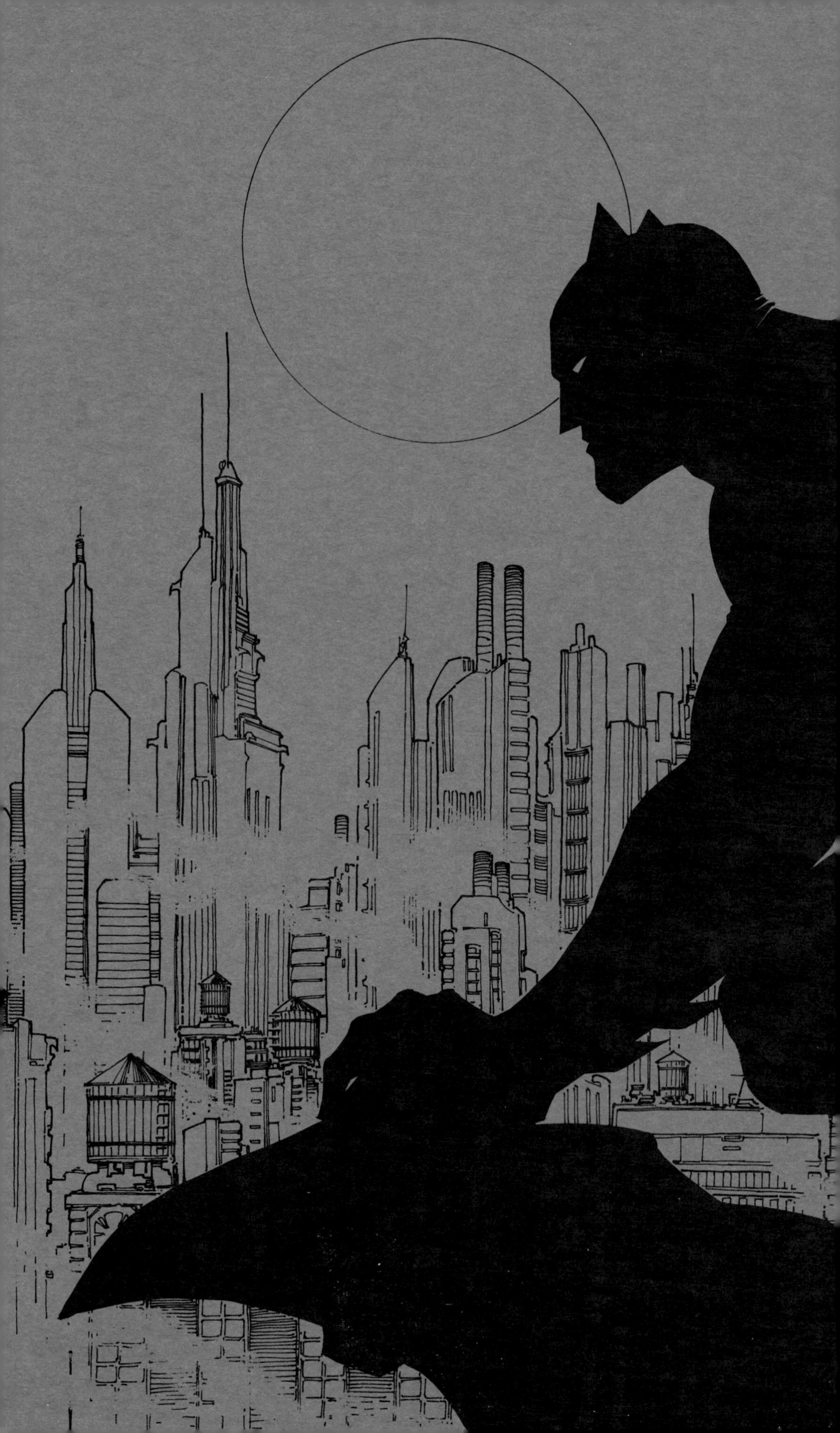